Bordered Writers

Bordered Writers

*Latinx Identities and Literacy Practices
at Hispanic-Serving Institutions*

Edited by

Isabel Baca, Yndalecio Isaac Hinojosa,
and Susan Wolff Murphy

Library of Congress Cataloging-in-Publication Data

Names: Baca, Isabel, 1965– editor. | Hinojosa, Yndalecio Isaac, 1971– editor. | Murphy, Susan Wolff, editor.
Title: Bordered writers : Latinx identities and literacy practices at Hispanic-serving institutions / edited by Isabel Baca, Yndalecio Isaac Hinojosa, and Susan Wolff Murphy.
Description: Albany : State University of New York Press, [2019] | Includes bibliographical references and index.
Identifiers: LCCN 2018036277 | ISBN 9781438475035 (hardcover : alk. paper) | ISBN 9781438475042 (pbk. : alk. paper) | ISBN 9781438475059 (ebook)
Subjects: LCSH: English language—Rhetoric—Study and teaching (Higher)—United States. | Hispanic Americans—Education, Higher. | Hispanic Americans—Ethnic identity. | Writing centers—United States.
Classification: LCC PE1405.U6 B67 2019 | DDC 808/.042071173—dc23
LC record available at https://lccn.loc.gov/2018036277

10 9 8 7 6 5 4 3 2 1

Contents

PART IV: WRITING CENTERS AND MENTORED WRITING

Foreword

Celebrating Bordered Writers

CRISTINA KIRKLIGHTER

I am honored and humbled to write the Foreword to *Bordered Writers: Latinx Identities and Literacy Practices at Hispanic-Serving Institutions* as one of the co-editors of *Teaching Writing with Latino/a Students: Lessons Learned at Hispanic-Serving Institutions* (2007). As a retired professor, one of the greatest rewards in this profession is to see three former graduate students, Drs. Yndalecio Isaac Hinojosa (co-editor and contributor), Candace de León-Zepeda (contributor), and Romeo García (contributor) carry on what their professors at a Hispanic-Serving Institution (HSI) started more than a decade ago. I am happy to see Susan Wolff Murphy as co-editor continue to follow through with this second book and Isabel Baca who wrote a chapter in the last book come on board as co-editor. I also find it rewarding to see members of the NCTE/CCCCs Latinx Caucus in this book with so many coming from Hispanic-Serving Institutions. As Latinx graduate students and professors at Hispanic-Serving Institutions increase in Rhetoric and Composition so too will the scholarship, teaching, and community outreach at these institutions.

Yemin Sánchez, Nichole Nicholson, and Marcela Hebbard mention in one of the book's chapters the following:

> For Latinx communities, *familismo* is the strongest core cultural value. . . . *Behavioral familismo* refers to the behaviors that reflect these beliefs, such as childrearing, taking care of an ill family member, living near or visiting kin, or providing support for close family and friends.

When we encourage a *familismo* approach to flourish in academia in the way Latinx students and faculty treat one another, especially at Hispanic-Serving Institutions, then we set the example for others to follow suit, thus increasing the chances of Latinx student success. From my observations after teaching at a Hispanic-Serving Institution in South Texas for thirteen years, those who tried to instill an individualistic instead of a *familismo* approach with Latinx students, staff, and faculty usually deterred Latinx success and ultimately fed into the Latinx academic challenges of isolationism and nonbelonging. These books are important in helping others understand what works at Hispanic-Serving Institutions and ensuring that Latinxs experience the familiar.

Something similar to the *familismo* approach is the *familia* approach described by Barbara Jaffe in the first book with California's community colleges' *Puente* Project Model focusing on counseling, writing, and mentoring. Ten years later Erin Doran, in this current book, describes how the *Puente* model from California is adopted in Texas as the Dream Catchers Program (whose name has been recently changed to Project Ascender). While Barbara Jaffe devoted most of her article to describing the *Puente* training workshops she conducted with faculty, Doran interviews and studies the faculty who are in the Dream Catchers Program and how it has influenced their teaching and effect on students. One facet of the program that shows its effectiveness was when Doran says this about her study: "Every faculty member provided stories of at least one student they clearly remember and have kept in touch with multiple years after the student left their class." Clearly, the *familia* and *cariño* for these teachers and students are evident.

When I reflect on the first book and after I read this book, I thought about the histories of Latinxs entering academia long before the HSI designation. I thought about Felipe Ortego de Gasca, one of the co-founders of the NCTE Chicano Teachers of English caucus back in the early 1970s, a WWII veteran who benefited from the GI Bill and became part of the first significant wave of Latinxs entering colleges and universities in the United States. No Mexican-American classes or studies were available for these WWII veterans after the war, but they had a presence. These WWII veterans paved the way for student activism in the '70s with a much broader understanding of what it meant to be Chicanos/as and activists. Felipe Ortego de Gasca was both a WWII veteran and later Chicano activist, so we see through his life experiences these changes, as I was privileged to discover almost ten years ago when I first interviewed him. Texas A&I, later called Texas A&M Kingsville, right down the road from where I worked and where our co-editor, Yndalecio Isaac Hinojosa, received his undergraduate degree, was a hotbed of Chicano/a student activism during the late '60s and '70s. In the undergraduate autobiography class I taught at Texas A&M Corpus Christi, students were always fascinated when they read Jose Angel Gutierrez's *The Making of a Chicano Militant*, where he spoke about Chicano/a student activism at Texas A&I. They craved to know these local historical HSI identities long before the official designation. So, if I write a foreword that oscillates between the first book on *Teaching Writing* and the second book, it is because I am a firm believer in following the historical trajectories of HSIs.

Even though it has only been a little over a decade since the first book was written, the co-editors and contributors of *Teaching Writing with Latino/a Students* were part of the first book in a discipline focused on HSIs. The definitive scholar on HSIs at that time, Berta Vigil Laden, came from another discipline, and we also relied on the data Deborah Santiago provided as part of *Excelencia* in Education's HSI initiatives. Back then, when we started in the latter part of 2004, there were fewer than 250 HSIs, and today we stand at around 472 (HACU 2017 Fact Sheet Hispanic Higher Education and HSIs). As faculty at an HSI, the book came about because we were searching for our HSI identities as writing teachers and thought we could better understand our identities by discovering what others were doing at other institutions. I saw some similarities and differences with Nancy Alvarez in "On Longing and Belonging: Latinas in the Writing Center," when she collected 17 *testimonios* from Latina tutors from different HSI colleges and universities. She felt validated after reading these like-minded *testimonios* and knew she belonged at a writing center. I was pleased to see the *testimonios* from Steven Alvarez, Christine Garcia, Heather Lang, Isabel Baca, and Kaylee Cruz, in this second book to further this sense of belonginess, and I wish we had had *testimonios* in the first book. In our case as co-editors in the first book, we either felt validated when we read submissions that spoke to our perceptions of this identity or horrified to read how some writing teachers researched and wrote about HSI Latinx students. This was to be expected when so little had been written on HSIs as we navigated these relatively uncharted waters. Although we were not part of the histories of returning WWII Latinx veterans or Chicano/a activists of the 1970s, we did see our HSI book as working toward discovering HSI identities in our writing profession and hoping we would set the groundwork for a building block of identities to follow. It takes time to form identities, and this second book was needed to continue HSI identity explorations.

As part of this building-block approach of identities, I was pleased to see chapters in the second book building on the scholarship of the first. Jen Lloyd's " 'One Foot on the Bridge and One Foot Off the Bridge': Navigating the Geographies of Access and Rhetorical Education at an HSI" with its case study approach on UC Irvine's Summer Bridge Program builds from Robert Affeldt's focus in the first book, where he studies and applies rhetorical theories to these personal narratives of a few Latina and Native American women from

University of New Mexico's Summer Bridge Program. Both chapters rely heavily on studying and interpreting the narratives, interviews, and experiences of these Summer Bridge students to ensure, as Lloyd explains, "that the bridges, the doors, and any other entry points to these multifaceted sites remain accessible to those willing to seek them out." Without the valuable insights from Summer Bridge students and our care in interpreting and understanding their words and experiences, access remains limited and possibly misdirected. Through these Summer Bridge student insights, we realize how access is not restricted to traditional notions of academic success as Monica, a Summer Bridge student at UC Irvine, explains but encompasses their ability to access familiar communities:

> . . . as we are growing academically and professionally, outside factors like the community are pretty much what makes us develop even further. There's a limit in the classroom.

In a similar vein, teachers of writing at HSIs must often depend on their students to help them understand and navigate the particular HSI communities, especially if the teachers are not from these communities. Four of the authors, Isabel Baca, Yndalecio Isaac Hinojosa, Kendall Leon, Beatrice Mendez Newman grew up in the communities they teach in, so they are very familiar with the cultures of their local HSI students, thus making it easier for them to apply theoretical and pedagogical practices familiar to many of their local students. However, as Dora Ramirez-Dhoore and Rebecca Jones discovered in the first book and Laura Gonzales discovers in the second book (all of who came from different geographic locations and backgrounds and thus were unfamiliar with the cultural complexities of their U.S–Mexican border HSI communities when they arrived), the traditional approach of teaching writing or technical communications was often at odds with the realities of their students and classroom approaches. In her chapter, "Teaching Technical Communication on the México/U.S. Border: A Brief Case Study," Gonzales builds on this unfamiliarity by discovering how the complexities and messiness of HSI Border institutions can benefit the diversity in the field of technical communications when she says

> . . . the border helped me understand the blurred lines between 'expert' and 'non-expert' discourses, between 'simple' and 'messy' design, and between what I may have considered 'mono' versus 'multi' lingual, highlighting the value and importance of messiness and complexity in communication design.

If we listen carefully to what local students know about their HSI communities, especially if we are not from the region, our HSI classrooms and practices will be better for it.

When technical writing professors do come from the region, as is the case with Diana Cárdenas from the first book and Kendall Leon from the second book, then a less traditional approach to technical writing comes into play. Both know the oppressive histories and challenges of their local communities and thus work with their technical writing colleagues to develop rhetorical and service-learning approaches to meet the technical writing needs of these communities.

As we search for ways to better understand our HSI students and their communities, we sometimes need to devise reflective assignments, so both students and teachers can better ascertain how to move forward. Lucas Corcoran and Caroline Wilkinson, in their chapter "Translingualism and ALP: A Rhetorical Model for Bordered Latinx Writers" do just that with their translingual autoethnography assignment for ALP students. By helping students reflect on their "different varieties of English . . . in direct response to the communicative exigencies of their environments," through "both personal narrative writing and the entirety of students' linguistic repertoires," Corcoran and Wilkinson helped students see how monolingual emphases in developmental writing disempowered them. Students were empowered to discover in rhetorical and linguistic ways their translingual identities rather than simply seeing themselves as students in need of remediation. Helping ALP Latinx students discover the value of their languages in academic classrooms goes a long way toward building their confidence and demonstrating their academic belongingness.

Beatrice Mendez Newman and Romeo García in their chapter entitled "Teaching with Bordered Writers: Reconstructing Narratives of Difference, Mobility, and Translingualism," write about a region of this country, the Lower Rio Grande Valley (LRGV), where translingualism is the norm. Therefore, as they say, student writers from this region as evidenced in their ethnographic study of these writers, "construct their stories and academic products from the macro position of dual embodiment in two cultures, two languages, and two mindsets." Both Mendez Newman and García are from this region and thus their identities are tied to creating a pedagogical approach "that celebrates 'intrusions' of Spanish as gems of authenticity and linguistic authority."

I was pleased to see my former graduate students Yndalecio Isaac Hinojosa and Candace de León-Zepeda contribute a chapter devoted to decolonizing composition classrooms through a Chicana feminist lens, more specifically through Anzaldúa, Sandoval, and later Pérez. Instead of following the traditional trajectory of composition classrooms, they encouraged students to employ rhetorical tools of enquiry "to reclaim their bodies and histories and to reimagine their identities through discursive practices, through acts of writing." Personal writing, especially the *autohistoria-teoría* encompassing many of the students' reflective writings, helps students participate in reclaiming and reimagining their identities. I know from personal experience as a personal essay scholar and teacher at a Hispanic-Serving Institution in South Texas how important it was for students to bring the personal into their writings as they searched for academic belongingness on their terms. Many of these students were first-generation and/or Latinx students experiencing much of what Hinojosa and de León-Zepeda experienced as undergraduate and graduate students. Hinojosa and de León-Zepeda also "reclaim" and "reimagine" as teachers and scholars and know how what they did not get as students should never be repeated in their classrooms.

We also have professors such as Isabel Baca in her *testimonio*, "English, *Español, or Los Dos*," who can say to her local HSI Latinx students how she values both of her languages and "If I can do it, you can too. *Sí se puede*." This is another level of empowering validation and mentorship. I remember writing a tenure letter for Isabel a few years ago as an outside reviewer and saying how lucky UTEP was as an HSI to have an English professor from the community who understood her students and community so well. My experiences co-editing the first book and observing professors at my university and others showed me how important it is for HSI colleges and universities to recruit and retain professors from the local area who grew up in these communities. This is especially relevant when many students come from the local area as is the case with many HSIs. In many instances, they are the bridge, the diplomats, the mediators, the connectors between the university and their surrounding community. These professors should be respected and valued for all they bring to their HSIs by students, faculty, staff, administrators, and their local community. When they have this respect and value, HSIs are better for it.

In the years since the first book was published, a number of articles and chapters have come out focusing on HSI STEM students and programs. Just google "HSI STEM" and page after page comes up on HSI STEM grants and programs at many HSIs. Not surprisingly, this is where the high-dollar HSI grants are coming from, and HSI universities are benefitting from this as are STEM students and faculty. However, as Heather M. Falconer illustrates in her chapter, "Mentored Writing at a Hispanic-Serving Institution: Improving Student Facility with Scientific Discourse," we, in Rhetoric and Composition, are benefitting as well with opportunities to study Latinx student writing in HSI STEM environments. With the Program for Research Initiatives in Science and Math (PRISM) at John Jay College of Criminal Justice as part of the CUNY system, Falconer had the opportunity to do a case study on Ruben and his mentor Marta. What is success for a Latinx student at an HSI? The answer for Falconer, after choosing to intensely focus on Ruben and his success, is that success comes in many different forms and does not necessarily follow the traditional trajectory of academic success. The most telling quote from this chapter that maybe the whole book followed is this last quote: "Thus, the exceptionalism that is embedded in science is not necessarily one of innate brilliance and daily breakthroughs, but of access."

How many of us at HSIs (and I was one of the many much to my shame) celebrated the achievements of Latinx students who furthered their education at the expense of other Latinx students who did not? How much of this was tied to our trajectory paths as academics and the validation we received in our navigation of traditional perceptions of "access" and "success?" When Sánchez, Nicholson, and Hebbard describe how Latinx students practicing the *familismo* approach are loyal to their classroom families to the point of knowing they will fail the class but sticking it out to the end to show these family loyalties to their classmates, isn't this a form of success that should be celebrated and doesn't it work against mandated drop date regulations that penalize students for persisting in their classrooms? Isn't persistence a form of access and success as described in the *familismo* approach? In the coming years, I hope to see more case studies such as this one. For if we wish to retain our HSI Latinx students, we must individualize for each student their specific contexts of "access" and "success."

As I close this Foreword, I want to express my gratitude to all of the authors and editors of both books. While the research on HSIs, especially in a discipline, remains scant, we must keep plugging away and not become discouraged. Some Latinx students will read these books and recognize themselves. Some faculty will read these books and say, "I can do better" or "I'm on the right track." Some administrators will read these books and say "I better understand what needs to be done at my HSI for Latinx students and what can I do to work with faculty, staff and students to make this happen."

As the number of HSIs increase, we have opportunities as established HSIs working towards our identities to show a path for emerging HSIs to make their identity paths less difficult. Books like these are part of these paths and journeys.

Acknowledgments

This collection would not have been possible without the amazing work, experiences, and personal journeys of all our contributors at HSIs. It takes courage to share these personal trajectories and challenges. It takes hard work and faith to believe that better times are coming, and changes are and will continue to take place for Latinx and other underserved minorities in higher education and in our nation today. *Thank you for placing trust in us!*

As co-editors, we are honored to introduce *Bordered Writers: Latinx Identities and Literacy Practices at Hispanic-Serving Institutions.* As a second volume to its 2007 predecessor, *Teaching Writing with Latino/a Students: Lessons Learned at Hispanic-Serving Institutions*, co-edited by Cristina Kirklighter, Diana Cárdenas, and Susan Wolff Murphy, this collection demonstrates the increased presence of Latinx scholars, practitioners, and students in higher education, and their work voices the urgency of acknowledging Latinx challenges, needs, and accomplishments in higher education. We thank artist Ronnie Dukes from DUKEScomics.com for providing the cover art for this book. His artwork entitled "En Route" illustrates ever changing and evolving obstacles to education and success. We thank the State University of New York Press for their continued support of our projects on the amazing work being done at Hispanic-Serving Institutions (HSIs). Collectively, as co-editors, we thank Rebecca Colesworthy, Beth Bouloukos, and Rafael Chaiken for their continued support throughout this project, and we thank Cristina Kirklighter for paving the way for us and opening the door to this second collection on HSIs. *Thank you, Cristina, for your mentoring, encouragement, and support.*

Isabel expresses gratitude to her co-editors (Yndalecio Isaac Hinojosa and Susan Wolff Murphy) for inviting her to serve as co-editor on this second volume. Collaborating with them has strengthened her knowledge on HSIs and has allowed her to see the incredible work being done by Latinx students, scholars, and practitioners. Working on this volume has also opened her eyes to how much work yet remains to be done if we indeed seek equality, access, and excellence in higher education. Latinx are the largest minority in the nation, and *we* are here to stay. This collection speaks volumes to this message, and Isabel is grateful for being given the opportunity to share this message. Isabel also thanks her institution, the University of Texas at El Paso, for standing firm on its open access policy and standards of excellence for Latinx students and faculty. She thanks her parents, Maria and Ricardo Baca, for raising her as an English-Spanish bilingual and providing her with an excellent education, and she thanks her son, Antonio, for making her a proud Latina mother. *Gracias, Toño! Sí se puede!*

Yndalecio expresses thanks to his co-editors (Isabel Baca and Susan Wolff Murphy), colleagues and writing group members (Glenn Blalock, Chuck Etheridge, Susan Garza, Frances Johnson, and Catherine Quick,) and mentors (Diana Cárdenas, Sue Hum, Cristina Kirklighter, and Laura K. Muñoz), for their assistance and support on this project. He also expresses special thanks to Jeremy Anderson, Elias Benavides, Larry Cantú, Norma Cantú, Candace de León-Zepeda, Sara Boone Mcandrew, Larissa Mercado-López, Julie Moore-Felux, Denise Tolan, and Ito Romo for their inspiration and motivation on this journey. *I would not be where I am today without all of you.*

Susan would like to thank her co-editors (Isabel Baca and Yndalecio Isaac Hinojosa) and her colleagues and writing group support members Susan Garza, Glenn Blalock, Chuck Etheridge, Diana Cárdenas, Catherine Quick, and Frances Johnson for their assistance on this project. For helping her to be attentive to language, identity, and equity, she acknowledges her mentors and friends, including Valerie Balester, Kathleen Ferrera, Mary Bucholtz, Barbara Johnstone, Barbara Hodne, and Michelle Hall Kells, as well as members of the profession who continue to pursue this work. *I could not do anything that I do without the belief and support of my family, including Tom, Sophia, Anna, and Elanor.*

Introduction

Isabel Baca, Yndalecio Isaac Hinojosa,
and Susan Wolff Murphy

In 2007, the volume *Teaching and Writing with Latino/a Students: Lessons Learned at Hispanic-Serving Institutions* by editors Cristina Kirklighter, Diana Cárdenas, and Susan Wolff Murphy, was published. At that time, the editors were responding to a need to address the increasing presence of Latinx students in higher education and the increasing number of Hispanic-Serving Institutions. The conversation in composition studies focused on how students transitioned, should transition, to academic discourses to reflect more on how students could navigate a broad range of discourse communities (communities of practice). Our volume, *Bordered Writers: Latinx Identities and Literacy Practices at Hispanic-Serving Institutions*, continues the work of the previous volume. Following the collections by Kells and Balester (1999) and Kells, Balester, and Villanueva (2004), as well as other scholarship on multilingual writers and students of color, the previous collection highlighted the scholarship of faculty of color and those working at Hispanic-Serving Institutions, many of which were two-year community colleges. In 2007, protests about immigration and English Only legislation were in the news; today, we face anti-Mexican/immigrant rhetoric, attempts to restrict voter access and disenfranchise people of color and the poor, and attacks on race in higher education admissions policies.

How Have Things Changed?

In the face of these eruptions, we find ourselves in higher education reflecting on similar questions of identity, race, and language, including how to teach writ-

1

ing in ways that do not privilege a monolingual, Standard or Edited American English measure of writing. But some things have shifted. Institutional racism in the form of profiling, inequitable treatment, and police-caused violence and death, and resulting protest have reemerged in mainstream awareness. On a more positive note, the legal rights of LGBT (Lesbian, Gay, Bisexual, Transgendered) people have expanded significantly. Questions of identity—and self-defined "identification"—have become more mainstream, and yet challenges of race and the related issues of language use and literacies continue, persistent and not easily dismissed. In our field of writing studies, scholars have shown how our classroom practices, placement decisions, and responses to student writing, among other things, have privileged Standard or Edited American English and "Western" rhetorical strategies and values (Inoue, 2015). Discussing writing teaching and assessment, Asao Inoue proposes "theorizing writing assessment in ways that can help teachers cultivate antiracist agendas in their writing assessment practices" (2015, p. 3). This collection expands this antiracist focus (translingualism, rhetorical dexterity, transcultural repositioning) to classroom practices, curricula, and program design.

Our purpose in this edited volume is to extend the conversations about student success, racial identity, and Latinx students that exist by providing work focused on the programs and experiences of students and faculty at Hispanic-Serving and Minority-Serving Institutions from across the country. We want to advocate for pedagogies and curricula that center on the culturally diverse populations being served at the nation's Hispanic-Serving Institutions (HSIs). We also want to give voice to past and present Latinx scholars, rhetoricians, and students in both academic articles and *testimonio* narratives.

We hope our collection will speak to graduate faculty and writing program administrators (WPAs) preparing graduate students to teach writing with culturally diverse students, students in graduate seminars on pedagogy/practicums, administrators seeking to innovate and/or build program designs, and centers for teaching excellence who might use the book in faculty development seminars/book clubs/discussions. As not all of our readers will teach or attend an HSI or a campus with a large population of Latinx students, our introduction provides some background by explaining the context and difficulties of the Hispanic-Serving Institution label. We explore the demographics of the Latinx student population in the United States in order to show some recent changes and to counter some stereotypes. In these sections, we refer to resources such as *Excelencia* in Education, which can be helpful to any scholars interested in this area.

Our introduction also discusses some of the terms we have chosen to use. Terms used to describe the population of peoples who originate from México, Central or South America are contentious and evolving. We explain our choice of Latinx and our use of "bordered writers."

Last, we have chosen to include *testimonios* as interludes between chapters. As this is somewhat of an unusual genre in academic work, we discuss it below. The collection as a whole is organized into four sections that arise from the different places where writing occurs in the undergraduate experience, and the sections appear chronologically in the students' experiences: developmental English and bridge programs, first-year writing, professional and technical writing, and writing centers and mentored writing. At the end of the introduction, we explain these four sections and some relationships we see between the different chapters.

What is a Hispanic-Serving Institution?

Hispanic-Serving Institution is a designation applied by the U.S. Department of Education to an eligible institution of higher education that enrolls at least 25% undergraduate, full-time equivalent Hispanic students (U.S. Department of Education). The Department, however, does not provide a list of HSIs for public use. As a result, organizations such as the Hispanic Association of Colleges and Universities (HACU) and *Excelencia* in Education create their own lists using government data. The most recent list compiled by *Excelencia* uses data from the Department of Education's Integrated Postsecondary Education Data System (IPEDS) from 2016–2017 and lists 492 two- and four-year institutions (*Excelencia*, 2018).

What being an HSI means to the identity and mission of an institution varies. As it is based solely on enrollment percentages, the designation does not necessarily reflect the mission or vision of an institution. As Cristina Kirklighter mentions in the foreword, it is the choices that administrators and faculty at an HSI make that determine whether the space of the university is a place where Latinx scholars and students can flourish and whether serving Hispanic students is actually a goal or a feature of that institution.

Student Demographics, Identity, and Language Use

This volume is deliberately titled, "Bordered Writers" for several reasons. We want to recognize that while identity is self-defined to an extent, it is also mandated by external forces and experienced in concrete, embodied terms. Students are bordered or marginalized for many reasons, not all of which relate to race or language. Not all students at HSIs are Latinx; not all Latinx students attend HSIs; not all writers at HSIs are bordered. Some of the elements of writers being bordered relate to their racial identity, language use, and country of origin; it may also relate to their gender, sexual orientation, physical abilities, etc.

Demographics of the United States population of traditional-aged college students (18–24 years) are shifting. While numbers of White and Black students have declined since 2012, numbers and percentages of Asian and Latinx students of the undergraduate population have increased (Stepler & Brown, 2016; Brown & Patten, 2014). Eighteen percent of 18–24 college students are Latinx, and their number has increased by 121,647 since 2012 (Stepler & Brown, 2016; Brown & Patten, 2014). Of U.S. born 18- to 24-year-old Latinx, 38.3% are enrolled in higher education (compared to 44% of White, 36% Black, and 65% Asian) (Stepler & Brown, 2016; Brown & Patten, 2014). As the largest minority and growing undergraduate population, Latinx students, their interests, needs, and goals, and those of their families will reshape the landscape of higher education in the United States, especially as colleges and universities compete for students and their tuition dollars in times when budgets are increasingly dependent on those funds.

One of the topics addressed in the chapters that follow is language use. While 72% of Latinx millennial students speak Spanish at home, the percentages are declining; more than one-quarter speak only English at home, and three-quarters of Latinx millennials are proficient English speakers (Patten, 2016). Those students who live along the U.S./México border, however, are more likely to be bilingual/translingual code meshers/mixers, and many are Mexican nationals who cross the border to attend a college or university. People who study multilingualism know that it is the norm for most humans on the planet; operating in more than one language provides many cognitive and social benefits. If colleges and universities can abandon their position as gatekeepers of monolingualism, perhaps we can help combat the generational linguistic acculturation of Latinx students, both in our students and in the teachers we prepare.

Regarding national origin, this anthology focuses mostly on the experiences of Mexican-origin Latinx in Texas, California, and Florida, with some representation from the New York/New Jersey area. This focus is reflective of the college-age population: 65% of Latinx Millennials are of Mexican origin, and 65% are born in the United States (Patten, 2016).

Why Latinx?

Latinx (pronounced "La-Teen-ex") is a modification of Latino/a, which is inclusive of all gender identities, including those outside the masculine and feminine binary, by avoiding the gender markers of -a/-o required in the

Spanish language. "The x [in Latinx]," as queer, non-binary femme writer Jack Qu'emi explains, "is a way of rejecting the gendering of words . . ." (qtd. in Van Horne, 2016). As part of a "linguistic revolution" on the Internet (Crystal), Latinx emerged online within left-leaning and queer communities in 2004 and gained momentum in usage by 2014 (Padilla, 2016). Social media platforms, advocates for LGBT community members, student groups, intersectionality scholars, journalists, and others use the term. Given that the use of Latinx is a move of advocacy, it has inspired resistance. Guerra and Orbea of Swarthmore College published several objections to the term (2015) which were countered by "The Case FOR 'Latinx': Why Intersectionality Is Not a Choice," by Maria Scharrón-Del Rio and Alan Aja (2015), who name the use of term as liberatory praxis. We are following their lead, and we hope this volume fulfills our goal of being inclusive and respectful of the identity choices of all people, including those who are bordered writers.

Who are Bordered Writers?

Academic spaces create many borders, and nowhere are these borders more evident than between college-ready and underprepared students, traditional and nontraditional students, academic and nonacademic lives, formal and vernacular discourses or literacies, as well as college and everyday literacy practices. These borders establish the foundation for *border literacies*, "the altered literacy practices that students are already familiar with which become relevant in a college context" (Carmichael et al., 2007, p. 79). Such altered literacy practices, bordered no less, are "reading and writing practices in *other* domains of students' lives—home, work, community—that are, or have the potential to be, situated also in the educational domain" (emphasis added, Ivanič et al., 2009, p. 22). Thus, we embrace the construct of *bordered writers* first to support such altered literacy practices in academic spaces, and second to broaden the scope of student writers considered bordered in academic spaces by hegemonic, conventional, monolingual discourses. We find such student writers, especially Latinx writers, are necessarily bordered no longer by geographical boundaries or defined solely by their ethnic or racial status. These student writers are bordered "because they have constructed spaces of linguistic and bodily performativity shaped by realities of literal and constructed place" as Mendez Newman and García claim and, as a result, are "*bordered subjectivities* . . . that highlight the embodiment of borders or bordered cultures," as Hinojosa and de León-Zepeda introduce. What these definitions reveal is how closely borderedness parallels with characteristics of otherness. Bordered literacies, so to speak, are more closely associated with those literacies, or participants for that matter, from nondominant categories, rather than dominant. This perspective would suggest, then, that the term *border* denotes what has been acknowledged as constituting otherness, a perspective that aligns with Brenda J. Allen (2011), who suggests difference usually "refers to how an individual or a group varies from, or compares to, the unspoken norm of the dominant group" (p. 4). As such, border literacies are more likely representational spaces of marginalized bodies. Therefore, in our attempt to address classroom/writing center practices and/or program design, we adopt bordered writers as a construct in order to reconceive of the purpose of the HSI and to complicate the ideas of Latinx students, staff, and faculty, especially at HSIs. Also, the phrase bordered writers is our attempt to connect a writer's identity and literacies to the concrete, material, lived experiences of a particular place, and, at the same time, to question the essentialized nature of ethnic and racial identity. These are concepts that have come from the new research and scholarship by Latinx/Chicanx scholars.

What are *Testimonios* and Why Do We Include Them?

In addition to the traditional scholarly chapters, we have interspersed *testimonios* in this volume. These firsthand, empowering personal narratives give voice to Latinx scholars and students who have personally experienced, in very concrete and material ways, education, language use, and literacy expectations in the United States. Kalina Brabeck (2004) describes a *testimonio* as "voices that speak from the margin . . . [that] offer an individual account that encompasses and expresses the reality of a whole people and can only be understood within the context of belonging to a community" (p. 43). John Beverly (2004) adds to this definition in *Testimonio: On the Politics of Truth*, stating that a *testimonio* is told in the first person by a narrator "who is also the real protagonist or witness of the events he or she recounts, and whose unit of narration is usually a 'life' or a significant life experience" (Beverly, 2004, p. 31). In *testimonio*, it is the "intentionality of the narrator that is paramount" (Beverly, 2004, p. 32). The "situation of narration in testimonio has to involve an urgency to communicate, a problem of repression, poverty, subalternity, imprisonment, struggle for survival, implicated in the act of narration itself" (Beverly, 2004, p. 32). *Testimonio* is concerned with "a problematic collective social situation in which the narrator lives" (Beverly, 2004, p. 33).

The *testimonios* in this collection include the voices of men and women, young and mature, first-, 1.5-, and second-generations of Mexican-Americans from Arizona, Texas, New Mexico, and California, and a *Cubana* from San Angelo, Texas. They all operate in translingual hybrid spaces with various levels of confidence and ability in code-switching/code-meshing and have found their ways into academia. In these stories, we can see the importance of mentoring and combating linguistic prejudice and racism. There are complications of skin tone and whiteness—the concrete and material experience of race and of being a minority in America, on a university campus, or in higher education in general (both in "allies" and Latinx). Themes of first-generationality for college students emerge, including challenges of acculturation, feelings of belonging and separation from home and school, and misunderstandings of the demands of college and family, both on the side of the family and student and those of higher education faculty and staff. These *testimonios* help both students and faculty/staff recognize the reality for these men and women and the issues they might be experiencing, and hopefully, reassure those attempting to join the academy that others have experienced what they have experienced, and been successful.

How is the Collection Organized?

This volume is organized in four parts, each providing a different location or perspective where questions of serving Latinx and bordered writers arise, which should appeal to different audiences with particular interests. These four spaces/perspectives are: developmental English and bridge programs, first-year writing, professional and technical writing, and finally, writing centers and mentored writing. Each part is paired with a *testimonio* written by Latinx authors who use that narrative form to talk about their experience. Grouping our chapters in these ways presents themes of translingualism and rhetorical dexterity in first-year composition, developmental English (ALP and bridge), identity and language in professional development, and Latinx identity in various institutional locations, including the writing program and writing center.

The collection as a whole is prefaced by the *testimonio* of Steven Alvarez, who speaks about his working-class, Spanish-speaking household in Arizona, earning a PhD in English, and the various moments of assimilation culturally and linguistically that he experienced. In doing so, he provides a glimpse of the transition many of our students are making as they move through the various levels of education and American (White/mainstream) culture.

Part I: Developmental English and Bridge Programs opens with Corcoran and Wilkinson's argument that we can promote multilingualism and rhetorical awareness among our students by assigning language autoethnographies. In this way, we can reduce the sense and/or need for the assimilative moves made by Alvarez. Another program that reduces assimilation to institutional norms is the successful "Dream Catchers" program (whose name has been recently changed to "Project Ascender"). Doran studied the paired-class first-year intervention that includes developmental courses in several community colleges in Texas. This program connects the classroom to families in several ways, including a family event called *Noche de Familia*. Dream Catchers also encourages using first languages and writing assignments that help faculty learn about their students.

Echoing Alvarez's *testimonio* is Lloyd's examination of the institutional rhetoric of transitional programs and how these impact students' perceptions of belonging (or not) in higher education. We close Part I with the *testimonio* by Christine Garcia who poignantly demonstrates the importance of the simple presence of people and scholars of color in our readings—graduate and undergraduate—that is necessary for students to feel respected and included.

Part II: First-Year Writing opens with a chapter that bends genre expectations by weaving the voices of Hinojosa and de León-Zepeda, narrating their experiences as students and scholars of color, with a theoretical discussion of how to bring Chicanx thought, Chicana feminist thought specifically, to bear on the first-year composition classroom, and what that would mean for students' cultural and political literacies. The embodied, concrete experiences combined with theorized consideration of identity connects strikingly to Alvarez and Garcia, as well as the lessons from the academic chapters that discuss institutional rhetoric and classroom pedagogies and assignments.

The next chapter also advocates for ways of teaching that are culturally sensitive, consider the whole student, and are sustainable. Sánchez, Nicholson, and Hebbard outline their *"Familismo Teaching"* approach, formed within the challenges and opportunities of teaching in the Rio Grande Valley. Also studying the students and faculty in the region, Mendez Newman and García argue for a celebration of "translingual hybridity" rather than an impulse to move students toward monolingual aptitude.

This first-year writing section closes with the *testimonio* by Heather Lang, who reflects on her role as a graduate teaching instructor in Las Cruces, New Mexico, and the student, Valeria, who challenged her to define her role as a teacher. Valeria is a student who "brought the border with her" into class, revisiting the questions raised by all the authors in this section. Lang critiques her decisions, her relationships, and her practices within this "bordered" teaching space, reminding us we are all in this "borderland" or contact zone of cultures, languages, races, etc.

Part III: Professional and Technical Writing expands our focus to technical and professional writing courses. Chapters by Leon and Enríquez-Loya and Gonzales consider how these courses and programs should be designed at HSIs, taking into account students' cultural and linguistic assets.

Leon and Enríquez-Loya, at a newly designated HSI, consider the design of their professional and technical writing course. Gonzales demonstrates how service-learning, cross-cultural communication, and translation activities can be incorporated into technical communication programs to highlight and develop the strengths of Latinx students, and how the students' cross-cultural and linguistic expertise is drawn out by those innovations. This section closes with professional and technical writing scholar Isabel Baca's *testimonio* which reflects on her own bilingualism and the loss of that which frequently occurs in second and third generations. This *testimonio* reminds us how investing institutional weight in bilingualism can help our students (perhaps) avoid that loss, and see bi- or translingualism as a strength, with economic reward.

The chapters in Part IV: Writing Centers and Mentored Writing provide rare glimpses into the importance of considering these spaces in our discussions of race, language, and writing. These spaces/activities can promote (or deny) inclusion. Nancy Alvarez's chapter both demonstrates how these spaces are traditionally exclusive and monolingual and suggests how they can be made more diverse and deliberately translingual/transcultural. Falconer's chapter on mentored writing in the sciences (a model many of us are unfamiliar with) demonstrates how our students' goals for education and constraints (i.e., supporting a family) can run counter to the ambitions of faculty who are promoting graduate school and more traditionally academic literacies. Falconer's chapter reminds us that we cannot define "success" for our students; they will define success on their own terms. Part IV closes with the *testimonio* of Kaylee Cruz, a first-generation Latina student and undergraduate writing center tutor. Cruz shows how her experiences at a peer-tutoring conference, among other things, demonstrated how not coming from a White, upper-middle-class background, not her academic preparation, is what made her "underprepared." Cruz's statement, "I was shocked too to realize that race and ethnicity had been at the center of my experiences in higher education, without me being aware," is a powerful statement of the pervasive impact that race, class, language, and ethnicity have on our students' (and our) lives.

As the ethnic/racial configuration of the United States shifts toward a "minority-majority," scholars and teachers must rethink their paradigms and move the margin to the center. We must also push back against the racist responses this shift is inspiring in our nation. We hope this volume will help writing studies researchers and scholars understand how WPAs and practitioners are changing the teaching of writing at Hispanic-Serving Institutions to be more inclusive and welcoming, how Latinx students, scholars, and researchers are experiencing both classrooms and the field of writing studies, and the lessons we must learn from student and activist Latinx rhetorics.

We see our book making a significant contribution to the conversation in writing studies about students of color, linguistic diversity, and pedagogies and practices. Bordered writers are being heard and are growing in numbers in higher education, while scholars of color and those located at HSIs are contributing to the fields of literacy, language, rhetoric, and writing studies.

It is our hope that this book connects to all bordered writers and educators, making higher education stronger and more representative of the nation's population. Bordered writers, in and outside Hispanic-Serving Institutions, have a voice that must be heard and should not be ignored.

Best,

Isabel, Yndalecio, and Susan

References

Allen, B. J. (2011). *Difference Matters: Communicating Social Identity.* 2nd ed. 2004. Long Grove, IL: Waveland P, Inc.

Beverly, J. (2004). *Testimonio: On the Politics of Truth.* Minneapolis, MN: University of Minnesota Press.

Brabeck, K. (2004). Testimonio: bridging feminist and participatiory action research principles to create new spaces of collectivity. In *Traveling companions: feminism, teaching, and action research* (pp. 41–54). Westport, CT: Praeger.

Brown, A., & Patten, E. (2014). Table 26: College Enrollment, by Race and Ethnicity: 2000 and 2012. In *Statistical portrait of Hispanics in the United States, 2012.* Washington, DC: Pew Research Center. http://www.pewhispanic.org/2014/04/29/statistical-portrait-of-hispanics-in-the-united-states-2012/

Carmichael, J., Edwards, R., Miller, K., & Smith, J. (2007). Researching literacy for learning in the vocational curriculum. In *The pedagogy of lifelong learning: Understanding effective teaching and learning in diverse context* (pp. 79–89). London: Routledge.

Crystal, D. (2003). "A Linguistic Revolution?" *Concord.* 6–7.

Excelencia in Education. (2018). Hispanic-Serving Institutions (HSIs): 2016–17. Washington, DC: *Excelencia in Education.* Retrieved from https://www.edexcelencia.org/research/data/hispanic-serving-institutions-hsis-2016-2017

Guerra, G., & Orbea, G. (2016, November 19). The argument against the use of the term "Latinx." *The Phoenix: Swarthmore's Independent Campus Newspaper.* Retrieved from http://swarthmorephoenix.com/2015/11/19/the-argument-against-the-use-of-the-term-latinx/

HACU. (2017). HACU Member Hispanic-Serving Institutions (HSIs) [data file]. Retrieved from: https://www.hacu.net/assnfe/CompanyDirectory.asp?STYLE=2&COMPANY_TYPE=1,5&SEARCH_TYPE=0

Inoue, A. B. (2015). *Antiracist writing assessment ecologies: Teaching and assessing writing for a socially just future.* Fort Collins, CO: The WAC Clearinghouse.

Ivanič, R., Edwards, R., Barton, D., Martin-Jones, M., Fowler, Z., Hughes, B., Mannion, G., Miller, K., Satchwell, C., & Smith, J. (2009). *Improving learning in college: Rethinking literacies across the curriculum.* London: Routledge.

Kells, M. H., & Balester, V. (Eds). (1999). *Attending to the margins: Writing, researching, and teaching on the front lines.* Portsmouth, NH. Boyton/Cook Heinemann.

Kells, M. H., Balester, V., & Villanueva, V. (Eds.). (2004). *Latino/a discourses: On language, identity, and literacy education.* Portsmouth, NH. Boyton/Cook Heinemann.

Padilla, Y. (2016, October 20). What does 'Latinx' mean? A look at the term that's challenging gender norms. Retrieved September 25, 2017, from http://www.complex.com/life/2016/04/latinx/

Patten, E. (2016). The Nation's Latino Population Is Defined by Its Youth. Washington, DC: Pew Research Center. http://www.pewhispanic.org/2016/04/20/the-nations-latino-population-is-defined-by-its-youth/

Scharrón-del Rio, M. R., & Aja, A. A. (2015, Dec. 15). The Case FOR 'Latinx': Why Intersectionality Is Not a Choice. *Latino Rebels.* Retrieved from http://www.latinorebels.com/2015/12/05/the-case-for-latinx-why-intersectionality-is-not-a-choice/

Stepler, R., & Brown, A. (2016). Table 21: College Enrollment, by Race and Ethnicity: 2014. In *Statistical Portrait of Hispanics in the United States, 2014.* Washington, DC: Pew Research Center. http://www.pewhispanic.org/2016/04/19/statistical-portrait-of-hispanics-in-the-united-states-key-charts/

U.S. Department of Education. White House Initiative on Educational Excellence for Hispanics. Retrieved from: https://sites.ed.gov/hispanic-initiative/hispanic-serving-institutions-hsis/

Van Horne, P. (2016, June 21). Writer Jack Qu'emi explains the meaning of 'Latinx.' Retrieved September 25, 2017, from https://www.pri.org/stories/2016-06-21/writer-jack-quemi-explains-meaning-latinx

Testimonio 1

A Family *Testimonio en Confianza*

Becoming *Pocho*

STEVEN ALVAREZ

I lived the first 18 years of my life in rural Safford, Arizona, population 10,000: a desert town nestled in the Gila Valley between the Piñaleno Mountains to the north and the Gila Mountains to the south. Safford's a desert town a few hours from the México–United States border, and I'm connected to that border through my mother, de los Navarro, a generation 1.5 Mexican American from Cananea, Sonora, and my father, a second-generation Mexican American with roots in Sinaloa and Durango. My father's family, los Alvarez, fled a Sinaloa rancho called Tetaroba during the bloody Mexican Revolution. Los Alvarez have been in the USA for over a hundred years, but there's a bunch of us still in Sinaloa.

I grew up in a Mormon cul-de-sac in a suburb called Hillcrest, the only Mexican family in a majority LDS neighborhood. My best friends were the Smith and Barney kids, and it was these white children I learned to identify with and befriend. I was an Eagle Scout in an LDS Boy Scout troop, the only Mexican American, and the only Catholic (a kind of Mexican default religion in my case). I was permitted to join the troop without any intentions of conversion and with deference for my beliefs. Don't get me wrong: I experienced racialized discrimination and slurs on a regular basis in the scout troops, from not being selected for certain positions based on assumptions about my abilities, to being called "wetback" and "dirty Mexican." I remember riding to summer camp in a crowded passenger van with scouts who taunted me with how we were packed like Mexicans on the way to work, and who joked about Mexicans having *tamales* for Christmas because they couldn't afford

13

real presents to unwrap. I was outnumbered, and I could either have laughed along or fought back. Instead, I did neither. I put my head down to focus on the book I brought for the trip, fastening on my headphones connected to my portable CD player. I tolerated them in this respect.

But I suppose I learned something about tolerance growing up among the white folks, and no doubt I met more nice people than bullies. I learned religious tolerance from the LDS community I lived among, but also tolerance for how the white kids saw me as a Mexican. For my parents, it was not important that our neighbors didn't resemble us. My father's wages from the copper mine and Army National Guard were enough to put a down payment on a house in Hillcrest, and the white folks, if nothing else, could respect that. Over time, our neighbors accepted us as a loving and hardworking American family, and we accepted them for the same. I'd say they tolerated us, but only so long as there was only one Mexican family in the neighborhood. When more *gente* began to move in decades later, many of these neighbors left.

In this context, then, I acknowledge how my contact with white people growing up has guided my language learning, and later my scholarship. That is, I was different from the white young people of my neighborhood, where I negotiated identity through different registers of English, and only English. I was also different from the Mexican American folks at my school, with whom I also negotiated my identity largely in English, but with some Spanish as well. This in-betweenness is still something I negotiate now as a professor, as a privileged Mexican American struggling to maintain and negotiate my Latinx and American cultural identities under constant cultural and linguistic confidences and insecurities. This is what I know of what I think I am, who I've become, and, of course, where it is I hope to go. But I must also check my privileges as well. Dealing with the social privileges I'm granted with being an assimilated American of Mexican descent permits me certain gifts: the ability to recast my challenges of my diminished Mexican identity and emergent bilingualism as gifts is one such privilege. My white skin and being a straight male have also helped too, *claro*.

My parents of course are fully bilingual; Spanish their home language. None of my four siblings speak Spanish. I speak Spanish with an *acento gringuense*, and mostly in the present tense. I'm ashamed of this. And when I speak to Spanish speakers, I censor myself in fear. My Spanish is a poor, *pocho* Spanish. "The *pocho*," explains Gloria Anzaldúa, "is an anglicized Mexican or American of Mexican origin who speaks Spanish with an accent characteristic of North Americans and who distorts and reconstructs the language according to the influence of English" (78). Anglicized, assimilated, culturally detached: *eso sí que es* (S : O : C : K : S—*pocho* trick). The larger picture for me is this: I've always been different from many of the Mexican-

American people whom I've known, but also slightly different from the Anglo people I've known as well.

"A sandwich," my cousin Marta in Mexico City once said about the situation.

"*Una torta*," I responded.

My parents learned English at elementary school in Bisbee, Arizona, where both grew up in blue-collar working families renting copper company homes. My parents both recall being punished into learning English; my father vividly tells of being forced to stand behind the classroom door until he "decided" to speak the "American way" (my father's words from an interview I conducted with him). Discrimination in Bisbee during the 1950s was so terrible that Mexicans who worked at the copper mine earned lower wages reserved for "non-whites." Yet there were rare spaces reserved in the "white" category for Mexicans who acculturated well, Mexicans who conformed to the dominant culture which emphasized monolingual English spoken with an American accent. Mexicans who looked and sounded like they spoke "the American way."

My parents, acting out of survival, internalized this model of speaking American domination, and as a result of their labors to be integrated and accepted as Americans, they fully participated in the U.S. acculturation of their children. That I'm of the one-percent of Mexican Americans who earned a PhD testifies to the generational success of my family's absorption of dominant social forces that continue to structure American culture into this century. This last privilege I'm granted is the reason for my research.

I have conducted long-term ethnographies of Mexican and Mexican-American families at after-school programs in New York City and Kentucky. I pursued a sociolinguistic examination of bilingual interaction and grassroots community organizing in order to better understand the literacy practices I observed, but also the intergenerational, transnational lives of families and their educational pursuits. At both sites, I witnessed how bilingual learning could be cultivated by parents despite English-only ideologies circulating among them and how trusted mentors could build sustained emotional connections to folks, what I describe as *confianza*. I experienced bilingualism in families instilling cultural confidence and also two-way relationships grounded in care.

For Mexican immigrant children, the process of becoming American largely happens via schooling. Immigrant parents understand that being in the United States means that their children will be raised by the nation's institutions to be American. Hard-working Mexican parents trust in schooling for cultivating educational capital amongst their children, later to be exchanged for economic advantages and greater chances for social mobility. This trust, however, is not always *en confianza*. Trust in schools can be difficult, especially when schools might not make the effort to build trust with students and their communities. Listen to the *jovenes*, you'll hear this story, one that has schools as sites of hope, fear, and pressure. Listen to these stories, they are the immigrant bargain that youth live.

My Mexican-American bargain has been different from the *jovenes* I have listened to in my research, but I can relate to the sense of being between. I can relate to the pressure felt by the children of immigrants feeling between cultures and social classes. When I tell people that my parents Robert and Anna clean offices for a living, and that I know what it feels like to work, really work, I remind myself that I'm nostalgic for my roots and the people and times in my life that shaped me. I'm constantly waging a battle within myself in regard to my class and culture and the class and culture I find myself occupying now, and its accompanying guilt for being someone so different from what I've known growing up. I've come a long way from my blue-collar, Arizonan upbringing to where I am, to be able to critique my *pochismo*. I fear that the values I gained from my working-class roots will resemble faint memories as I vault ahead of the superficial expectations of me, a Mexican-American academic, in a discipline, English, where Latinx *gente* are largely underrepresented. And yet, the pride I have for learning more about where my family came from, about their struggles, especially the struggles of my grandparents who migrated for a better future for me before I was ever born, makes me grateful for the opportunities I have had and the experiences I can share with youth and families with powerful hopes guiding them in the uphill battles they face, *en confianza*.

References

Alvarez, R. (2011, June 6). Personal interview.

Anzaldúa, G. (2007). *Borderlands/La frontera: The new mestiza* (3rd ed.). San Francisco, CA: Aunt Lute Books, 2007.

PART I

DEVELOPMENTAL ENGLISH AND BRIDGE PROGRAMS

Chapter 1

Translingualism and ALP

A Rhetorical Model for Bordered Latinx Writers

Lucas Corcoran and Caroline Wilkinson

Introduction

At New Jersey City University (NJCU), over one-third of the student population identifies as Hispanic or Latinx. Although the university's mission statement relates directly to "cultivating an understanding of community diversity"
("Mission Statement," 2016), monolingual assumptions regarding language and
literacy remain embedded in the developmental writing program through
institutionalized attitudes about grammar and Standard Written English (SWE).

The English department has labeled its developmental writing curriculum as an "Accelerated Learning Program" (ALP), a title that hopes to align
this curriculum with innovative pedagogical models developed primarily for
two-year colleges. However, as composition instructors who regularly teach
NJCU's version of ALP, Caroline, as junior full-time NJCU faculty, and
Lucas, as part-time NJCU faculty and a doctoral candidate in Composition/
Rhetoric Studies at the Graduate Center, CUNY, we believe that this writing
curriculum does not acknowledge the rhetorical and linguistic expertise of
NJCU's multilingual students with assignments or discussions about being
multilingual. Rather, it tacitly treats students' linguistic repertoires that fall
outside the range of SWE as deficits. By implicitly, and oftentimes explicitly,
disregarding students' multilingualism, we argue that this iteration of ALP,
despite its progressive aspirations, still operates within a monolingual framework that continually reverts back to default developmental writing pedagogy:

19

students must first learn grammar "correctly" before they can learn rhetorical strategies and genre-based writing skills.

This "default" approach to developmental writing stands in contrast to the Conference on College Composition and Communication's 1974 statement, reaffirmed in 2014, "Students' Rights to Their Own Language" (SRTOL), which states: "Language scholars long ago denied that the myth of a standard American dialect has any validity. The claim that any one dialect is unacceptable amounts to an attempt of one social group to exert its dominance over another." As much as this statement directs instructors and writing program administrators to acknowledge students' linguistic repertoires, other national statements guiding WPA work, such as the "WPA Outcomes Statement for First-Year Composition," do not address the linguistic diversity of students, but rather concentrate on the technological advancement that transforms first-year writing (Council, 2014). In contrast, our approach to ALP, and to developmental writing in general, is a translingual one that hopes to realize the goals of SRTOL. We question the default division between language and rhetoric in the composition classroom by demonstrating the educational benefits of developing a critical awareness of how rhetoric informs students' diverse language and literate identities.

This chapter explores one writing assignment—what we call a language autoethnography—in the ALP English Composition I classroom. We explain how this assignment provides instructors with a simple way of introducing translingual practices to language and literacy in their classrooms, although monolingual ideology might remain operative throughout their writing program or university. In terms of assessment, this assignment stresses a labor-based paradigm: since we asked students think beyond the borders of what might count as acceptable language in a writing classroom, we did not assess students' work qualitatively, but rather in terms of the work they put into writing, revising, and reflecting critically on their drafts.

This chapter also recognizes that contingent labor staffs the majority of composition sections in U.S. colleges. Pedagogies and assignments that outright challenge status quo methods of teaching can often pose a serious risk to the livelihood of part-time faculty. Thus, we have designed this assignment model with the hope that it might become easily incorporated in a variety of curricula, ranging from default current-traditional ones to more progressive approaches to composition/rhetoric pedagogy. In order to contextualize this assignment, we describe NJCU's history, the student population, and the university's writing program. Taking recent scholarship on translingualism as a starting point, we argue that rhetoric and language are symbiotic and co-constitutive. A move that, we hope, reframes our Latinx students as rhetoricians, and distances language pedagogy from a reductive focus on a narrowly defined notion of grammar. Drawing from student essays and interviews with two student writers who identify as Latinx in our two ALP English Composition I courses, we demonstrate how the translingual focus of the language autoethnography assignment can begin to relocate the learning goals of a "default" developmental writing curriculum away from a monolingual pedagogy focused solely on the transmission of a singular variety of English and toward a dialogic, student-centered pedagogy predicated on the development of students' meta-linguistic and meta-rhetorical awareness.

New Jersey City University: "Self-Made Starts Here."

New Jersey City University (NJCU), a public university based in Jersey City, New Jersey, is located in the second most populous city in New Jersey behind Newark. Situated in the shadows of Manhattan's financial center, Jersey City itself is a unique metropolitan area, with many of its residents living in New Jersey but commuting daily to work in New York. It is a diverse and linguistically heterogeneous city where 54.5% of Jersey City citizens are speakers of a language other than English (LOTE). At least one-fifth (20.5%) of the population speak Spanish, with Tagalog, Hindi, and Arabic being the three most common languages after English and Spanish (United States Census, 2015).

A smaller state school, with 6,317 undergraduate students, NJCU itself displays the same level of diversity as Jersey City: Thirty-five percent of its students identify as Hispanic, 23% as White, 21% as African American, 14% as Other, and 7% as Asian ("Profile," 2016). However, NJCU keeps no records of the language diversity present on campus. Because of the diverse population it serves, it has been classified as a Minority-Serving Institution and a Hispanic-Serving Institution, as well.

NJCU was founded in 1927 as a teacher training college under the name New Jersey State Normal School at Jersey City, and it adopted its present name in 1998. Its mission statement focuses on providing "a diverse student population with an excellent university education," and it pledges that NJCU "is committed to the improvement of the educational, intellectual, cultural, socio-economic, and physical environment of the surrounding region and beyond" ("Mission Statement," 2016). Hence, the university's constitutive identity depends upon the local community, as so many of the students come from the Jersey City area. On its website and on billboards and buses across downtown Jersey City, the university's slogan tailors to Jersey City's working-class population by advertising to potential students that "Self-made starts here." Most of the students attending NJCU indeed are first-generation college students with 76% of them receiving financial aid for college ("Profile,"

2016). Accordingly, NJCU represents itself as a place for students from diverse backgrounds to come and thrive, so they can receive a quality education and also enhance their upward social mobility.

The Composition Sequence at NJCU

Through a university-wide mandate to use SAT scores as the placement procedure, NJCU categorizes the majority of its students as developmental writers. In past iterations of NJCU's developmental writing program, when students were identified as developmental, they were placed into a class called Reading and Writing Across the Disciplines (RWAD). A remedial six-credit class, with only two of these credits counting toward students' graduation, RWAD served as a gate-keeping prerequisite to English Composition I and English Composition II. RWAD was only for developmental writing students, and, in order to pass the class, students had to pass a test referred to as the Writing Proficiency Exam, or WRAP. A two-hour timed test, students were given a reading and then had to answer a prompt about that reading. If students passed the WRAP exam, and RWAD in general, they would move on to the "regular" English Composition I class. Students all together could end up taking up to 14 credit hours of composition at NJCU. Like many institutions, in the last five years NJCU decided to decrease the number of developmental courses both in composition and math because they are seen as bottleneck courses—by administrators and students alike—that hamper both student recruitment and retention. Therefore, the English department eventually cut RWAD from NJCU's composition sequence.

In order to retain a developmental writing course in our writing program in response to the English department's belief that developmental writing is needed and the administration's belief in retention, NJCU's Composition Committee decided to implement an Accelerated Learning Program (ALP), modeled on the ALP sequence at the Community College of Baltimore County (CCBC). According to CCBC, the ALP model should function as "a form of mainstreaming" that works to "raise the success rates and lower the attrition rates for students placed in developmental writing" ("What is ALP?," 2016). A progressive approach to teaching composition to a diverse student population, CCBC's ALP program focuses on having a variety of students who are in mainstream first-year composition. Administrators at CCBC designed their ALP program so that half of the class would be "regular" composition students, and half of the class would be developmental writers as designated by the institution. At CCBC, ALP students meet in the English composition class with the "mainstream" students *and* a companion class only for them that "functions as a workshop to provide the support the basic writers need to succeed in English 101" ("What is ALP?," 2016). According to CCBC's model, students pay for six credits, but only receive three credits on their transcripts.

NJCU's ALP class differs significantly from the CCBC model. At NJCU, any student whom the institution deems as a developmental writer is accordingly placed in an ALP course. On the other hand, any student who is labeled a "mainstream" composition student takes a 4-credit English Composition 101 class, without the ALP lab model attached. Therefore, NJCU students do not receive one of the main benefits of the CCBC model because they do not take classes with more advanced student writers. ALP students at NJCU end up taking classes *only* with other developmental writers. In addition to this, they also take and pay for six credits of courses but receive only four credits for the course.

NJCU's ALP model also continues to retain some of the "developmental" features of its ill-fated RWAD course: in order to receive credit for ALP English Composition I, students no longer must pass a high-stakes timed writing test, but they have to receive a passing grade for their coursework from their instructor, as well as submit a final portfolio made up of two revised essays. These revised essays are graded according to a rubric that NJCU's Composition Committee created, which focuses on thesis, evidence, organization, and grammar, and which also clearly assumes the five-paragraph essay as the paradigmatic academic genre. The rubric gives equal weight to each of the four categories, so each part is 25% of the final grade, and, thus, we feel that it inevitably shifts an assessor's attention away from writers' overall rhetorical efficacy and toward writers' adherence to or deviance from institutionalized stylistic norms. This assessment's technique reinforces a norm that writing comprises the decontextualized deployment of a singular language variety that does not need to be rhetorically situated. Although NJCU's ALP model was an improvement over the past course sequence that included the remedial RWAD course, since developmental writers now take fewer courses overall, it still functions as a gate-keeping method to keep multilingual students on the wrong side of the "mainstream" composition border.

The Historical Advent of Monolingualism

Although composition/rhetoric scholars working under the banner of "translingualism" disagree over the precise meaning of the term, they remain united in their critique of monolingualism. Embedded in pedagogical practices, educational institutions, and language policies, monolingualism conceives of languages as homogeneous and discretely bounded entities primarily tied to geographies and cultures. Monolingualism constitutes what sociolinguistics have described as a "metadiscursive regime": any widely circulated method of representing language that, combined with material occurrences of everyday language usage, provides a mechanism for defining language in such a way that supports *status quo* hierarchical distributions of cultural and material capital (Makoni & Pennycook, 2007, p. 2).

Metadiscursive regimes are discourses that have the power to mark both overtly and subtly some language practices as legitimate and others as marginal. The term "monolingualism" points to a metadiscursive regime developed in conjunction with European colonialism and emerging capitalism in the early modern era that sought to codify the linguistic practices of the ideal bourgeois subject and to juxtapose these linguistic practices with the those of the inferior non-European Other. As Flores and García (2013) have argued, the "creation of a standardized language shifted the focus of language from its communicative aspects toward a focus on correct form as an expression of a static superior national identity" (p. 244). As European colonialism continued to perpetuate the metadiscursive regime of well-defined language categories as a tool to classify and subjugate colonized peoples, monolingual ideologies worked to define language not as a sociocultural practice continually remade in manifold speech acts, but instead as stable codes that speakers could either follow properly or improperly. The codification of language provided (and continues to provide) an effective and subtle procedure for inscribing subaltern distinctions into the very nature of speakers' subjectivity, by marking their linguistic repertoire as "functional" but not "correct."

Translingualism interrogates what Horner (2011) has highlighted as monolingualism's continued maintenance of discrete language codes, even in conceptions of language that acknowledge the existence and the validity of "non-standard" varieties. In Horner's (2011) terms, this "Archipelago Model of Linguistic Heterogeneity" conceives of both national languages (e.g., English and Spanish) and varieties of languages (e.g., "college" English and "street" English) as separate linguistic islands, so to speak, that language users can shuttle between but can never inhabit simultaneously. In this metaphor, each "island" has its own language ecology, and travelers between them remain well advised not to introduce a foreign language species from one into another.

Within a pedagogical framework, the "archipelago model" that Horner critiques acknowledges the validity of different linguistic codes that students bring with them into the classroom but insists that they learn to use each code in its so-called appropriate context. Each code "has its specific, fixed, and appropriate sphere of use: French in France, English in the U.S., academic writing in school, texting for cell phones" (2011, p. 13). Continuing the legacy of monolingualism, this "archipelago" way of thinking about language inevitably splits up students' language and literate identities into arbitrary linguistic categories, and, even while acknowledging the legitimacy of these categories, stigmatizes a large variety of students' language practices as inappropriate for academic settings.

A Translingual Perspective

The translingual turn in composition/rhetoric studies has challenged writing instructors and writing programs in U.S. universities and community colleges to interrogate pedagogical practices and student assessment strategies that install a privileged variety of English while enacting an erasure of all others. Teacher-scholars hoping to implement a translingual approach have advocated for a "disposition of openness and inquiry" toward language difference in the classroom (Horner, Lu, Royster, & Trimbur, 2011, p. 311), which moves beyond monolingual ideology and its codified linguistic boundaries established by the continuing influence of European colonialism. Situating itself in direct contradistinction to the fixity of monolingualism, translingualism argues that "the seeming regularities of language can be best understood not as the pre-existing rules determining language practices, but, rather, as the products of those practices: an effect of the ongoing process of sedimentation in which engagement of language practices participates" (Lu & Horner, 2013, p. 588). Translingualism re-conceives of languages not as firmly anchored codes but as *practices*: the day-to-day communicative activities in which people take part in order to make meaning in their respective lifeworlds (Pennycook, 2010). Within this practice-based orientation, language becomes an iterative and improvisatory performance in which speakers and writers convey themselves in response to the affordances that obtain within the dialogic interplay between their subjectivities and rhetorical situation—a process which Lorimer Leonard (2014) has labelled as "rhetorical attunement."

A translingual approach to language and literacy has also strongly critiqued traditional models of bilingualism that conceive of bilingual speakers as "switching" between two different and mutually independent language systems, and that consider bilingual speakers as fluent insofar that they can operate each language system as a "native" speaker without any interference from the other. This "dual" notion of bilingualism, however, has given way to a "dynamic" model that positions bilingual speakers as continually operating from a *singularly unified* repertoire that contains linguistic features traditionally associated, through the processes of geopolitical territorialization, with particular nation-states. The dynamic model of bilingualism argues that, from the perspective of bilingual individuals, no hard-and-fast boundary obtains between the languages that they speak. Instead, "dynamic bilingualism is like an all-terrain vehicle (ATV) with individuals using their entire linguistic repertoire to adapt to both the ridges and craters of communication in uneven (and unequal) interactive terrains" (Garcia & Wei, 2014, p. 16). In this sense, *all* individuals, including monolingual ones, possess a single array of heteroglossic language resources that they can strategically employ in order to adapt to different communicative environments. Thus, the denial of dynamic bilingualism can have particularly harmful effects on multilingual students in the college writing classroom. By not allowing students to have access to the *full* range of their language resources—including those traditionally associated with LOTEs—institutions prevent multilingual writers from accessing their full linguistic potential in their written work. A translingual approach to writing, then, would recognize the entire range of multilingual students' linguistic repertoires as a valid semiotic resource in the composition process and as a useful tool in creating a rhetorical effective text.

Critical Rhetorical Awareness, Multilingualism, and Language Autoethnographies

Developmental writing at NJCU has separated, both implicitly and explicitly, linguistic knowledge from rhetorical knowledge in the implementation of its ALP composition course sequence. Although, in CCBC's original version, ALP pedagogy hoped to create more inclusive writing classrooms by "mainstreaming" developmental writers, NJCU's version of ALP has functioned so far as a subtle form of what Matsuda (2006) has described as "linguistic containment." The university misuses ALP courses to cordon off the language of students whom it has deemed as lacking the appropriate variety of English to participate in academic life. NJCU's use of ALP's progressive pedagogy to re-deploy subtly the remediation strategies of developmental writing glosses over the rich linguistic diversity on NJCU's campus. It also can disadvantage NJCU's large multilingual student population. The placement mechanism endorses the tacit but pervasive belief that students must first develop certain *linguistic* proficiencies before they can begin to develop "higher order" *rhetorical* proficiencies. Embedded in this assumption resides the idea that rhetorical strategies in the writing process depend essentially upon a more elementary linguistic knowledge, that students need to acquire the linguistic "building blocks" of vocabulary and grammar before they can move onto to the more complex study of genre and rhetorical situations.

In contrast, our approach to ALP, and to developmental writing in general, questions this division between language and rhetoric. Following current scholarship in translingualism, we contend that language and rhetoric co-construct one another, and that the rhetorical nature of daily language practices—especially those of multilingual students—take place within highly nuanced language ecologies that require both skilled linguistic and rhetorical dexterity in order to communicate effectively. Our approach has thus led us to articulate new learning objectives for ALP at NJCU. Instead of a developmental writing course with an exclusionary focus on the mastery of a singular variety of English ("College" English, "SWE," "Academic" English, etc.), we see ALP as a space where students can begin to develop critical rhetorical and critical linguistic awareness. Our model aims to help students refine their ability to write on an abstract level about their language and literacy practices and to reflect critically on how these practices relate to wider social, cultural, and political contexts on both a local and global scale.

In order to shift away from a code-acquisition model of developmental writing, Lucas created a "language autoethnography" assignment that asks students to analyze their everyday language as a series of highly contextualized rhetorical situations in order to discover how audience, genre, medium, goal, and voice influence their language usage in a variety of communicative situations. Drawing on Alim's (2007) notion of "Critical Hip-Hop Language Pedagogies" along with scholarship on "translanguaging" in the K-12 setting (Hesson, Seltzer, & Woodley, 2014), we pose the language autoethnography as a student-centered method for teaching rhetoric and meta-linguistic vocabularies to developmental writers through emphasizing the rhetorical expertise and linguistic creativity that students already have in hand.

Before assigning students the language autoethnographies, we first introduced a module on rhetorical situations in each of our classes. Based on our own teaching practices, we examined with our students' various texts—ranging from memes found on the internet to poems about the environment—in terms of how the authors of these texts composed in response to their particular rhetorical situations. We distributed handouts to our students that broke the rhetorical situation down into the five separate categories of purpose, audience, genre, stance, and media/design, so students could quickly begin to compare and contrast a variety of rhetorical situations in class by utilizing concrete and repeatable terminology. Once we felt that our students had a firm grasp on the notion of the rhetorical situation, students during in-class discussions began to break down their own daily language and literacy practices as a series of rhetorical situations and to use the same terminology of purpose, audience, genre, stance, and media/design in describing how their language shifts, as they move about between home, work, and university life.

For their written language autoethnographies, we asked our students to connect a series of 2 or 3 concrete examples of rhetorical situations into

a single narrative in which they could see themselves using different varieties of English or LOTEs in direct response to the communicative exigencies
of their environments. The assignment page that we distributed to students
asked them to make two major rhetorical moves in their writing. First, it
invited each student to:

> reflect in detail about how **audience, purpose, genre, stance,**
> **medium/design** shape your language use and choices in these
> concrete episodes. Please feel free to use these rhetorical terms,
> and also feel free not to use them. However, if you chose *not* to
> use them your story should still illustrate to your reader how
> **audience, purpose, genre, stance, medium/design** influence your
> language use and language choices.

Second, the assignment page explicitly and directly encouraged all students
to use their complete linguistic repertoires, and it especially encouraged multilingual students to use LOTEs in order to express their linguistic creativity
and linguistic accomplishments. Furthermore, it asked students to reflect
on what kind of rhetorical decisions "codemeshing" (Canagarajah, 2011)
prompted them to make:

> This is your language story. So please feel free to use any elements
> of your language repertoire to tell it. This means that you have
> every right to include languages other than English (LOTEs) and
> "non-standard" varieties of English. This assignment gives a chance
> to showcase your language talent and your language expertise,
> even if people don't usually consider this talent and expertise as
> "school" English, or even if this talent and expertise is in a LOTE.
> When you include LOTEs or a "non-standard" variety of English
> you should ask yourself:
>
> • How can I incorporate these elements into my writing so that
>   they are rhetorically effective?
>
> • Should I "translate" or will context clue the reader into the
>   meaning?
>
> • Should I italicize words from LOTEs or "non-standard" variet-
>   ies of English?
>
> All of these questions are yours to answer as a writer. The deci-
> sions that you make in response to these questions will show

both your creativity and your understanding of the assignment's particular rhetorical situation.

By prompting students to reflect on how language and rhetoric interact in meaningful ways (with often very real material consequences) in their lives, we hoped to implement an assignment readily accessible for students that utilized both personal narrative writing and the entirety of students' linguistic repertoires in order to place language and rhetoric in a symbiotic relationship with one another, while, at the same time, positioning students as language experts by having them draw on their own authentic linguistic experiences. Thus, through this assignment, we aimed to foster a rhetorical awareness with students that could bridge the "gap" between their pragmatic language and literacy practices and those that the university will come to expect from them. In this manner, the language autobiography also draws on the work of critical pedagogy. Shor's (1992) idea of a "third idiom" sought to find common ground between students' discourse communities and those of instructors, by setting aside as much as possible the received expectations of what counts as "proper" and "improper" language in the composition classroom. By stressing the ubiquity of rhetoric in all language acts, including the ones that occur outside of the classroom, this assignment constructs rhetoric as a "third idiom" through teaching a rhetorical meta-vocabulary that helps establish a shared terminology between students and instructors, which allows them to describe a wide variety of texts and language acts. Thus, the language autoethnography asks students to practice the necessary critical thinking skills that can locate rhetoric as a meta-concept large enough to describe language and literacy practices ranging from the hyper-condensed textual and visual literacies on apps like Snapchat to translingual language practices to the discursive norms of college-level research paper. This assignment looks to situate students' prior expertise in language and rhetoric on a continuum with academic literacies and discourses instead of walling it off as something inappropriate for the university. We believe that this helps shift the paradigm of developmental writing away from a pedagogical agenda of linguistic formalism centered on the transmission of "correct" forms to students and toward the development of students' acuity in understanding, analyzing, and writing in diverse rhetorical situations.

Two Student Experiences

Alicia

A sophomore majoring in Finance, Alicia speaks and writes in both English and Spanish. She speaks English at the university and at work but speaks both English and Spanish at home with her family, specifically since she is trying to help her mom learn English. Alicia grew up learning mostly Spanish from both her parents until she began primary school. In her language autoethnography, Alicia focused on the differences in language that make up her extended family:

> When I talk to my grandmother on my mother's side, I speak differently than I would to my grandmother on my father's side. The reason is because my mom is Dominican. There are certain words that are hard to translate to English because it might be 'Dominican slang' or just words that Dominicans use. When my grandmother comes to my house [. . .], I begin to speak Spanish better because she does not understand English so my vocabulary has to match hers in order for her to understand me.

Alicia explains how much of this concentration on language deals with the audience of her grandmother. It was a habit for Alicia to begin to speak Spanish, so her grandmother would feel more comfortable. In her interview, Alicia states that the shifting of languages relates to the audience of her mother as well: "I speak English and Spanish at home, but my mom is Dominican so she is fluent more in Spanish so she speaks to me in Spanish and I respond to her in English so she can like learn." Alicia explains how she speaks English to her mother for the purpose of helping her mother learn English better. This purpose is so Alicia's mom will eventually lean on her less when they are out in public. Through class discussions and writing the language autoethnography, Alicia discovered how both the rhetorical notions of purpose and audience apply to her daily language life. In the interview, she explained that being able to work with different audiences effectively was a major benefit of being multilingual.

Alicia also explains her experiences of being multilingual in a local grocery store: "If I'm shopping and I see someone like needs help like saying a certain word in English and they can't really get it out so I'll help them. For example, at the register, if they have an issue or something, I'll usually help out if I see them really struggling." Alicia saw that she was able to work with different audiences depending on language because she was multilingual. She also explained she had empathy for these customers because her mom had been in similar situations. Thus, Alicia perceived a benefit of speaking multiple languages in that she was able to help people more than if she was monolingual in situations such as in the grocery store. Multilingual students seeing their uses of multiple languages as a benefit would probably seem obvious to composition scholars. However, Alicia and many other students in Caroline's class did not see themselves as being multilingual as a benefit until they talked about this assignment in this course. Many of Caroline's students did not explicitly tell her they were multilingual because some of them worried she would think they were ESL and that they struggled with grammar. The conversation on students' multilingual identities occurred in conferences and class discussion after the language autoethnography assignment and toward the end of the semester when there was a level of trust developed between the instructor and students. Students' reluctance to disclose their multilingualism reveals both the entrenched stigmatization that comes along with ESL and developmental writing courses and students' warranted reluctance to get caught within a complex dragnet of remedial courses. It also exhibits a common assumption regarding the role of instructors in the writing classroom: their default job remains the surveillance and segregation of students based on perceived linguistic difference. Both of us as educators assumed, though, that if we gave our multilingual students a chance to use their whole linguistic repertoires, they would be excited to do so and actively participate. Yet what we found in this assignment is that students are ready to admit that they speak a LOTE but remain completely hesitant to produce anything besides SWE or anything that highlights their multilingual experience. Monolingual ideology influences not only educators' but also students' attitudes toward multilingualism.

Alicia's essay also concentrated on the way she looks compared to the languages she speaks. Alicia wrote, "When I talk to my friends, they begin to tell me that I have an accent because the Spanish language tends to linger, but when I'm not speaking Spanish, no one ever knows that I understand it because I do not look Hispanic." The connection Alicia recognized between Spanish and her identity was part of the reading associated with the autoethnography assignment. The class discussion of Gloria Anzaldúa's "How to Tame a Wild Tongue" influenced Alicia where she acknowledged the argument behind Anzaldúa's work that language and identity are connected, but Alicia also saw through a rhetorical analysis of how Anzaldúa wrote her own article. The Spanish in Anzaldúa's writing worked as a way to invite more audiences who speak Spanish but also to marginalize audiences that only understand Standard Written English because they would not have knowledge of the Spanish words used in the essay. Alicia determined the connection between language and identity in Anzaldúa's article through her rhetorical analysis of it, which demonstrates the contribution of the language autoethnography assignment to students not only expressing themselves, but also analyzing other texts and identities.

José

José, a 19-year-old freshman, moved with his mother from Costa Rica to New Jersey ten years ago. Although he feels technically proficient in Spanish, José prefers to speak English, since he uses it the most with his friends at school and his coworkers at his job at a local supermarket. José has one younger sister, born in New Jersey, who, according to him, does not put much effort into keeping up her Spanish. As a result, José often finds himself language brokering between his sister and his Spanish-speaking mother, translating his sister's school and medical forms for her. José says that this role in his family has helped him keep up his Spanish, and in his language autoethnography, he regrets not having had someone perform the same role for him when he first arrived in New Jersey and began going to school in English for the first time. He reflected on the problems that he initially had with schoolwork: "Starting school in a brand-new language meant that I would be on my own and have to figure out the assignments and work on my own. As much as she would want to help me my mom just was not able to help me with homework as much as she would have wanted to due to this language barrier that was being built." José's rhetorical choice here of describing his new educational environment in New Jersey as actively constructing a language barrier between his mother and him subtly points to the language hurdles that he and his mother would have to overcome together in the years ahead. To cope with the lack of language support at home during his early schooling, José developed new strategies for achieving academic success: "Often my main source of information to figure out how to do my assignments would be my memory. I would have to recall specific actions or words from the lesson that day in school. It would often be hard to recall these moments because starting out I wouldn't understand what they would say in class." Eventually, José began to feel comfortable using English to the point where now he has developed his language resources into a form of dynamic bilingualism, seamlessly using a single repertoire of both English and Spanish. He explains in his interviews: "it's not like I have to think: 'Oh how am I gonna say this in Spanish.' I just kind of do it. Like, if I go to talk to someone in English right after I'm talking to someone in Spanish, I don't have to think about like a translation. It just kind of happens." José, however, sees his early difficulty with language in an educational setting as having a lasting effect on his writing process. He described himself as always having trouble starting a persuasive essay, especially timed ones for standardized tests: "I always try to look at things from like different angles [. . .] With the persuasive essay, I would try to look at one point of view, then from the other, and then try to compare it, and then I would waste time on that." When asked if he thought his desire to give equal weight to different sides of an issue might have anything to do with his bilingualism, José responded:

> I just kind of like looking at it from all different angles to see basically how someone might feel about it. It kind of goes back to back when I didn't know English. It was like weird someone talking to me in English, because I didn't know what they were saying [. . .] That's why I don't like to talk to someone in English if they don't speak it because I'm like I know how you feel. It feels bad. So I want to look at how someone might feel about a situation.

José resists composing pro/con persuasive essays, precisely the ones that the ALP portfolio rubric mandates and assesses, because this *monologic* form of argumentative writing also silently endorses a *monolingual* orientation. José's past lived experiences of communicative struggles as a linguistic outsider have led him to resist rhetorical strategies that aim to invalidate others' points of view. Instead his multilingual background has compelled him to prefer a *dialogic* approach to argumentation and rhetoric:

> Like you know how they say like there's two sides to a coin? I want to see both sides because I know what it feels like to be on the other side. When you think like someone else doesn't understand you, you're just trying to get your point across. But it's like talking to a wall. They just don't understand. So I try to look at it from their point of view, and like see their thought process and figure out so we can come to an agreement.

José's comment here reveals how traditional college essay writing might implicitly favor monolingual students, not only linguistically but rhetorically as well. In contrast, the language autoethnography intends to provide students in a developmental writing course with an assignment that positions them as already established expert language user and rhetoricians. It does this by inviting them to think critically about their language and literacy practices and by asking them to give an explicit account of their embedded rhetorical and linguistic dexterity. José continued on to reflect that the language auto-ethnography "shows that there are different ways that you speak to different people. Regarding how you want to sound and come across you use those different ways to talk."

Conclusion

There were similarities in Alicia's and José's responses to the language auto-ethnography assignment in that both students mentioned a purpose to help their family members with English. Both also recognized the rhetorical strategies inherent in negotiating multiple languages in their everyday lives from talking with friends and family members to writing a paper for their English class to assisting a stranger in the grocery store. The assignment offered both Alicia and José, and many other students in the classes, a chance to reflect on their linguistic repertoires and connect with other students in the course who also speak multiple languages through class discussion.

This reflection was helpful, but it also demonstrated the extent to which multilingual students in NJCU's composition courses seem to be more comfortable not sharing that they are multilingual for fear of the assumptions made about their proficiency in Standard Written English and their own literate identities. This reticence demonstrates a culture of monolingualism not only in higher education, but prevalent for most of these students' school experiences. Our university represents a unique space to combat these attitudes because of its status as an HSI and an MSI. However, because of the histories of how composition, particularly developmental writing courses, have been taught in the past, it is difficult to change instructor attitudes on the place of language in the composition classroom and its connection to rhetoric. At a site like NJCU where the majority of the instructors who teach writing are adjuncts, monolingualism really is an *ideology*, in the sense that there are no top-down controls mandating a certain way of treating student language and literacy. Instead, it is an embedded belief system that keeps perpetuating itself.

Although most developmental writing programs, and writing programs in general, will continue to approach composition from a monolingual point of view, this assignment offers one point of resistance, where students can fully demonstrate their linguistic repertoires and reflect upon their embedded rhetorical expertise. By beginning with an assignment like this, instructors can use the approach as a catalyst for longer assignment sequences and to generate further discussions on the connections between language and rhetoric. Assignment modification acts as a way to resist the monolingual tendencies of writing programs, especially for tenure-track and part-time faculty who are not in a position to change the curriculum or assessment of the writing program as a whole. For instructors and writing program administrators, this assignment offers a place to begin to approach students as experts in their own right, and it has the potential to renew conversations in writing programs and universities about what it might mean for a department with the word "English" written above the door to serve a primarily multilingual student population.

References

Alim, H. S. (2007). Critical hip-hop language pedagogies: Combat, consciousness, and the cultural politics of communication. *Journal of Language, Identity, and Education, 6*(2), 161–176.

Anzaldúa, G. (2007). *Borderlands/La frontera: The new mestiza* (3rd ed.). San Francisco, CA: Aunt Lute Books, 2007.

Canagarajah, S. (2011). Codemeshing in academic writing: Identifying teachable strategies of translanguaging. *The Modern Language Journal, 95*(3), 401–417.

Conference on College Composition & Communication (CCCC). (1974). Students' Right to Their Own Language. Retrieved from http://www.ncte.org/library/NCTEFiles/Groups/CCCC/NewSRTOL.pdf

Council of Writing Program Administrators (2014). WPA Outcomes Statement for First-Year Composition. Retrieved from: http://wpacouncil.org/positions/outcomes.html

Flóres, N. & García, O. (2013). Linguistic third spaces in education: Teachers' translanguaging across the bilingual continuum. In D. Little, C. Leung, & P. Van Avermaet (Eds.), *Managing diversity in education: Languages, policies, pedagogies* (pp. 243–256). Bristol, UK: Multilingual Matters.

Garcia, O., & Wei, L. (2014). *Translanguaging: Language, bilingualism, and education.* London, UK: Palgrave Macmillan.

Hesson, S., Seltzer, K., & Woodley, H. H. (2014). *Translanguaging in curriculum and instruction: A CUNY-NYSIEB guide for educators.* New York: CUNY-NYSIEB, The Graduate Center, CUNY.

Horner, B. (2011). Relocating basic writing. *Journal of Basic Writing, 30*(2), 5–23.

Horner, B., Lu M., Royster, J. J., & Trimbur, J. (2011). Language difference in writing: Toward a translingual approach. *College English, 73*(3), 303–321.

Leonard, R. L. (2014). Multilingual writing as rhetorical attunement. *College English, 78*(3), 227–247.

Lu, M., & Horner, B. (2013). Translingual literacy, language difference, and matters of agency. *College English, 75*(6), 582–607.

Makoni, S., & Pennycook, A. (2007). Disinventing and reconstituting languages. In S. Makoni, & A. Pennycook (Eds.), *Disinventing and reconstituting languages* (pp. 1–41). Clevedon, UK: Multilingual Matters.

Matsuda, P. K. (2006). The myth of linguistic homogeneity in U.S. college composition. *College English, 68*(6), 637–651.

NJCU Mission Statement. (2016). Retrieved from http://www.njcu.edu/about/mission-statement NJCU Profile and Accreditations. (2016). Retrieved from http://www.njcu.edu/about/njcu-profile-and-accreditations

Pennycook, A. (2010). *Language as a local practice.* New York, New York: Routledge.

Shor, I. (1992). *Empowering education: Critical teaching for social change.* Chicago, IL: University of Chicago Press.

United States Census Bureau. (2015). Retrieved from http://www.census.gov/quickfacts/table/PST045215/3436000

What is ALP? (2016). Retrieved from http://alp-deved.org/what-is-alp-exactly/

Chapter 2

Developmental Instructors in the Contact Zone

Perspectives from Hispanic-Serving Community Colleges

Erin Doran

The scholarship on Hispanic-Serving Institutions has grown tremendously over the last five years (e.g., Cuellar, 2014; Contreras & Contreras, 2015; Núñez, Hurtado, & Calderón Galdeano, 2015; Garcia, 2016). Considering that more than half of Latinx[1] students enrolled in postsecondary institutions in the United States attend these institutions (Núñez, Crisp, & Elizondo, 2015), this is no accident. Hispanic-Serving Institutions (hereafter HSIs) are defined as two-year or four-year institutions with an undergraduate student body that is at least 25% Latinx (Núñez, Hurtado, & Calderón Galdeano, 2015).

As of the 2014–2015 academic year, there were approximately 409 HSIs in the United States (Santiago, Taylor, & Calderón Galdeano, 2016), up from approximately 189 institutions when the federal designation was created in 1992 (Calderón Galdeano, Flores, & Moder, 2012), a sign of the increase of the Latinx demographic in higher education. Hispanic-serving community colleges enroll about two-thirds of all Latinx students enrolled in the two-year sector (Santiago, Taylor, & Calderón Galdeano, 2015). Despite comprising 18% of two-year institutions in the United States (Santiago, Taylor, & Calderón Galdeano, 2015), there remains a striking dearth of research on specifically community colleges that qualify as HSIs.

Among the multiple missions of community colleges and broad access four-year institutions, including HSIs, is the mission to provide developmental education courses and services to students who arrive at their institution below college readiness levels (Boylan, Bohnam, & White, 1999; Cohen, Brawer, &

37

Kisker, 2013). Despite the intention to prepare students for college-level courses as quickly as possible, students often get stuck in developmental courses and are kept from enrolling in credit-bearing courses. In Texas, for example, only 9.5% of the cohort who entered in the fall of 2011 had graduated from their two-year college by 2014 (Texas Higher Education Coordinating Board, 2015). The purpose of this study is to present data from Project Ascender, a college success intervention for students who place into developmental education that currently operates at a number of Hispanic-serving community colleges in Texas.

Project Ascender

In the 1980s, Patricia McGrath and Felix Galaviz collaborated to address the disparities in persistence and achievement at Chabot College between Latinx students and other racial/ethnic groups ("About the Puente Program," 2018). After combing through thousands of students' transcripts, McGrath and Galaviz noticed a pattern: developmental writing was a course that Latinx students routinely struggled to complete (McGrath & Galaviz, 1996). In order to address this problem, McGrath and Galaviz developed a model that combined intensive reading and writing courses, intrusive advising, and strong mentoring to developmental students, especially Latinx students (McGrath & Galaviz, 1996). The program was called the Puente (Bridge) Project. The program now operates in 61 community colleges in California ("About the Puente Program," 2018).

In 2012, the Puente Project expanded to Texas, another state with a large Latinx population through a nonprofit organization called "Catch the Next" that oversees the program in Texas. That same year, it was reported that more than a third of Latinx community college students in the state required some type of developmental education (Complete College America, 2012). The program began with three participating colleges in the fall of 2012 and has steadily expanded each year since. Project Ascender (whose name has been recently changed to "Project Ascender" from "Dream Catchers") has provided training to 9 institutions across Texas, including one four-year institution.

The Puente model developed by McGrath and Galaviz in California and adopted in Texas is a literacy-based intervention that attends to students' writing skills, their college knowledge (Conley, 2005), and provides students with experiences aimed at increasing their likelihood to transfer to a four-year institution and complete a bachelor's degree or beyond (Our Program, n.d.). In order to carry out the program, faculty members, advisors, and program coordinators from each college undergo intensive, ongoing professional development in the form of mini-conferences, monthly conference calls with featured speakers, and support through Catch the Next. Faculty members receive training in culturally relevant pedagogy that includes exposure to various Latinx authors (e.g., Sandra Cisneros, Sergio Troncoso, and Benjamin Alire Sáenz) and specific teaching tools such as writing prompts they can use in the classroom. Regardless of their position in the program, personnel who work with Ascender students learn about two key concepts to the program: *familia* (family) and *cariño* (affection). Faculty, advisors, and mentors specifically teach with the mindset that the program is an on-campus family there to support students in the Ascender program, and through an intentional use of *cariño*, students can learn how to be successful in a college environment.

Students are recruited to the Ascender program during summer orientation sessions at the college. Faculty members and program advisors provide information to the students about the program and its commitment to providing extra support to students in their first year and beyond. Students are advised of the need to take specific paired courses in their first year as well as the out-of-class activities that are required while they are in the program. For example, most students in the program take a developmental-level integrated reading and writing (INRW) course and an education course (Learning Frameworks) their first semester. In the second semester, students take credit-bearing Composition I, and colleges differ on whether they require a second course in the spring semester.

Additionally, the program holds an evening or weekend event called *Noche de Familia* (Family Night) for students, faculty, advisors, and special guests (e.g., family members invited by the students, campus administrators, and community mentors) to celebrate the program and for family to gather more information about the program, the transfer process, and related issues such as financial aid. Students are also notified about field trips to area universities that could also entail an overnight stay in a dormitory. After the first year, the program encourages students to stay connected to the program through the Ascender Club, a student organization that participates in campus-wide activities.

Developmental Classrooms as Contact Zones

Pratt (1991) introduced the concept of the contact zone, or "social spaces where cultures meet, clash, and grapple with each other, often in contexts of highly asymmetrical relations of power, such as colonialism, slavery, or their aftermaths as they are lived out in many parts of the world today" (p. 34). Pratt mentioned the push for increased multiculturalism in education and engaging the relationships and differences among cultures in the classroom. Lu (1994) applied this metaphor specifically to the developmental writing and ESL classrooms, noting that many instructors adhere to traditional notions of correctness and error without helping students, especially those from minoritized backgrounds, develop their own ideas by drawing on the wealth of their own cultural backgrounds.

McCook (2016) expands the previous literature on contact zones, arguing that the understanding of such spaces necessitates an understanding of how these are "set within the contexts of history, language difference, orality, and power differentials" (p. 62). This project is limited by its data in that it cannot take into account how orality plays into the developmental classrooms. However, the purpose here is to understand how a historically underserved population within community colleges such as Latinx students in developmental education engage with diversity and difference on their campuses and how these interactions contribute to long-term persistence and success in college.

The community college setting is filled with contact zones as these institutions fulfill a multitude of needs and missions, including adult and basic education services (including English as a Second Language programs); transfer programs for students who want to pursue a four-year degree; career and technical education; community education for lifelong learning; and shorter certificate programs. Even Hispanic-serving community colleges are not homogeneous institutions; in this study, some of the faculty work in colleges with 90% or higher Latinx student populations (e.g., El Paso Community College and South Texas College) while others in the Gulf Coast region of Texas, specifically in the Houston area, work in colleges with large numbers of students from other racial/ethnic groups including international and immigrant populations from all over the world. Developmental students engage with a power structure—that is, the potentially gatekeeping policies and courses that restrict their enrollment (Bailey, Jeong, & Cho, 2010). Students of color in developmental writing and reading courses contend with academic discourse (Lu, 1994), and faculty who teach these students must learn how to address these literacy needs without committing the aforementioned "linguistic terrorism" (Anzaldúa, 1987, p. 58).

At the intrapersonal level, students, especially students of color and students in developmental education, arrive at college with their own identity contact zones. It is well-documented in the research literature that a large proportion of students who are placed in developmental education in college attended under-resourced K-12 schools (Gándara & Contreras, 2009; Hodara, 2015; Ignash, 1997). Students can experience a stigma with placement in developmental education, whether intentional or not (Deil-Amen & Rosenbaum, 2002), so students may be contending with feelings of being physically in college but enrolled in courses that do not actually carry college credit. Recent work on the transition from high school to college shows that the transition is a confusing one, and not all students successfully navigate the two-year and four-year systems and balance their personal lives that may include jobs and/or families with their academic ones (Ruecker, 2015). Given this complexity, it is novel to look at a program like the Ascender program that addresses students' academic skills and their ability to navigate the college environment in order to boost their likelihood of transferring to a four-year institution and completing a bachelor's degree or higher. Through the concept of the contact zone, this project looks at the ways in which the Ascender program engages various spaces of students' lives, the backgrounds of students, and the diversity of the classroom to create experiences that help students through their first year of college and beyond.

Methods

This study utilizes a basic qualitative approach (Merriam & Tisdell, 2016) to address the following research questions: First, how do Ascender faculty describe the contact zones within their classrooms, especially in relation to Latinx students? Second, how do Ascender faculty make sense of this complexity in order to boost their students' success in college-level courses?

The goal of this type of approach to the research questions is to uncover the experiences and perceptions of faculty who teach in this program and make meaning out their stories in relation to how students are served by this program. To answer these research questions, interviews were conducted with two-year college faculty teaching within the Ascender program across sites in Texas who had taught at least one class within the program in the last two academic years. Table 2.1 offers information on the faculty participants, particularly what subject area they taught.

Table 2.1. Faculty participant information

Faculty participant name	Region	Subject area taught within the Ascender program
Anthony	Border region	Integrated Reading and Writing, Composition I
Allia	Border region	Integrated Reading and Writing, Composition I, Learning Frameworks
Cynthia	Border region	Learning Frameworks
Valerie	Border region	Learning Frameworks
Frank	Border region	Learning Frameworks
Gustavo	Border region	Integrated Reading and Writing, Composition I
Nicholas	Border region	Integrated Reading and Writing, Composition I
Natalie	North Texas	Integrated Reading and Writing, Composition I
Raquel	East Texas	Integrated Reading and Writing, Composition I
Mary	East Texas	Integrated Reading and Writing, Composition I
Vivienne	East Texas	Integrated Reading and Writing, Composition I
Gloria	East Texas	Learning Frameworks

After IRB approval was received, faculty across all the participating colleges were sent a recruitment email inviting them to participate in this study. Participants were also recruited at two professional development meetings, a monthly webinar and the Ascender Fall Institute. Approximately 35 faculty members were approached for interviews, and 12 responded to participate in this study. Interviews lasted on average one hour and took place in person or via Skype or telephone. A semi-structured interview protocol was used to guide the meetings (Merriam & Tisdell, 2016), and these meetings were audio-recorded once informed consent (written and verbal) was received. After the interviews, the audio files were transcribed, and to ensure trust-worthiness, the researcher utilized member-checking (Hays & Singh, 2012) by providing the participants with the opportunity to review and edit their own interview transcripts.

Transcripts were analyzed in two phases using an a priori technique based on the concept of contact zones. Initial coding (Saldaña, 2015) was used in the first phase to get a sense of the contents of the interviews and what connections emerged between them. More specifically, codes were developed around discussions of students' identities and identity development, engage-ment with difference, and instructors' awareness and descriptions of how they address students' needs and interactions. Pattern coding (Saldaña, 2015) was used in a second round in order to break down the codes into categories or patterns (e.g., classroom practices, attitudes, teaching philosophies).

Findings

Acknowledging the Contact Zones

The first step in engaging with the contact zones of a developmental writing classroom is to acknowledge and understand where the zones actually are and what they mean. Put another way, instructors need to understand who the students in their classroom are as well as what their backgrounds and past experiences are. Each participant was asked to describe the students who enrolled in Ascender on their campus. These students were representative of their mainstream student body, and many categories were repeated across the sites: First-generation, students who work, English Language Learners, students in families that are migrant and/or undocumented, students of all ages, and some of whom have specific familial obligations like parents they care for or children of their own. Instructors close to the Texas-México border noted that some of their students lived in México and crossed the border each day to attend college. The faculty from North and East Texas acknowledged the racial/ethnic and cultural diversity in the classes, including Ascender classes on HSI campuses where Latinx students were actually the minority in the classroom.

What is noteworthy about the Ascender program is its emphasis on acknowledging the backgrounds of the students and finding ways to treat diversity and differences as assets that can be used as learning tools in the classroom. For Mary and Vivienne, this diversity required a thoughtful consideration of how a Latinx Studies-based curriculum could be broadened to include some of their students from African and Asian backgrounds. They incorporated a textbook that, though challenging (Ronald Takaki's *A Different Mirror: A History of Multicultural America*), appealed to the variety of racial and ethnic backgrounds in order to have something for everyone. In the same way that Latinx students were not used to seeing their culture represented in the education system, Vivienne explained, "My Asian students are so interested in the book, but I think a lot of it has to do with that they've never read anything from Asian history."

One issue that was brought up by five participants was the use of Spanish in the classroom. Frank and Valerie attributed this to having a group of students in their classes from México, pointing out that students were speaking a distinctly native Mexican dialect. Gustavo and Nicholas brought up several issues related to language usage. First off, Gustavo acknowledged his lack of training in Teaching English as a Second Language. Though he is an English Language Learner himself, he expressed a level of discomfort with teaching writing to students who are Spanish-dominant. Nicholas discussed his students' use of Spanish inside and outside the classroom and described using Spanish himself as a way to make them feel comfortable. For example, he conversed with students in Spanish during one-on-one meetings in his office and also allowed students to quote Spanish passages in their own writing: "When it comes to their own writing . . . they're free to use direct quotes in Spanish. I have to make that concession for them to get them invested in the material . . . This seems to make a difference for some of my students." Nicholas admitted that he has coworkers who do not feel that speaking in Spanish is appropriate, but he described it as a way to get students to buy into his class.

Engaging the Contact Zones

The Ascender curriculum encourages faculty members to learn about their students' backgrounds and experiences outside of college. For example, faculty learned through their training about various writing prompts that ask students to write about the origins of their names or to bring in family photos that can be used in reflective essays. These in-class activities, however, served as a starting point for connecting students' home lives with their school lives, another interaction between the contact zones in students' lives.

Throughout the interviews, the concept of *familia* emerged in every interview, as a pedagogical tool both inside and outside the classroom. Gloria, an education instructor, explained that the college experience is often not new just to the student, but to their families as well: "A fair number of Latino students tend to stay at home longer than other student groups. Their family is going to be a large part of them succeeding in college." She went on to say, "If the family [knows the demands of college] and we invite the families to come in and work with us and know who we are, then they have a clearer understanding and can support the student more." Given that other faculty note that some students may work one or multiple jobs while attending college to add to their family's income, the process of enfranchising families with information about the college experience and helping them to support their student was potentially life-changing for the student.

In an interesting interaction regarding her college's *Noche de Familia*, Natalie told the story of a student who stood up and apologized to her and the rest of the class in the class meeting following the *Noche de Familia* event. The student's sisters had pointed out her cold treatment of her peers at the event. Their intervention prompted a significant change in the student's attitude toward the program. Cynthia indicated that *Noche de Familia* also impacted the family's role in a student's college experience. She joked, "I've had several students who have told me, 'Aye, Miss, I wish you'd have never said that at *Noche de Familia*. Now my mother's always reminding of me of what you said.'" Cynthia said that she explains the program to family members, including parents and spouses, and explicitly tells relatives that the program needs their help in supporting their student.

Within the classroom, the use of small groups, or *familias*, is a key part of promoting active and collaborative learning. Students used their *familias* to peer review each other's work and to complete assignments in Raquel's classroom, for instance. Multiple participants also noted that the community built in the classroom through the use of *familias* promoted interaction and accountability inside and outside the classroom. Anthony found that as students got closer to one another, they kept tabs on one another, especially when they did not come to class.

Sometimes students can also be there to help each other in emergencies. Valerie recounted a time when a female student collapsed in her classroom after giving blood. What she and the students quickly realized was that the student had not eaten breakfast prior to coming to campus that day. However, they also found out that she regularly has nothing to eat for breakfast. Valerie said that, "It became a social issue. We took care of that. At that point, class isn't important whenever the safety and well-being of a student [is threatened]."

With regard to students' own contact zones, or the spaces of their lives, the Ascender program expanded the boundaries of students' zones. The purpose of the campus visits to four-year university campuses in nearby areas and away from students' homes is to help students realize their transfer potential. Valerie cited a student who, upon visiting the Texas State University campus in San Marcos, Texas, said, "This is where I want to go." The experience of being on campus gave him a tangible goal to work toward, and as Valerie proudly reported, the student achieved it.

Another common experience students have across the campuses is some sort of community event. Nicholas described his students going to a play on the local university's campus and pointed out that even going to a different side of town is new for some students, especially if their transportation options are limited. Valerie's students visited a local art museum and were allowed to bring their families, and she revealed that for some students and their families, this visit was the first time some had ever visited a museum. Raquel's students went across campus for a multiple-course dinner at the college's culinary arts building. As part of the dinner, a hospitality instructor walked through the etiquette of the dinner, including what silverware to use.

Mindfully Teaching Through the Contact Zones

Throughout the course of the academic year, Ascender students receive in- and out-of-class experiences that help them succeed in their critical first year of college and beyond. As noted, events were held to engage students' families as well as to broaden students' aspirations for what they can achieve beyond the community college campus. Opening up the spaces of students' lives required sustained effort on the part of faculty over the course of the academic year.

In her Learning Frameworks class, Cynthia asked students to carefully consider the question, "What is college success?" Several students in past terms gave responses that went beyond graduating and getting a good job; for them, part of being successful in college was having instructors who cared about them. Gloria argued that the faculty instructors who opt to teach in the program are more sensitive than others given the active, arguably intrusive, approach the program takes to foster student success. Raquel put this argument another way:

> Education already is a lot of work, and it's a challenge. Being a
> good teacher is hard work . . . This program, I think, is not for

the faint of heart. It's not for those who aren't motivated to be with students or to take the time to really listen to them and provide them the support that they need.

From fully executing a learning community with paired courses to planning the out-of-town university visits, each participant noted various aspects of this program that require significant investments of time and effort from both the students and the instructors.

However, Frank pointed out that programs like the Ascender program enabled him to return to the type of teaching that drew him to the community college in the first place. He told of the assessment and accountability movements that increasingly invaded higher education over the past ten years:

> We started out with small classrooms that would hold no more than 25 students so you could have an intimate environment. That's when the word community was in the name of our college, community college. It has since been removed. [Before Ascender,] We were just so engaged in that data driven [evidence]. We lost everything. We were doing it [teaching] cognitively, nothing affective.

Once the Ascender program arrived at his college, Frank told of his colleague in the program who remarked, "The program is giving us permission to go back and do what we wanted to do 25 years ago . . . It's going to give us permission to continue with the mission that we've lost sight of."

While Frank described a return to a long-abandoned mission, others spoke of teaching content that has fallen out of the curriculum. Both Natalie and Mary expressed the power of storytelling and of narrative writing in their classes, especially in the first weeks of the year in getting students to find their confidence to begin writing. As Mary put it,

> We get hung up on what the learning outcomes of the course are and preparing them for the next course. As a writing instructor, I know how important it is to do narrative writing. It was like Ascender was just going, 'Yeah, it's okay.'

A narrative approach to writing and teaching was something that Natalie described moving away from, and by bringing that back to her classroom, storytelling became "an analogous primer for [students] figuring out what the lesson is." In that sense, Mary and Natalie depicted a return to their natural instincts for good teaching that they felt students best respond to.

When asked what students get out of the Ascender program, both Gustavo and Frank described hope for long-term impact. In the short-term, Gustavo hoped that by the end of the school year, each student is still in college and have skills that can be applied in other courses. Looking forward, Gustavo remarked, "I would hope that they become mentors to their little brothers and sisters and other students . . . I hope that they still remember their time in the Ascender program, that they still keep that family going even if they go their separate ways."

Discussion

At the individual level, the work of the Ascender faculty is perhaps not unique in that many community college instructors understand the challenges of their students and work their hardest to help their students be successful. What is unique about this program, however, is the institutional commitment to the developmental student population and the program's way of formalizing best practices (e.g., connecting with their students, providing students with content reflective of their backgrounds) that make a difference. An expectation of the faculty who teach in the Ascender program is that they will meet students' relatives, learn their narratives, accompany their students on four-year campus visits, and help students to think about what they want to accomplish past the two-year degree. The investment in students extends far past the semester or academic year.

Programs like Ascender reveal various strengths about teaching Latinx students, such the powerful positive influence that family members can have on college-going experiences when they are invited into the process. These programs can also reveal what areas of teaching and serving Latinx students are ripe for improvement. For example, it is worth noting that creating and maintaining these types of programs are very labor intensive for the colleges. Faculty members, advisors, and program coordinators have to commit to the professional development, which the colleges pay for. Course enrollment minimums must be met, and most of the interviews indicated that out-of-course activities and mentoring provided various challenges at each college that had to be overcome. For instance, coordination between the developmental writing course and the Learning Frameworks course requires time and effort to ensure the content of the courses is appropriately reinforcing the other. Most programs struggle with finding enough community mentors to match up with small groups of students. This type of program is time-intensive for students who are juggling other courses and their obligations outside of school.

Though the Ascender professional development addresses some of the best practices in teaching, it does not explicitly address the English as a Second Language needs that instructors mention needing. The program's many moving parts also necessitate various staffing challenges, including people who are responsible for coordinating mentoring, advising, and out-of-course activities. Since all the faculty members in this study teach various other courses besides their Ascender courses, it is ideal if a dedicated staff member can oversee these peripheral tasks.

Despite requiring a great deal of investment in terms of time, resources, and money, the long-term payoff appears to be worth it. Every faculty member provided stories of at least one student they clearly remember and have kept in touch with multiple years after the student left their class. In fact, one faculty member (Allia) reported that she would be walking the stage for her doctoral graduation at the same ceremony where a former Ascender student would receive their bachelor's degree. Each professional development institute for faculty includes a panel of students who attest that their participation in the program played a critical role in helping them graduate with their associate's degree and transfer to a four-year institution.

Limitations

The most glaring limitation of this study is the lack of students' voices. Considering the dearth of research on Latinx students in developmental education, more work must be done to capture their experiences and what parts of programs like Ascender specifically worked or did not work for them in their educational journeys. The Ascender program does administer multiple surveys over the course of the academic year, but the survey instrument does not allow students to reflect on their experiences in the program and to provide feedback on what worked and what did not. Work that is more dynamic should also include entering developmental classrooms and seeing what successful teaching looks like in a naturalistic setting. The continuation of work on Latinx students, especially in the community college sector, those who are placed into developmental education, and Hispanic-serving community college will continue to generate new ideas for policy, practice, and research.

Implications and Conclusions

Despite these flaws, this study offers some important implications for policy, practice, and research. The need to support HSIs and Latinx students who attend them is a critical economic issue as this population continues to grow nationwide. Programs like Ascender that target Latinx students at a point in their educational journeys where the system is likely to lose them are crucial and should be properly supported financially so they can be scaled up to more colleges and universities. As Frank said in his interview, "Our [Latinx] culture's success is going to be everybody else's success."

Finding spaces to incorporate additive practices with intention, meaning that these become a regular part of interactions with students, is an important takeaway from the Ascender program. College instructors are undoubtedly stretched thin in their professional lives with classes, service activities, office hours, and their own personal lives. The Ascender approaches of *familia* and *cariño* are not original, but the fact that they are intentional elements of the program contributes to its impact. The program takes various best practices like targeted advising and culturally relevant teaching in order to blend them into a targeted intervention for students.

Hispanic-serving community colleges like the ones participating in the Ascender program in Texas juggle multiple missions and student needs. Their distinctiveness often comes directly from the diversity of students who con-verge on their campus with a wide array of aspirations. This makes catering to one specific group, like Latinx students, challenging but not impossible. The program demonstrates how an intentionally cultural program can serve a multicultural campus.

Notes

1. The term "Latinx" is used to be inclusive of gender diversity (Molina, 2016). The term "Hispanic" is only used in this chapter when referring to Hispanic-Serving Institutions as this is a federal designation.

References

About the Puente Program. (2018). Berkeley, CA: Center for Educational Partnerships, University of California at Berkeley. Retrieved from http://puente.berkeley.edu/about

Anzaldúa, G. (1987). *Borderlands/la frontera: The new mestiza.* San Francisco: Aunt Lute Books.

Bailey, T., Jeong, D.W., & Cho, S. (2010). Referral, enrollment, and completion in developmental education sequences in community colleges. *Economics of Education Review, 29*(2), 255–270. doi: 10.1016/j.econedurev.2009.09.002

Boylan, H. R., Bonham, B. S., & White, S. R. (1999). Developmental and remedial education in postsecondary education. *New Directions for Higher Education,108*, 87–101. doi: 10.1002/he.10806

Calderón Galdeano, E., Flores, A. R., & Moder, J. (2012). The Hispanic Association of Colleges and Universities and Hispanic-Serving Institutions: Partners in the advancement of Hispanic higher education. *Journal of Latinos and Education, 11*(3), 157–162. doi: 10.1080/15348431.2012.686352

Cohen, A. M., Brawer, F. B., & Kisker, C. B. (2013). *The American community college* (6th ed.). San Francisco, CA: Jossey-Bass.

Complete College America. (2012). Remediation: Higher education's bridge to nowhere. Washington, DC: Complete College America. Retrieved from http://www.completecollege.org/docs/CCA-Remediation-final.pdf

Conley, D. T. (2005). *College knowledge: What it really takes for students to succeed and what we can do to get them ready.* San Francisco, CA: Jossey-Bass.

Contreras, F., & Contreras, G. J. (2015). Raising the bar for Hispanic serving institutions: An analysis of college completion and success rates. *Journal of Hispanic Higher Education, 14*(2), 151–170.

Cuellar, M. (2014). The impact of Hispanic-serving institutions (HSIs), emerging HSIs, and non HSIs on Latina/o academic self-concept. *The Review of Higher Education, 37*(4), 499–530. doi: 10.1353/rhe.2014.0032

Deil-Amen, R., & Rosenbaum, J. E. (2002). The unintended consequences of stigma-free remediation. *Sociology of Education, 75*(3), 249–268. Retrieved from http://www.jstor.org/stable/3090268

Gándara, P., & Contreras, F. (2009). *The Latino education crisis: The consequences of failed school policies.* Cambridge, MA: Harvard University Press.

Garcia, G. A. (2016). Complicating a Latina/o-serving identity at a Hispanic serving institution. *The Review of Higher Education, 40*(1), 117–143. doi: 10.1353.rhe.2016.0040

Hays, D. G., & Singh, A. A. (2012). *Qualitative inquiry in clinical and educational settings.* New York, NY: Guilford Press.

Hodara, M. (2015). *What predicts participation in developmental education among recent high school graduates at community college? Lesson from Oregon* (REL 2015-081). Washington, DC: U.S. Department of Education, Institute of Education Sciences, National Center for Education Evaluation and Regional Assistance, Regional Educational Laboratory Northwest. Retrieved from http://ies.ed.gov/ncee/edlabs

Ignash, J. M. (1997). Who should provide postsecondary remedial/developmental education? *New Directions for Community Colleges, 100*, 5–20. doi: 10.1002/cc.10001

Lu, M-Z. (1994). Professing multiculturalism: The politics of style in the contact zone. *College Composition and Communication, 45*(4), 442–458. Retrieved from http://www.jstor.org/stable/358759

McCook, N. (2016). Literacy contact zones: A framework for research. *Literacy in Composition Studies, 4*(1), 50–72. Retrieved from http://licsjournal.org/OJS/index.php/LiCS/article/view/116

McGrath, P., & Galaviz, F. (1996, November–December). In practice: The Puente Project. *About Campus*, 27–28, 30.

Merriam, S. B., & Tisdell, E. J. (2016). *Qualitative Research: A guide to design and implementation* (4th ed.). San Francisco, CA: Jossey-Bass.

Molina, A. (2016, August 31). *Latina, Latino, Latinx. What is this new term Latinx?* Student Affairs Administrators in Higher Education: Latino Knowledge Community. Retrieved from https://www.naspa.org/constituent-groups/posts/latina-latino-latinx.-what-is-this-new-term-latinx

Núñez, A., Crisp, G., & Elizondo, D. (2015). Hispanic-serving community colleges and their role in Hispanic transfer. In A. Núñez, S. Hurtado, & E. Calderón Galdeano (Eds.), *Hispanic-serving institutions: Advancing research and transformative practice* (pp. 47–65). New York, NY: Routledge.

Núñez, A., Hurtado, S., & Calderón Galdeano, E. (2015). Why study Hispanic-serving institutions? In A. Núñez, S. Hurtado, & E. Calderón Galdeano (Eds.), *Hispanic serving institutions: Advancing research and transformative practice* (pp. 1–24). New York, NY: Routledge.

Our Program. (n.d.). New York, NY: Catch the Next. Retrieved from http://catch-thenext.org/our-program/

Pratt, M. L. (1991). Arts of the contact zone. *Profession,* 33–40. Retrieved from http://www.jstor.org/stable/25595469

Ruecker, T. (2015). *Transiciones: Pathways of Latinas and Latinos writing in high school and college.* Logan, UT: Utah State University Press.

Saldaña, J. (2015). *The coding manual for qualitative researchers* (3rd ed.). Thousand Oaks, CA: SAGE Publications.

Santiago, D. A., Taylor, M., & Calderón Galdeano, E. (2016). *From capacity to success: HSIs, Title V, and Latino students.* Washington DC: *Excelencia* in Education. Retrieved from http://www.edexcelencia.org/gateway/download/23582/1471381888

Texas Higher Education Coordinating Board. (2015). Developmental education accountability measures data: Graduation and persistence of developmental education students [two-year institutions]. Austin, TX: Texas Higher Education Coordinating Board. Retrieved from http://www.txhighereddata.org/reports/performance/deved/

Chapter 3

"One Foot on the Bridge and One Foot off the Bridge"

Navigating the Geographies of Access and Rhetorical Education at an HSI

JENS LLOYD

Expanding access to higher education is a motivating purpose for many who teach and learn at HSIs, with the Hispanic Association of Colleges and Universities, an advocacy group that promotes the HSI designation, identifying the expansion of access as one of its primary goals ("HACU 101," n.d., para. 5). Likewise, access motivates the work of many rhetoric/composition teacher-scholars, and, as such, the discourse of access is rightly scrutinized by those committed to making it serve a meaningful role in defining the field. Tom Fox (1999) contends that, though progress has been made in recent decades with regard to supporting students from underrepresented backgrounds, "lack of access remains our most crucial problem" and an enduring impediment to realizing the "democratic purposes" of higher education (p. 1–2). Responding in part to Fox's contention, Pegeen Reichert Powell (2009) poses a succinct question that is worthy of extensive contemplation: "[T]o what, exactly, are we asserting that we should provide students access?" (p. 670). This question opens up the discourse of access to various perspectives about what, exactly, "access to higher education" means.

In this chapter, intent on opening up this discourse to include the perspectives of students, I present a case study of Monica.[1] I interviewed Monica over the course of her first year as an undergraduate at UC Irvine (UCI), a large Southern California research university that, in addition to recently being designated an HSI by the Department of Education, has the highest number of Latinx freshmen applicants among all UC campuses (Watanabe, 2017). Monica immigrated to the United States from a Central American country when she was a child. As a young adult entering college, she had left her family's home in the Los Angeles area to take up residence on a campus about an hour's drive to the south in Orange County. I first interacted with Monica during the summer of 2015 as part of my research into UCI's Bridge Program, a residential summer transition program for "first-generation, low-income students and students from disadvantaged backgrounds/circumstances" ("FAQ," n.d., para. 2). I have taught in the program since 2013. The six-week program, which typically enrolls around 90 incoming students, revolves around three courses. Two are large, lecture-style courses: a university studies course and philosophy of science course. The other is a small, workshop-style course: the writing lab. This is the part of the program with which I have been involved. In discussions with Bridge administrators, I have been told that the writing labs, capped at around 20 students, are essential to the course of study because students need to be confident about confronting a variety of writing and communication situations. Given this combination of factors, as with most summer transition programs, UCI's program is a critical site for researching the overlap between postsecondary writing and rhetoric instruction and efforts to expand access to higher education.

After recruiting Monica for my research project in the summer, I continued interacting with her throughout the 2015–2016 academic year, interviewing her in fall quarter, winter quarter, and spring quarter. Our discussions encompassed a range of topics, including Monica's experiences as a first-generation college student, her successes and struggles with postsecondary writing and rhetoric instruction, and her involvement in cocurricular activities. We also talked about bridges. To be more specific, we talked about *the bridge*, the metaphor at the heart of the summer transition program in which Monica had participated. "Where are you in relation to the bridge?" I posed this question during each of my three interviews with Monica. By concretizing the metaphor, I hoped to gain insight into how access is experienced as a spatiotemporal phenomenon by students like Monica. Ostensibly, by enrolling at UCI and arriving on campus, Monica had achieved access to higher education; she was off *the bridge*. Tellingly, though, in response to my questions about the metaphor, Monica responded with an ambivalent geographical portrait. This was most apparent during our winter quarter interview. "I think I'm off the bridge," she responded initially. But then she self-corrected. "Maybe one foot on the bridge and one foot off the bridge. . . . I'm in the school, but I'm still not there yet." Though it suggests a structure that affords linear, steady progress, *the bridge* for Monica was not a straightforward point of entry into higher education. As I detail in this chapter, Monica's talk about her experience of access reveals an uneven, multi-step journey.

This is a stark contrast to the relatively straightforward way that Powell (2009) talks about access in her aforementioned article. "Once students are in our classrooms," Powell writes, "they have already, by definition, achieved access to higher education" (p. 673), and, thus, she encourages rhet/comp teacher-scholars to focus on what comes after access, namely retention. Yet, talking about access simply in terms of *getting in* reduces what can be a vexing, enduring experience for students like Monica and a difficult process also for the instructors and institutions intent on assisting them. I think that we would do well to recognize that access is and always has been a matter that is "far from settled" (Fox, 1999, p. 2). Furthermore, while the discourse of access often centers around the socioeconomic factors that enable or constrain students' pursuit of higher education, there are inescapable geographical implications insofar as access to higher education often involves residing in or commuting to a campus. I am interested in sharing Monica's experiential narrative because, eschewing the simplicity of *getting in*, it highlights how access entails a more complicated process of *taking up residence* as a writer and rhetor on a college campus.

Relying on Monica's own words to compose a narrative of her efforts to take up residence at UCI, I use this chapter to elucidate the complexities, both metaphorical and material, of her self-assessment that, for much of her first year, she had "one foot on the bridge and one foot off the bridge." In addition, I detail how Monica resists evaluating her progress solely in terms of academic success and, instead, emphasizes involvement in cocurricular activities that prompt civic engagement on campus. After reviewing research on summer transition programs and explaining my methodology, I show how the metaphor of *the bridge* permits Monica to articulate a complex understanding of what it means to have access to higher education, and then I consider how she narrates her opportunities for a campus-based rhetorical education. Ultimately, I argue that such opportunities are not confined to curricular spaces and that, by linking the prospects for a campus-based rhetorical education to the discourse of access, rhet/comp teacher-scholars at HSIs and elsewhere can think more dynamically about what, exactly, access can mean for underrepresented students and for the instructors and institutions intent on assisting them.

Researching Summer Transition Programs

While summer transition programs come in many forms, ranging from on-campus, credit-bearing programs to online remediation programs, many of them have a common link: writing and rhetoric instruction. Accordingly, rhet/comp teacher-scholars should be eager to study these programs. Yet, the extant scholarship from rhet/comp and adjacent fields deals only indirectly or briefly with summer transition programs, considering them in conjunction with broader institutional assessments of accelerated courses (McLeod, Horn, & Haswell, 2005), broader networks of support services for refugee students (Hirano, 2014), and broader calls for assigning personal narratives (Affeldt, 2007). In a notable example of sustained inquiry, Barbara Jaffe (2007) reflects on her involvement in the Puente Program at California community colleges, which started in the 1980s "to address the low rate of academic success among Mexican American and Latino community college students" (p. 170).[2] Jaffe, though, chooses to focus on instructors instead of students, identifying the potential for the program to instigate "teacher transformations" (p. 174). While an email chain circulating on the Writing Program Administrators listserv, the WPA-L, during the spring of 2015 revealed a robust assortment of writing and rhetoric curricula for summer transition programs, there is a discernible need for research, particularly research that considers the effects of these programs on students.

Recently published studies on the effects of summer transition programs are more common from sociologists and scholars of education interested in or involved with student support services. Using standard academic measures such as GPAs (Cabrera, Miner, & Milem, 2013) and degree completion rates (Douglas & Attewell, 2014), these studies show a positive correlation between participation in summer transition programs and academic success. However, some complications are worth noting. Cabrera et al. (2013) studied the New Start Summer Program, or NSSP, at the University of Arizona and, while their conclusion about the program's benefits is based in part on nearly two decades of student data, they postulate that "the most significant effects of NSSP participation are indirect" (p. 491). This hints at a methodological problem for researchers interested in studying programs that are designed to acclimate students to college, as such an acclimation process is not reflected entirely in academic measures. Douglas and Attewell (2014) note a similar problem in their comparative analysis of two datasets: data from a large-scale survey conducted by the National Center for Education Statistics and data from an unspecified community college system. Douglas and Attewell surmise that "it may be the case that bridge programs are only contextually beneficial" (p. 88), and they suggest that future studies, rather than scrutinizing large agglomerations of quantitative data, might concentrate on gathering qualitative data (p. 103). So, although studying summer transition programs in the aggregate is important, there is a need to disaggregate, as it were, what makes participation in such programs beneficial by considering qualitatively the experiences of specific students in specific programs. Accompanying this, I would add, is the need to think about how participation in summer transition programs affects students in ways that are not reflected in standard academic measures.

Latty L. Goodwin's (2002) ethnographic study demonstrates a commitment both to qualitative inquiry and to examining the range of effects that result from participation in summer transition programs. Goodwin focused on a group of roughly 20 students at a university in New York who participated in the Higher Education Opportunity Program, or HEOP. The study encompassed the students' first year in college, which included a period of time spent in a summer transition program. Though Goodwin found that many of her subjects appreciated the program, she discerned an unintended effect: "The program is not only for racial and ethnic minority students, but because HEOP's population is overwhelmingly composed of underrepresented students, it has all the outward appearances of a minority summer program" (p. 87). About this unintended effect, Goodwin explains that some of her subjects "recognized the irony of their situation, that the very program that provided them a safe haven and compassionate understanding on this campus was also one of the major sources of stigmatizing stereotypes" (p. 207). This effect and others like it are not readily discernible in standard measures of academic success or in large agglomerations of quantitative data.

In the hopes of prompting students to "narrate their experiences during this time [of transition to college]" (Goodwin, 2002, p. 23), I followed a methodological impulse similar to Goodwin's when I designed the research project that included Monica. Less interested in the effectiveness of the program overall and more interested in the program's effects on students, I recruited students during the Bridge Program and collected data, first, by surveying participants and, second, by conducting semi-structured interviews throughout the academic year, giving special care to how they talked about becoming writers and rhetors in residence on a college campus. The inspiration for this approach derives from Nedra Reynolds's (2004) claim that, when it comes to how rhet/comp teacher-scholars study students "as agents who move through the world . . . we haven't yet tapped their spatial imaginations or studied their moves." To counteract this, she continues, "we should investigate encounters with place and space and reconsider the kinds of movement (and stillness) that characterize acts of writing and places for learning" (p. 176). With my research into the UCI Bridge Program, I sought to build extensive experiential narratives with my participants, cultivating qualitative richness in the hopes of drawing out the connections between the geographies of access and rhetorical education. I focus exclusively on Monica in this chapter because, of all my participants, her narrative offers the most richly varied account of a student taking up residence at an HSI.

"Still a Few Steps Away": Metaphors, Materiality, and Access

The UCI Bridge Program is a residential program. It takes place on campus, and this place is central to its purpose. As a researcher, while I realized that asking about *the bridge* could initiate a discussion about the residential nature of the program, I was hesitant to ask about it. It seemed too playful, and I worried that it might degrade the tone of the interviews. But I was encouraged by Monica's responses and by her willingness to take the metaphor seriously. As she told me in her final interview, "I like this metaphor."[3] I assured her that I, too, liked the metaphor. I grew to appreciate the metaphor because it provided a spatially evocative way for Monica and me to talk about her experience of access. The metaphor provided what, in summarizing George Lakoff's work on metaphors, Christy Friend (2002) describes as "a basis for shared understanding" (p. 179). But, importantly, in facilitating this "shared understanding," *the bridge* did not simplify or homogenize Monica's experience. Instead, Monica used the metaphor to illuminate her uneven, multi-step journey.

Initially, Monica used the metaphor to reflect on her past, extending the span of *the bridge* to include her time in high school. In her first interview, she told me that, "during high school, I just wanted to get over the bridge." She continued reflecting on her high school experience in her second interview, mentioning the "limited" resources she had to assist with college preparation. "I didn't have a main factor for learning about college," she told me. "So, in the end, I ended up doing things by myself," which included researching colleges and completing applications. This seemed to influence her perception of where she was in relation to *the bridge*. During fall quarter, she reported the following: "I want to say that, at this point, I have crossed the bridge, but [I know] I am still a few steps away from the school itself." Though eager to complete the journey, Monica intuited that she was still in the midst of the transition. In her second interview in winter, during which she remarked that she had "one foot on the bridge and one foot off the bridge," she surmised that her undecided/undeclared status was "slowing [her] down" and she tied this status directly to her lack of preparation for college.

When I asked Monica in her first interview to unpack the metaphor, she provided a dynamic interpretation that revealed to me that *the bridge* can represent isolation just as much as inclusion. Monica told me that *the bridge* metaphor carried "[a] positive aspect" because it signaled "[a] new phase in your life." Yet, as Monica continued to explicate the metaphor, she explained that it "[could be] seen as negative . . . because . . . other people think 'Oh, those people [in the Bridge Program] need extra help.'" Because *the bridge* creates a passageway that is not commonly available, it stands out and, as such, people on it stand out, too. Monica's critical interpretation, an interpretation gleaned from her firsthand experience, echoes Goodwin's disconcerting insight about the stigma that can come with participating in a summer transition program.

At their best, critical interpretations like the one offered by Monica can lead to transforming or replacing metaphors. Musing about this prospect, Friend (2002) argues, "if we admit that figurative language shapes our thinking and behavior in powerful ways, how can we use this knowledge to our advantage? In short, . . . should we actively strive to replace these metaphors with more positive ones?" (p. 188). This is exactly what Monica did in her final interview with me in spring quarter. I asked her where she was in relation to *the bridge* and she responded, "I think, as of right now, I'm on the front porch or front area of the school. I'm knocking and waiting for someone to open. Or more like I have my hand on the handle of the door and [I'm] trying to get in." This change of metaphor was unprompted. I did not ask for a new metaphor. I asked about *the bridge*, and I found myself facing *the door*. When I asked her to unpack it, Monica explained that *the door* is a better indication of her experience because the metaphor allows her to claim some control over a process that might otherwise seem out of her control. "I know I'm off the bridge," she told me confidently, "because I have a better sense of myself professionally and personally." What is important about *the door*, Monica insisted, is "that symbolism of me trying to get in." Via this metaphor, access becomes something for her to claim actively rather than something for her to accept passively. But *the door* is also an obstacle. Whereas *the bridge* might imply linear, steady progress, *the door* reinforces the idea that there are obstacles to access that endure long after students get in.

For those seeking to advocate for access and to advocate on behalf of students seeking it, we would do well to think critically about the metaphors that saturate the discourse of access. We would do well to remember that, as Reynolds (2004) cautions, "spatial metaphors—from how writers find a way 'in' to where the boundaries are for different discourses—are not meant to be overcome, only recognized for the power they wield over our imaginations and for their frequent neglect of material conditions" (p. 177). The "power" of any spatial metaphor used to talk about access, to talk about having a place on a college campus, should be judged for its potential to heighten, not dampen, our sensitivity to the geographies of access. At UCI, for instance, the newly gained HSI designation will not do away with the "culture shock" that many students face in "moving from largely Latino neighborhoods and schools to the university, where only a quarter of students share their ethnic background" (Watanabe, 2017, para. 18). Thus, while we should acknowledge milestones like HSI designations and what they signify for the large-scale expansion of access, we should strive to be just as attentive to access as a spatiotemporal phenomenon experienced on a smaller scale by individual students. Furthermore, the language used to explain the experience of access should not be inaccessible to those most affected by it. We should reside with students at the intersection of metaphor and materiality, lingering long enough so that students can tell us what they know about access and about the bridges, the doors, and whatever else they encounter along the way.

Such a strategy of residing with students and listening to them tell us what they think we should know about access might also go a long way in helping us answer Powell's question: "[T]o what, exactly, are we asserting that we should provide students access?" I take this up in the next section by exploring how residing with others on campus presented Monica with opportunities for a conspicuously campus-based rhetorical education.

"Learning Doesn't Just Happen in Classroom Settings"
Rhetorical Education on Campus

In addition to formal coursework, the UCI Bridge Program entails a range of cocurricular and extracurricular activities because, as explained on the program's website, Bridge is about ensuring that students "make the best possible academic and social transition to UCI" ("Program Information," n.d., para. 4). Regarding these various activities, Monica told me that the program helped her realize that "learning doesn't just happen in a classroom setting." She talked about the significance of an assignment in her university studies class that asked her to research clubs and organizations using an institutional database. As Monica described how this assignment influenced her vision of the campus, I recognized that her vision epitomizes an "involving college," a concept advanced by George D. Kuh et al. (1991) to explain "[the] blurred, fuzzy lines between what, where, and how students learn in college" (p. 3). An involving college is one where a student's education exceeds curricular spaces and where every interaction is latent with pedagogical potential.

The notion that inhabiting a campus should entail interactions with others speaks to the belief that college is an opportunity for students to grow and mature as participants in broader cultural, social, and political flows. Campus planner and architect M. Perry Chapman (2006) captures this well when he argues that a campus provides "a multitude of venues and encounters that amplify the learning experience through inquiry, direct observation, debate, action, and social exchange from the playful to the very serious. Being there [on campus] is learning the choices and challenges of a complex society" (p. xxxii). Though certainly an ideal portrait, it speaks to the civic aims of higher education. UCI Chancellor Howard Gillman (2017) invoked these aims when, in celebrating the institution's HSI designation, he outlined his hope to faculty, staff, and students that the new title, in addition to generating opportunities to vie for federal grants, would "enable UCI to serve as an engine of social mobility for all Californians and empower us to create a more brilliant future for everyone in the state" (para. 3). If UCI or any HSI is to achieve such lofty aims, we must consider how the campus facilitates academic *and* civic engagement. We must consider how an HSI functions as a site for rhetorical education that, to repurpose Jessica Enoch's definition (2008), "*develops* in students a communal and civic identity and *articulates* for them the rhetorical strategies, language practices, and bodily and social behaviors that make possible their participation in communal and civic affairs" (p. 7–8).

Monica's recognition that the campus is more than just a place for classroom-based learning manifested in her cocurricular commitments. From the start, Monica presented herself as an involved student, frequenting campus events and considering how best to get involved with clubs and organizations. In her third interview during the spring, she told me that she joined an organization that advocates for immigrant rights. "I never thought I would be in such a group," she explained, especially because, with regard to the activist dimension of the organization, "I'm not that type of person." An instructor in an anthropology course, a graduate student studying migrant women, told Monica about the organization and encouraged her to attend a meeting. "I went there awkwardly," Monica told me, making it clear that she would not have attended without the encouragement from her instructor. But, upon seeing the extent to which it is a "student-led [organization] . . . trying to grow without much help from the school," Monica felt compelled to participate. Tying her personal connection as an immigrant to the organization's pedagogical potential, she explained in spatially evocative language that "[things] are happening and they are related to you, but you just never notice unless you put yourself in a space where you learn those things." This organization, in other words, prompted Monica to take notice of and to intervene in broader cultural, social, and political flows.

Serendipitously, Monica and I met for our third and final interview during "No Human Being Is Illegal Week," a weeklong series of actions and demonstrations led in part by Monica's organization. She was eager to tell me about it and, in the process, she revealed to me how her involvement advanced her rhetorical education. Monica explained that the organization strives to secure resources and support for immigrant students by communicating with others on the UCI campus and beyond. Part of the organization's mission, Monica told me, is to circulate the "full information" about the challenges faced by immigrant students. As for her role in the organization, she said, "I really want to be the communications person, . . . because I really like being the in-between person between two groups of people." Her role came up again later in the same interview when I asked about what she learned from the writing and rhetoric instruction she received in the Bridge Program. She explained that it helped her recognize the "underlying foundation of . . . know[ing] what to do, how to do it, and the limits or the things I shouldn't be doing." Drawing upon an example to explain what she meant, she turned not to a curricular situation, but rather to a cocurricular writing and communication situation related to the immigrant rights organization. Telling me about "volunteer[ing] to write a letter to other organizations to help us," Monica explained that, with this letter, she knew she could not sound "too desperate" and that she had to keep it "professional" in the hopes of convincing her readers. I interpret the opportunity to compose this letter as a significant extension of Monica's rhetorical education because, as demonstrated in her description of the task, it allowed her to exercise rhetorical flexibility and genre awareness, two terms that she likely encountered in her writing and rhetoric courses at UCI.

Quite clearly, Monica was not interested in confining her activities as a writer and rhetor to curricular spaces. However, this proved troublesome for her. In spring, as she got involved with the immigrant rights organization, Monica was enrolled in a lower-division writing and rhetoric course. Calling her experience in this research-intensive course "bittersweet," she expressed concern about the group work assigned in the course, which included creating an awareness campaign on social media. She was in the midst of working on this assignment when I interviewed her and, seeming very dissatisfied, she talked about the challenge of being in a group with procrastinating, unmotivated peers. Strikingly, as I documented above, Monica was, at this very same time, engaged in a weeklong series of actions and demonstrations to raise awareness about immigrant rights on campus. I asked her about the coincidence and whether she saw any advantage to participating simultaneously in these two similar activities, albeit one curricular and one cocurricular. She told me, in a resolutely dejected tone, that she had to forgo more substantial involvement with her organization's activities in order to work on the awareness campaign for her course, "which is unfortunate," she said, "because I really wanted to be a part of [the actions and demonstrations on campus]."

Monica's struggle to juggle curricular and cocurricular commitments is one faced by many students, especially those, like her, that seek to maximize opportunities to get involved. The research on involving colleges (Kuh et al., 1991) argues that getting students involved in a range of activities is vital for their success in college. This suggests, though, that to succeed students just need to do more. They need to do extra. But doing more is not always easy. Doing extra is not necessarily a sustainable way to take up residence on a college campus. Monica faced challenges with this throughout her first year. She told me in her second interview that she faltered academically during fall quarter and, as a result, was put on a form of academic probation. By her third interview in spring quarter, her curricular and cocurricular commitments were in direct competition for her time and attention, despite the fact that, to me, they were similar in nature. Monica's experience reveals that the demands of inhabiting an involving college can be overwhelming and even detrimentally so.

In response to her frustration, one might advise Monica to concentrate on her curricular commitments. That is certainly the message sent by the administrators who decided to put her on academic probation. Yet, I do not think Monica would abide by such a relatively restricted notion of residing on campus. She wanted access to more than just academic success. In her third interview, she explained that, "as we are growing academically and professionally, outside factors like the community are pretty much what makes us develop even further. There's a limit in classrooms." Monica was convinced that residing with this "community" on campus was essential to her success at UCI and beyond. "If you're not really willing to go out into the community, you're not able to learn as much," she concluded. While in rhet/comp scholarship the impulse to "go out into the community" often signifies escaping the proverbial ivory tower to engage with people and places beyond campus, in this instance, Monica was talking explicitly about people and places on campus. For her, the community to engage with consists of fellow campus inhabitants and the limitations to exceed are those of the curriculum.

Conclusion
Bridges, Doors, and Other Entry Points

I find myself returning to Powell's question: "[T]o what, exactly, are we asserting that we should provide students access?" Only this time, instead of asking it of rhet/comp teacher-scholars, I ask it of students like Monica: to what, exactly, do you want access? What happens to discussions of access and rhetorical education if we add in student self-determination? It strikes me that, in Monica's case of conflicting commitments, faced with two similar activities, one curricular and the other cocurricular, she might push for some combination. She might want to see, in the words of Jonathan Alexander and Susan C. Jarratt (2014), "the curricular and the cocurricular, the formally sponsored and the self-sponsored, as mutually informing resources" in her rhetorical education (p. 542). Rather than having to choose one over the other, Monica might want access to both and support in figuring out for herself the extent to which they are, indeed, "mutually informing."

I do not mean to advocate for the conflation of the curricular and the cocurricular. What I suggest, contra Kuh et al., is that we not see the lines demarcating where students learn on campus as "blurred" and "fuzzy," as this risks erasing the important distinctions that students, instructors, and administrators make between curricular and cocurricular activities. Instead, we should recognize and call attention to these demarcations as a means of appreciating that the campus, more than an assortment of curricular spaces, functions as a multifaceted site of rhetorical education for those who seek to inhabit it as such. If, as Alexander and Jarratt (2014) urge us, rhet/comp teacher-scholars are "to think more capaciously about the many different spaces in which rhetorical education might take place" (p. 528), then I am interested in attending to *where* students learn on campuses, not in some vain effort to record and catalogue every space, but in a hopeful effort "to think more capaciously" about the campus geographies to which students like Monica want access. To that end, emphasizing the convergence between the geographies of access and rhetorical education, I conclude this chapter with some suggestions for writing and rhetoric instruction in summer transition programs.

Importantly, I do not see students' experiences in these programs as isolated from the rest of their time in higher education. A summer transition program designed to be a one-stop, fix-it shop that helps students only with *getting in* disregards the extent to which these programs can influence students' expectations for college. Furthermore, as Lucas Corcoran and Caroline Wilkinson forcefully articulate in a previous chapter of this collection, implementing instruction that emphasizes above all else what students lack in terms of college preparation should be rejected, especially as this might reinforce a detrimental adherence to monolingualism in academia. We should build proactive rather than reactive curricula for summer transition programs, and, in this spirit, I think we must also consider how such a program can authentically inform students about the range of activities they might explore as writers and rhetors in college. If we frame it as "a kind of academic 'boot camp,' providing reviews of basic math, writing, or reading skills" and "a way of quickly resolving skill deficits without losing academic momentum" (Douglas & Attewell, 2014, p. 90), then, inevitably, the program suffers from seeming inauthentic to students and instructors alike. Summer transition programs must balance the goal of preparing students for academic rigor with the goal of supporting social cohesion by having a relatively small cohort of students participating in a curated selection of courses. This is, of course, different from what the students are likely to experience when they begin their first academic term. What can be done to diminish the sense that a summer transition program is merely an easy warm-up to the real college experience that is to come?

Certainly, we can examine the language we use to describe summer transition programs. We can avoid framing these programs as preparatory boot camps, which, aside from turning instructors into drill sergeants and students into new recruits, dictates that curricula for summer transition programs should consist of nothing more than academically oriented skill-and-drill exercises. For this reason, I appreciate the description of UCI's Bridge Program as a program "designed to help . . . [students] make the best possible academic and social transition to UCI" ("Program Information," n.d., para. 4). If we frame students' experiences in summer transition programs as the first steps toward taking up residence on a college campus, then we can think dynamically about the writing and rhetoric instruction offered in such programs and how this instruction can aid students in navigating the geographies of access and rhetorical education. For instance, in writing and rhetoric courses affiliated with summer transition programs, we might take up the metaphors of access as objects of study. We might linger with students at the intersection of metaphor and materiality in order to think critically about how, in the words of Friend, "figurative language shapes our thinking and behavior in powerful ways." Such a project seems especially relevant at HSIs, campuses that, following Gillman, can be figured ambitiously as "engine[s] of social mobility." We can do our students and ourselves a favor by scrutinizing the (dis)connections between the discourse of access and the material conditions of access, extending this discussion by inviting students to consider how access metaphorically and materially shapes their expectations for facing a variety of curricular and cocurricular writing and communication situations.

In conjunction with this critical scrutiny of language, we might prompt students in summer transition programs to speculate about their immediate futures as writers and rhetors in college. We might make residing amidst what Chapman (2006) calls a "habitat of learners" (p. 64) a key consideration. For instance, taking inspiration from an assignment that I highlighted as influential in Monica's narrative, we can ask students to research and analyze the rhetoric of campus clubs and organizations. Extending this further, we can encourage students to strategize for how to go about engaging in curricular and cocurricular activities that are, in Alexander and Jarratt's words, "mutually informing." This is hardly a straightforward proposition given the challenges that come with juggling the demands of residing on a campus. As we help students consider how to become, through ways curricular and cocurricular, writers and rhetors in residence, we can ourselves learn to better appreciate and constantly reevaluate how our campuses function as multifaceted sites of rhetorical education. My interest, as I hope to have demonstrated in this chapter, is in making sure that the bridges, the doors, and any other entry points to these multifaceted sites remain accessible to those willing to seek them out.

Notes

1. This name is a pseudonym. Also, to further protect anonymity, I refrain from providing highly detailed demographic information.

2. See Erin Doran's chapter in this collection for a more thorough description of the Puente Program, including a discussion of how it has been implemented in Texas.

3. To avoid cluttering up the text, I forgo parenthetical citations for my interviews with Monica. But, where possible, I distinguish between the interviews I conducted with her over the course of the 2015–2016 academic year.

References

Affeldt, R. J. (2007). The politics of space and narrative in the multicultural classroom. In Kirklighter, C., Cárdenas, D., & Murphy, S. W. (Eds.), *Teaching writing with Latino/a students: Lessons learned at Hispanic-serving institutions* (pp. 193–210). Albany, NY: State University of New York Press.

Alexander, J., & Jarratt, S. C. (2014). Rhetorical education and student activism. *College English, 76*(6), 525–544.

Cabrera, N. L., Miner, D. D., & Milem, J. F. (2013). Can a summer bridge program impact first-year persistence and performance?: A case study of the New Start Summer Program. *Research in Higher Education: Journal of the Association for Institutional Research, 54*(5), 481–498.

Chapman, M. P. (2006). *American places: In search of the twenty-first century campus.* Westport, CT: Praeger.

Douglas, D., & Attewell, P. (2014). The bridge and the troll underneath: Summer bridge programs and degree completion. *American Journal of Education, 121*(1), 87–109.

Enoch, J. (2008). *Refiguring rhetorical education: Women teaching African American, Native American, and Chicano/a students, 1865–1911.* Carbondale, IL: Southern Illinois University Press.

FAQ. (n.d.). Retrieved from http://sss.uci.edu/summer-bridge/program-information/

Fox, T. (1999). *Defending access: A critique of standards in higher education.* Portsmouth, NH: Boynton/Cook.

Friend, C. (2002). Seeing ourselves as others see us: The maternalization of teaching in everyday talk. In Fleckenstein, K. S., Calendrillo, L. T., & Worley D. A. (Eds.), *Language and image in the reading-writing classroom* (pp. 177–190). Mahwah, NJ: Lawrence Erlbaum Associates.

Gillman, H. (2017, May 22). UCI named Hispanic-serving institution for 2017–18. Retrieved from http://chancellor.uci.edu/engagement/campus-communications/ 2017/170522-uci-named-hispanic-serving-institution.php

Goodwin, L. L. (2002). *Resilient spirits: Disadvantaged students making it at an elite university*. New York: Routledge.

HACU 101. (n.d.). Retrieved from http://www.hacu.net/hacu/HACU_101.asp

Hirano, E. (2014). Refugees in first-year college: Academic writing challenges and resources. *Journal of Second Language Writing, 23*(1), 37–52.

Jaffe, B. (2007). Changing perceptions, and ultimately practices, of basic writing instructors through the *familia* approach. In Kirklighter, C., Cárdenas, D., & Murphy, S. W. (Eds.), *Teaching writing with Latino/a students: Lessons learned at Hispanic-serving institutions* (pp. 169–192). Albany, NY: State University of New York Press.

Kuh, G. D., Schuh, J. H., Whitt, E. J., & Associates. (1991). *Involving colleges: Successful approaches to fostering student learning and development outside the classroom*. San Francisco, CA: Jossey-Bass.

McLeod, S., Horn, H., & Haswell, R. H. (2005). Accelerated classes and the writers at the bottom: A local assessment. *College Composition and Communication, 56*(4), 556–580.

Powell, P. R. (2009). Retention and writing instruction: Implications for access and pedagogy. *College Composition and Communication, 60*(4), 664–682.

Program Information. (n.d.). Retrieved from http://sss.uci.edu/summer-bridge/faq/

Reynolds, N. (2004). *Geographies of writing: Inhabiting places and encountering difference*. Carbondale, IL: Southern Illinois University Press.

Watanabe, T. (2017, June 9). UC Irvine's rare distinction: It's an elite research university that's a haven for Latinos. *Los Angeles Times*. Retrieved from http://www.latimes. com/local/ lanow/la-me-uc-irvine-latino-20170609-story.html

Testimonio 2

Finding Anzaldúa

A West Texas *Testimonio*

CHRISTINE GARCIA

I am a West Texas woman: raised, educated, challenged, and nurtured by the people and land of San Angelo, Texas. My hometown is small, antiquated, and tough. The tallest trees are cottonwoods, we let our cactus grow wild, and we often measure time by the roll of the tumbleweed. Geographically, San Angelo is at the crossroads of big sky plains to its west and rolling hill country to its east. To the west, the *Llano Estacado*, a massive land escarpment that stretches down into México, presents an unforgiving expanse, with almost 40,000 square miles of grassland plains and not much else. To the east unfold the rolling hills of Central Texas. If compelled to do so, a short drive southbound will lead you straight to the border crossing into Ciudad Acuña, Coahuila, México, where many San Angelo residents go each weekend to visit family, shop, and partake in border nightlife. San Angelo is at the juncture of these southwestern ecologies.

We West Texans are an eclectic group; a sundry mix of our long and complicated history. We are and always have been Indigenous Native land, Northern México, and around 200 years ago we entered our Wild West period as a Republic. These ebbs and flows of land ownership eventually led to our current status as the biggest and decidedly best state in the contiguous United States. When San Angelo was founded in 1867, the zeitgeist of the Wild West era was still in full form, and our town embraced this spirit with zeal. In these early days, San Angelo was considered the county seat of banking and ranching as well as of brothels, saloons, and gambling. Though we would like to think ourselves good Christians, these vices still haunt our town's day-to-day existence.

Like most small Texas towns, San Angelo has legacy families that settled during early land grabs that followed Texas statehood in 1845. Often, these are the names you will see on the election signs and civic donation placards throughout the city. We also have a vibrant *barrio* that runs from Avenue M. to Avenue U., and boasts some of the most excellent *menudo* in the world, which is especially necessary to cure neighborhood revelers' Sunday morning *crudo*. And, as a relic to the past but window to the present, San Angelo is also home to "Blackshear," a historically African-American neighborhood on the north side of town. Though there are definitive separations of people based on socioeconomics and ethnicities, these separations are porous and it would be misleading to say that San Angelo is not often progressive in terms of race relations. It would be just as misleading to say that San Angelo is not free of troubling racial incidents. During my first year of college at Angelo State University, a young Black man was found shot to death and set afire in his car. This young man was dating the daughter of the White county sheriff, who vocally disapproved of his daughter's choice in lover. His murder was never solved.

San Angelo was my home and my neighbors, teachers, family, and friends alike constituted my entire world until I went to Albuquerque, New Mexico, for graduate school. I grew up outside the city limits on a multi-acre pecan farm that consisted of rows and rows of trees with an occasional dotting of sage and cacti. My childhood home was framed by endless blue horizon, storms in the distance, and, at night, a heaven full of stars. The weather was no less magnificent. Throughout the year, San Angelo typically has over 100 days of over 100-degree heat and then another 30-plus days of below freezing cold. Our land is beautiful, but extreme. You have to have physical mettle and mental fortitude to survive this place.

I was raised in this land as the daughter of a blue-eyed Anglo and a red-headed *Cubana*, and this strange mix had no counterpart in San Angelo. The Anglos knew I wasn't completely White and the Tejanos knew I wasn't completely Latina. Luckily, being *Cubana* in West Texas was unique enough that both factions of my youth could not quite figure out where to place me, and thus I made friends across the battle lines. Growing up in the rural outskirts of town meant that my closest companions were the kids from the other small farms and ranches nearby. We were a mix of first-, second-, and legacy-generation kids of varying ethnicities who came together through proximity and our mutual love of four-wheeling, hunting, and late-night bonfires. Living outside of the city limits meant a certain type of quiet freedom. I recall summers being long and lazy, scattered with slow evening walks, wind chimes, and the space, both physically and mentally, to roam and grow. San Angelo was, for me, a great place to grow up.

This San Angelo of my youth was not all bucolic, though. While the town's isolation kept us moving at a slow, steady, and safe pace, it also meant something more sinister in terms of inaccessibility. Innovation, progress, or novelty of any kind that manifested in a public way was often viewed as suspicious if not downright dangerous, and those who chose to deviate from the norm were effectively reprimanded, ostracized, or silenced. To be a non-conforming voice in San Angelo, a person had to be capable of engaged conversation, armed with knowledge both religious and secular, and altogether aware of the atavistic views that residents often held regarding race, gender, and sexuality. And that person had to be bold and self-assured, two traits that I find common to most West Texans. From a young age, I was a vocal feminist and anti-racist. In San Angelo, this meant being a tireless listener and interlocutor, being aware of community conventions of respect and deference, and then knowing when to rhetorically turn all the rules upside down. It also meant occasionally angering friends, family, and neighbors with views that were not conservative, traditional, religious, or politely racist. Language was my conduit for pushing back against the ills I saw in the community I loved, and my growing lexicon and rhetorical acuity was a definite reflection of these complicated intersections of my daily life.

I spoke a combination of Standard English and Tex-Mex as I navigated my different discourse communities, moving seamlessly between and around different formalities, tones, and codes as the audience and situation demanded. From the earliest age, I knew when and with whom to use "*elote*" over "corn," to allow, as a sign of respect, older ranchers to tell their stories in their unending entirety, and to always use the honorific terms "Sir" and "Ma'am." My primary education teachers included Ms. Alschwede, who instilled in me a respect for clarity, and Señora Perez who taught me the power of word, sentence, and paragraph organization. Our schools were not bilingual mandated, but my teachers always allowed, encouraged, and even expected competency in English and Spanish because it reflected our communities' language practices. Hearing both Spanish and English growing up, day in and day out, in home and community alike, was my linguistic reality. This pragmatic approach to language use and instruction, coupled with growing up in the bubble of West Texas, meant that my linguistic world was inhabited by no-nonsense, multilingual speakers and teachers. School was focused on formal English and Spanish instruction, and home and community interactions were multilingual as well with just a bit more color and raucousness. My language and literacy practices were honed within these verbally vibrant discourse communities.

Looking back, I took for granted that this was a typical upbringing in language use. Were not all kids instructed by diverse teachers in diverse language practices? Latinas were my lexical mentors, my guides in the standards and norms of syncopation and prosody. They were my inspiration. They were my teachers, my community leaders, my family, my friends. They were me. My love of language came from these eloquent women's insistence on precision and perfection. Latinas were my rhetorical paradigm. And what excellent teachers they were.

The moment I realized that this paradigm was, to some, nothing but an anomaly, an unimportant disruption in the otherwise monochromatic and tightly closed field of English language cultivation and teaching, was a moment of brutal realization. It was like a punch to the gut. The type of punch that expels every molecule of air from the diaphragm and takes one to their very knees in atonement. This moment came, not as one would expect, within the tense confines of my West Texas world, but rather in the much more metropolitan, much more progressive city of Albuquerque. And it did not come by a rusty old rancher or antiquarian English teacher, but rather from an advanced professor of language.

As a neophyte graduate student in Rhetoric and Composition, I was invited to be the graduate research assistant for Core Writing and my major task was to draft an updated reading list for our upcoming composition theory course. I was elated and went to work with the tenacity of someone with something, everything, to prove. I scoured anthologies and readers. I asked around. I deconstructed bibliographies. I analyzed, I synthesized, I prioritized. And, finally, I collated a list of readings that included Gloria Anzaldúa and Jacqueline Jones Royster, Lisa Delpit and bell hooks. I included the always cutting-edge work of Min-Zhan Lu and Bruce Horner. I respected the time-honored names and made sure to also include up-and-coming scholars. I balanced topics and approaches and ranged the included pedagogies and praxes. I was excited to have a voice in shaping this reading list. I was honored that my language practices held weight and that my scholarship could add to other's learning. I worked diligently to create a diverse yet balanced list that any new grad student could turn to as a starting point for comp theory. I knew not to get too attached to the list, as the first rule of writing is that our work is never a calcified artifact and is always a candidate for revisioning and rewriting. I knew this. Yet, I handed that list of composition theorists over as any proud mama would hand over her child and sit back to wait for the accolades to roll in. It was as if I'd given birth to the most beautiful bibliography of scholars the field of Composition Studies had ever seen. As a newbie doctoral student and one of the only Latinas in my department (graduate student or otherwise) I felt my voice validated and my scholarship important.

I walked into class that first evening with a little pep in my step. As expected, the first order of business was the passing around of the syllabi and the semester reading list. I immediately flipped past the course description, required materials, and accommodation statements. Though I expected to read "Anzaldúa" in shining glory as the first entry, in her place was the name "Bartholomae." The dissonance between my expectation and the reality of what I was seeing left me momentarily unable to compute a single letter on that page. None of my suggested readings had made the cut. It seemed, in fact, that my work had been altogether crumpled up and tossed in the garbage and the old reading list, which included no scholars of color, few women, and favored the professor's antiquated and narrow pedagogy, was once again the go-to list of "standards." I was livid. I was genuinely hurt. I asked my professor why none of the readings I suggested, specifically the texts by scholars of color, were being used and I listened, hollowed, as I was told, blatantly, that these particular readings were not important to learning the basics of composition theory and pedagogy. I pressed on, asking her why these scholars could not be included on the syllabus even as suggested or supplemental readings so that their names and works could get into the hands of the other doctoral students in the course. "Christine," she said, "get over it. This is just the way it is."

And at this moment, I understood what it felt like to be silenced. I had moved west, away from conservative rural West Texas to a major, progressive city, to enter an institution of higher learning whose student population was comparable to the population of the town I had grown up in, only to confront one of the most ignorant and bold attacks on language use I had ever experienced. At least in Texas, racism and sexism were apparent. This was an intellectual woman that I admired. I trusted her guidance and felt honored to work under her tutelage. Little did I know that the real lesson she was teaching me was that of polite White racism.

I'd like to say that I reacted with vigor against this silencing. That I printed and distributed illicit "Composition Scholars of Color" bibliographies. That I held alternative comp theory study groups that gave voice to the Anzaldúas and Delpits of Composition Studies and the voices, theories, and approaches they represent. Hell, I'd even like to say that I followed up with my professor and fought back against my silencing, demanding that the comp theory list be diversified, or I would protest! Organize! Mutiny! But, I did not. I was a vulnerable graduate student in a tenuous position, and I lacked the confidence in my own work that would have compelled such bold actions. I stayed silent and followed the rigmarole of the course. I completed the readings and did the writings in the way the professor expected. I made the right rhetorical moves in class and in my assignments and I finished the class with the lousiest "A" I've ever received.

I was down, but I was not out. In fact, I was down low enough to be able to take root and, like the seeds of Ayotzinapa, I grew. During this period of growth, I found a focus in Latinx Rhetorics and Latina Writing Program Administration. During this period, I also researched and wrote a dissertation on Chicana rhetors, focusing on the *chingona* labor and civil rights activist Dolores Huerta. And, during this period of growth, I began to confront and call out racism couched as standard language practices or "academic English" expectations. Through this process of growth and cultivation, I came to comprehend what César Chávez meant when he said, "You cannot un-educate the person who has learned to read. You cannot humiliate the person who feels pride. You cannot oppress the people who are not afraid anymore." My growth and cultivation, from my West Texas upbringing to my Albuquerque reckoning, taught me that language knowledge is power. I am no longer afraid.

References

César Chávez laid out his vision for farm workers and Latinos in 1984 Commonwealth Club address. (2018). Retrieved November 04, 2018, from https://ufw.org/research/history/cesar-chavez-laid-vision-farm-workers-latinos-1984-commonwealth-club-address/

PART II

FIRST-YEAR WRITING

Chapter 4

Rhetorical Tools in Chicanx Thought

Political and Ethnic Inquiry for Composition Classrooms

YNDALECIO ISAAC HINOJOSA
AND CANDACE DE LEÓN-ZEPEDA

> We are creating ways of educating ourselves and younger generations
> in this mestiza nation to change how students and teachers think and
> read by de-constructing Euro-Anglo ways of knowing: to create texts
> that reflect the needs of the world community of women and people
> of color; and to show how lived experience is connected to political
> struggles and art making.
>
> —Gloria Anzaldúa (2009), "The New Mestiza Nation"

¿Quién somos? Who are we? But, more importantly, why does that matter?

When we teach, we "project the condition of [our] soul onto [our]
students, [our] subject, and our way of being together," according to Parker
J. Palmer (1998), so, in essence, teachers teach who they are (p. 2). How a
teacher chooses to define him- or herself and the lived experiences he or she
brings into the classroom, therefore, matters. We, the authors, made rhetorical
choices in this chapter that declare and express the ethnicities and identities
which are parts of our souls and our work teaching first-year composition
courses. So, without further delay, who are we?

We are scholar-teacher activists, persons of color, and first-generation
scholars. We are advocates who speak against social inequities or inequalities.
We are writing studies practitioners teaching writing, working and continuing
to work with first-year students. These identities are just a few we choose

to adopt to demonstrate who we are as teachers. As educators, we each dedicate ourselves to raising consciousness and to creating opportunities for self-reflection as methodologies in taking pride for one's ethnic and cultural background. That work matters the most to us because ethnicities or cultural identities in educational spaces matter, especially concerning equal access and attainment for minoritized groups.[1]

Hispanic. Tejano/a. Latino/a. Mexican-American; hyphenated or not. Each is an identity we encountered or endorsed during our educational journeys in rural south Texas, but as politically conscious subjects of Mexican descent and born and raised in the United States, we choose to self-identify as working class Chicanx. We adopt the *x* not only to emphasize gender neutrality in replacing the *o* and *a* endings but also to underscore the inclusivity of all gender identities. Also, we use this term, pronounced CHi kän eks, as an indication of our self-determination and ethnic pride, and we adopt this moniker with the *x* to signify simultaneously Chicano and Chicana (and even Chican@).[2] *Somos Chicanx!*

Stylistically, our chapter is unlike any other in *Bordered Writers* because we want to change how practitioners, as well as students, think and read by creating new ways of educating ourselves and others, like Anzaldúa (2009) tells us. So, in what is to follow, we share lived experiences interrupted by *testimonio-like reflections*, describing encounters with Hispanic-Serving Institutions (HSIs) and pedagogical practices implemented in first-year composition classrooms. By speaking collaboratively and independently as writers, students, practitioners, and scholars, we evoke a linguistic polyvocality to construct discursive spaces that reflect the complexity of our identities as well as the sense of our borderedness. As Chicanx feminists, we create our own discursive spaces through a "rhetoric of difference," revealing "ethnicity" and "repudiating mainstream discourse" (Flores, 1996, p. 145). There are many rhetorical tools in Chicanx thought, especially from Chicanx feminists. So, in this chapter, we also present how Chicanx thought may offer practitioners rhetorical tools; tools as modes of inquiry that enable first-year students in composition classrooms, especially in classrooms situated along the U.S. – Mexico border, to reclaim their bodies and histories and to reimagine their identities through discursive practices, through acts of writing.

Experiences Lived at HSIs in the Borderlands

Nudge a Mexican and she or he will break out with a story.

—Anzaldúa (1987/1999c), "Tlilli, Tlapalli"

All we need is a little nudge, speak about HSIs, and we easily break out with not *a* story but many. We want to present a few of these stories to affirm what we experienced at HSIs situated in the borderlands. Todd Ruecker (2015) says that "many Latina/o students and their families have been beaten down with discourses labeling them as lacking capital, unprepared for college, or in other ways failing education institutions" (p. 148). As practitioners who teach first-year writing, we chose not to ignore this reality, because discourses aid in establishing power relations (Gee, 1987/2006; Tileagă, 2006). Within educational environments, rules or codes for what determines literacy are often imposed onto marginal cultures by those cultures who hold power, who typically adopt Western conceptions of literacy and who usually are white, Western European descendants (Street, 1985; Delpit, 1995).[3] To the extent that those with power do not maintain the status quo or limit access with exclusionary standards, marginal cultures who seek literacy, that involves "building access to literate practices and discourse resources," need only to acquire the skill set necessary—to gain access or to participate in social mobility—by choice (Luke, 2000, p. 449). However, to choose is easier said than done, especially for Latinx or underserved students of color. For instance, like Ruecker describes, throughout our educational journeys, we have been called the *remedial writer*, the *basic writer*, the *academically underprepared student*, the *culturally deprived* student, the *student on financial aid*, the *first-generation student*, the *developmental student*, the *provisional student*, or, worse yet, the *at-risk student*. Such deficit-based discourses describe many other Latinx or underserved students of color (Rendón, Nora, & Kanagala, 2014). Over time, these labels and the identity politics such discourses draw forth made a significant impact on us that has been difficult to overcome as writers, as minoritized people, and as first-year composition practitioners. These labels have branded our brown bodies as Othered or bordered based on our "altered literacy practices" (Carmichael, Edwards, Miller, & Smith, 2007, p 79). However, we attribute their use also to that which led us to embrace our "ethnic consciousness," our racial and ethnic pride and our solidarity and unity to give back to our families and communities (Padilla, 1985). This form of consciousness provided us with a relational understanding, that is to say the knowledge "*grounded in [our] bodily existence*," we needed to carry with us into educational environments (Emphasis in original, Shapiro, 1999, p. 41). It played a crucial role, shaping us into the teachers we meant to be and the practitioners we became upon entering first-year composition classrooms. To help communicate new identities that spoke to how we understood ourselves and our sense of Otherness in educational environments, we chose to call ourselves Chicanx rhetoricians.

Hinojosa: Soy Chicanx, y me llamo Chicanx porque Anzaldúa (1987/1999c), que descanse en paz, helped me to understand that I am my language and how the words I write on the page are like "carving bone," "creating my own face, my own heart" (p. 95). So, on these pages, I carve out the bones from my brown body to reveal a more vivid bordered face and heart.

When I look back at my undergraduate and graduate studies, I recall every intensive writing course I enrolled for felt like a first-year composition course all over again. To be honest, I despised such courses. I lacked any self-confidence that I knew how to write ~~good~~ *well. In my eyes, I never truly mastered the skill set required of a first-year composition course, especially when I failed—several times—developmental and first-year composition. At that time, I could not recognize how writing varied substantially from context to context. To engage in all acts of writing (or reading for that matter) terrified me, and I felt bordered from others, especially from those who did not have the same problems I encountered as a Spanish speaker with the English language. Instead, skills in math or science were strengths I possessed, and I loved science.*

Estrellas. Planets. Galaxies. I dreamed that maybe one day I would be a physicist. I thought I would find work in genetics, botany, microbiology, anything but English. But, my lab reports were under par compared to other student reports. My calculations. Correct. My illustrations. Amazing. My writing. Incomprehensible. Composing a well-organized and grammatically "free from error" (as defined by formal English rules) piece of writing was difficult. No doubt, this inability was tied directly to my less than below average writing skills I heard so much about from my white teachers. Embarrassed and at times ashamed, I steered away gradually from my love of science and headed straight toward the arts, theatre arts to be exact. There, as an actor, I learned first how to fake it and second how to hone in on my body. I developed a sense about my body on a stage or in any space, not only by listening closely but also by paying close attention to movement. Ironically, playing the part, so to speak, is what guided me toward learning more about my brown body and its voice.[4]

My feelings about writing and writing pedagogy led me to consider how I might be of some use to students, who like myself may have felt bordered. I thought that perhaps as a composition instructor I could help these students perform better than I had performed. To learn more about how students as well as instructors interact, negotiate, move, and transgress across borders with and in that space, the space where writing takes place, offered me the opportunity to "do work that matters," as Anzaldúa (2015) pleads, within the disciplinary field of writing studies (p. 22).

de León-Zepeda: Y yo soy Chicanx. Me llamo Chicanx porque, Anzaldúa (1987/1999c), un alma amada, taught me that I too can reclaim what I had been told was bad, sin verguenza, and how I can make or recreate my soul as well as my identity "through the creative act" (p. 95). Fear. Anxiety. Both feelings embody my earliest memory of entering higher education. Why would a brown girl like me need a college degree? As a first-generation college student, I often dealt with unwelcoming feelings in academic settings. As a result, a self-imposed silence ensnared my tongue from my mind and my body from others. Feeling inferior. Ignorant. I convinced myself that I did not belong in what I had branded a smart place occupied by smart people. I felt invisible. I struggled to find the strength to express myself in any way in any classroom, especially those classrooms where writing was required.

My borderland. Academia. With little to no avail at the time, I straddled this new academic borderland, bordered between my peers and professors. If I could not help myself, then whom could I help? What would I know if called upon? What could I offer anyone? How was this place a better place for me? Only later did I discover a handful of professors that created student-centered classrooms or included multicultural literature on their syllabi, but even then, I must say that I never saw myself reflected in the required literature. On top of that, my writing failed to meet expectations set by my professors, especially those who were uninviting or who failed to understand any of the cultural or familial influences that made an impact on my success or failure. Avergonzada. Many times, I left class shamed by my professors. I recall one professor, specifically, who found it difficult to accept that I did not have the financial resources to own a personal computer, let alone all the overly priced books required for the course. Other professors criticized my essays harshly; not outside of class but during class to prove a point about what makes bad writing bad.

As an undergraduate, I did not have opportunities to write about issues or content that was important or relevant to my brown existence. My professors supplied essay prompts with assigned unrelated topics that were outside of my cultural upbringing. One such assignment asked me to provide my perspective on the greenhouse effect. I didn't understand what that meant. I asked, "Do you mean as in the effects of living in a house painted "green," and the professor mocked me in front of the class. When I asked for a new in-class essay topic, he did not offer a new one. I did not complete my assignment as a result. The first time I chose to use lived experiences in my writing was as a graduate student, and I can never forget how that professor labeled my writing as being too culturally colorful for such academic settings. He insisted my writing could be improved easily if I removed myself and modeled myself after a strong form of writing. Academic discourse. Objective. These experiences are only just the few that made me want to teach writing and to develop pedagogies that empower traditionally marginalized students, who may find themselves bordered, like me, in unfamiliar and uninviting academic spaces.

As Chicanx, we ask for social justice and equality, and as rhetoricians, we ask that rhetoric involve both the study and strategic use (and placement) of spoken, written, and visual languages. Together, we stand as Chicanx rhetoricians to attest how our bordered brown bodies, our identities, and our lived experiences all serve as affirmation that the personal is political.[5] We are interconnected to specific places, such as rural south Texas, *barrios*, *colonias*, community colleges, or universities, and the material realities such places imposed, such as manual labor, economic hardships, limited resources and access, remediation, or alienation. The interconnectedness with these felt places is constituted by our interactions with such places and mediated by the material effect in languages to render our identities as well as our bodies to such places (Alcoff, 2006; Anzaldúa, 1987/1999a; Arreola, 2002; Babino & Stewart, 2016; Brady, 2002; González, 2001; Massey, 1994, 2005; Martínez, 1994; Selzer, 1999; Volk & Angelova, 2007). We acknowledge that languages have a material aspect and that material realities have a rhetorical dimension, as Jack Selzer (1999) argues. For us, the material realities of living in the borderlands has influenced our bodies rhetorically, in more ways than one, in that rhetoric "acts on the whole person—body as well as mind—and often on the person situated in a community of other persons" (Blair, 1999, p. 46). Thus, there exists a "rhetorical counterpart to the corporeal body" that also produces a "spatial body," causing language to occupy space when that language is placed into a specific context (Hinojosa, 2016, p. 107). So, when we say that we are bordered brown bodies, we evoke then an "embodied rhetoric," where we as writers "inextricably link" our bodies "to specific places and physical realities (Hinojosa, 2016, p. 107).

Our lived experiences have taught us how identity and its politics are multifaceted and complex. But, we do not stand alone in recalling the complexity of identity politics (Comas-Díaz, 2001; Murakami-Ramalho, Núñez & Cuero, 2010; Oboler, 1995). Identity politics are further complicated and play a more central role inside institutions of higher education, especially within those institutions designated as Hispanic-Serving Institutions (HSIs). Often, institutional mission statements do not directly address Latinx or student of color needs (Contreras & Bensimon, 2005; Lane & Brown, 2003). Also, Latinx experiences or persons of color ethnicities tend to go unnoticed at these institutional spaces. Drawing from New Mexico State University student experiences, Christina A. Medina and Carlos E. Posadas (2012) assert that "what HSIs should be challenging and altering is the 'Whiteness as norm' underlying structure that often serves to excludes non-Whites implicitly, if not explicitly" (p. 183).[6] To some degree, our lived experiences in Texas are comparable to those experiences expressed from students in New Mexico. There were a few times where we stood out, broke away from the Whiteness as norm structure, by bringing awareness to or making visible our racial or ethnic pride, but when we did, those times were more often than not met with resistance. However, despite having faced resistance, we each earned multiple degrees from HSIs, and in our solidarity, we confided in one another (and others), confessing to each other the microaggressions we encountered at HSIs.

Hinojosa: As a student, I will never forget my first day in English 1301, a freshman composition course, when on day one the white instructor declared his sole purpose to "weed out" everyone he felt did not belong at the university, and he would achieve that goal with our first assignment. It came as no surprise that most of my Latinx brothers and sisters, including myself, were the ones to leave. We dropped, failed, or withdrew.

When I first started teaching as an adjunct for a community college, I had a student, an older Latina maid, who waited over 20 years to attend college. She waited because her white employer taught there as an accomplished English professor and because he had embarrassed her repeatedly when she first enrolled 20 years earlier. She chose—out of fear—not to re-enroll until he retired from that place.

Later, when working on my PhD, I recall the Graduate Advisor on Record advising me to sell my car to make ends meet and insisting that while I completed my PhD I would not accept any employment from the local community college that wanted to

employ me as a full-time tenured track instructor. She insisted that
I do these things if I wanted to take the graduate program seriously.
But, I needed my car in a new city, and I needed to work full-time.

In what ways do HSIs serve students, like us, in the borderland? In a previous publication, based on our lived experiences, we labeled these institutions *Hispanic-Shaming* (Hinojosa & Zepeda, 2018). We criticized how some participants at these sites shamed—consciously or unconsciously—marginalized students. But clearly, that may not always be the case. As other chapters in this collection illustrate, those who work at HSIs are moving forward, improving inclusivity with language and ethnic diversity and serving the needs of all students. The Hispanic-Shaming declaration was made to align with our experiences, the predispositions we found ourselves in academic environments that were governed mostly by that *discourse of shaming*, a discourse entrenched in the borderlands and ingrained into our brown bodies.[7] Social institutions, especially academic institutions, are vehicles that govern what literacy and its practices mean for all participants involved. Embedded with other hegemonic discourses (e.g., ethnocentric, nationalistic, capitalistic, and Americanization), we see how along the U.S.–Mexico border a discourse of shaming plays a part in the common socialization processes for literacy and literacy practices. As a result, HSIs situated in the borderlands (like those we were so fortunate enough to attend) will tend to wield hegemonic discourses in a manner that perpetuate the marginalization of minorities, especially for Latinx, as our narratives indicate. These socialization processes, which merit injustices and inequalities for Latinx, reach as far back as the Treaty of Guadalupe Hidalgo in 1848 that ended the U.S.–Mexico War and persist.[8] For example, in response to the enactment of the North American Free Trade Agreement (NAFTA), Char Ullman (2005) points to El Paso's "long history of educational inequity that has circumscribed the economic options of minoritized peoples, benefited majority populations, and shaped the parameters of identity for everyone involved" (p. 241). Ullman maintains public school systems in El Paso "played an important role" in the production of Latinxs as laborers for corporations (p. 249). "On the border," she asserts, "the cultural production of the docile manual laborer has long taken precedence over the production of educated Americanized citizens" (p. 249). This cultural precedent to produce docile manual laborers along the U.S.–Mexico borderland is very much a precedent that was self-evident for us both based on what we experienced. There were clear demarcations placed on us about where we belonged, so to speak, especially when it came to what constituted an academic life versus a private life.

de León-Zepeda: As a student, I remember a tenured male professor explaining to us (mostly Latina women) that we should not get married, file for divorce, or have any children when starting our academic journey because any of those events might distract us from our pursuit and deem us—in his eyes—as not taking our scholarly activities seriously.

When I first started teaching as an adjunct, I was excited to use Gloria Anzaldúa's "How to Tame a Wild Tongue" in a writing class. But, I can never forget those words uttered by my community college American literature professor, who lectured us on the importance of white male writers like Whitman, Emerson, and Twain. He said only their work alone could teach us how to write like that and for all of us to disregard completely any person of color's work on the reading list.

When I was completing my PhD, I learned from a member on the Graduate Admissions Committee that incoming graduate students were ranked—without notification—subjectively by members on the committee. Their ranking designated successful applicants worthy of merit or academic protégées worthy of attention. Full-time workers and single mothers, like me, who were trying to complete their PhDs, fell to the bottom of that list. Thus, it came as no surprise then as to why I received no financial assistance and my presence in the program was barely known to other faculty members on campus.

So far, as our experiences show, we are marginalized, or rather bordered, in academic environments in ways that do not always necessarily relate to race, ethnicity, class, or language. We each voiced what we encountered separately at HSIs to show how these experiences visibly marked our bodies and influenced identities we either rejected or embraced. Our experiences may seem similar, but we acknowledge also that these lived experiences are different, no less. However, not so different that we could not recognize interrelatedness. And, not so different that we could not empathize with the realities embodied in each of us as well as in the rhetoric articulated on these pages. So, with that, we say we are bordered writers, constructing "spaces of linguistic and bodily performativity shaped by realities of literal and constructed place," as Beatrice Mendez Newman and Romeo García define. We materialize these spaces from our "*bordered subjectivities . . .* that highlight the embodiment of borders or bordered cultures" (Emphasis in original, Hinojosa, 2016, p. 102). "Our bodies are geographies of selves," like Anzaldúa (2015) claims, "made up of diverse, bordering, and overlapping 'countries'" (p. 69). Therefore, our language exemplifies a polyvocality, where we speak as writers, as students, as practitioners, and as scholars. All positions articulate our sense of borderedness that comes from being situated amid borders. Borders underscore our cultural backgrounds, our academic environments, and our psyches as brown bodies.

Rhetorical Tools for Modes of Inquiry

As we experienced, when it comes to writing instruction or pedagogies, we fear Latinxs occupying U.S.–Mexico borderland areas are often marginalized, if not alienated, by dominant discourses and ideologies, especially from inadequately trained instructors who see themselves as curricula gatekeepers. Despite progress, most first-year writing classrooms continue to privilege Standard English ideology in writing instruction and in writing pedagogies, especially in regions where language diversity is prevalent (Adger 1997; Ruecker 2015; Wheeler and Thomas, 2013). To offer clarity, we turn to education specialist Eunsook Hyun (2006), who offers a clear distinction between writing instruction and pedagogies. Writing instruction refers to instruction-oriented teaching that "focuses on identifying and delivering knowledge as timeless truths, social rules and laws, and a fixed-core curriculum mostly within the Western paradigm and values" (p. 144). In stark contrast, writing pedagogies involve pedagogy-based teaching "representing context-specific processes sensitive to the evolving needs of individuals, the learning community, and the society" (Hyun, 2006, p. 144). This pedagogy-based teaching is the kind of teaching we aim to learn and implement. In helping us fulfill that role we found *Teaching Writing with Latino/a Students: Lessons Learned at Hispanic-Serving Institutions*, edited by Cristina Kirklighter, Diana Cárdenas, and Susan Wolff Murphy, instrumental. As students immersed in doctoral work and as practitioners who work with first-year students, this text spoke to us, not only because we identified then as Latino/a students but also because we saw practitioners addressing our lived experiences and how best to serve our needs.

We drew inspiration from Beatrice Mendez Newman (2007), a contributor for *Teaching Writing with Latino/a Students*. She said instructors with little to no experience at Hispanic-Serving Institutions (HSIs), typically located in borderland areas along the U.S.–Mexico border, "quickly discover that traditional training in rhetoric and composition inadequately addresses the impact of many Hispanic [sic] students' sociocultural, socioeconomic, and ethnolinguistic makeup on performance in the writing class and on acculturation into the larger academic community" (p. 17). What Mendez Newman described is what Hyun called instruction-oriented teaching, "composed of parts . . . that eventually combine to educate the learner as a whole" (p. 144). At that time, Mendez Newman encouraged instructors to resist hegemonic practices that have become the norm in the classroom: a linguistic hegemony, explained Michelle Hall Kells (2002), "implicitly and explicitly shapes classroom practices" (p. 7). Thus, as practitioners who teach writing at HSIs, we endorsed the call made by Mendez Newman, who says that instructors "must look to their students and must truly listen to their voices to understand who their students are and how to respond to their needs" (p. 33). Pedagogically, this call requires an ecological orientation, where students' bodies in the classroom are situated within their particular locations, their representations of reality, or rather their own lived spaces. We connected this orientation with what Hyun referred to as pedagogy-based teaching, which "values subjective interpretation of meaningful facts and meaningful truths as well as epistemologically varied ways of knowing that are logical and holistic, interconnected, intuitive, emotional, and empathetic within and among learners, including teacher as learner" (p. 144). Pedagogical practices that align with such an approach to teaching could transform "HSI classrooms into sites of learning," as Mendez Newman argued back in 2007, "where teacher and student collaborate to reach new understandings about writing, self, culture, and identity" (p. 33).

To help us reach new understandings, we placed trust in our ethnic consciousness and turned to Chicanx feminists, who articulate a "theory of difference" (Sandoval, 2000) and a "rhetoric of difference" (Flores, 1996) that acknowledges and permits the visibility of race, culture, class, gender, or sexuality. Because they implicate the "production of space in the everyday, in the social," they also offer an alternative "theoretics of space" (Brady, 2002, p. 6). These core thoughts encourage us to improve writing pedagogies in alternative ways that validate culturally diverse students; validation is "an enabling, confirming and supportive process initiated by in- and out-of-class agents that foster academic and interpersonal development" (Rendón, 1994, p. 44). As a caring space, composition classrooms house opportunities for students to develop deeper understandings of their realities. The kind of discursive practices, acts of writing, we ask students to perform can offer validation and opportunities for students to engage in self-reflexivity. These actions can awaken forms of consciousness or the self. As part of our pedagogies, we implement rhetorical tools that Chicanx feminist thought provides for modes of inquiry. We believe the following two tools may serve students, especially Latinx students, in composition classrooms situated along the U.S.–Mexico border.

1. Reclamation: Awakening an Ethnic Consciousness
for Political Inquiry

> Like the ancients, I worship the rain god and the maize goddess,
> but unlike my father I have recovered their names.
>
> —Anzaldúa (1987/1999b), "La Conciencia de la Mestiza"

Reclamation, actions to reclaim bodies and their histories by discursive practices, is the first rhetorical tool we draw from Chicanx feminist thought. Reclamation aids processes of awakening ethnic consciousness for political inquiry, for only when we reach consciousness can we recover those parts of ourselves that have been lost. Chicanx feminist thought disrupts heteronormativity, mainstream discourses, traditional paradigms, and Eurocentric understandings of history (Alarcón, 2002; Bernal, 1998; Flores, 1996; García, 1997; Rendón, 2009; Pérez, 1999; Sandoval, 2000). Chicanx feminist Emma Pérez draws our attention to the histories, or lack thereof, of marginalized bodies. For Chicana/o history, she refers to a "decolonial imaginary," a theoretical tool, for "uncovering the hidden voices of Chicanas that have been relegated to silences, to passivity, to that third space where agency is enacted through third space feminism" (1999, p. xvi). To develop her interpretation of "historiography," Pérez borrows Foucault's language of 'excavation' or 'archeology' (p. 9). She advocates that we must write our own stories in order to overcome colonizing discourses. To recover or reclaim such histories, she argues for marginalized people to write their own histories. This action is something we both build upon as we design writing assignments for our students. Like Pérez, we provide a space where students can reclaim their bodies as a historical text in order to find where gaps exist. Reclamation encourages students to self-actualize their personal histories, including cultural and literacy practices. In the process, students reclaim the erasure of their bodies and their histories through discursive practices.

The Autohistoria-teoría Path to Conocimiento Assignment

We admit, students find the sound of the autohistoria-teoría path to conocimiento assignment frightening, if not threatening to what they are accustomed to hearing. It's different, and the title is in a tongue most students, even Latinx students, describe as alien. However, we choose to use this assignment as a learning opportunity for students to reclaim aspects of themselves by placing students on Anzaldúa's path to conocimiento. A path which asks them to tap into their lives and histories, moments of significance or moments of uncertainty. To embark on a journey where they will shift realities and write how they plan to act out that new vision. This assignment is modeled after Anzaldúa's (2002) "Now let us shift . . . the path of conocimiento . . . inner work, public acts" essay[9] and Caren S. Neile's (2005) essay titled "The 1,001-Piece Nights of Gloria Anzaldúa: Autohistoria-teoría at Florida Atlantic University."[10] We ask students to walk, like Neile, with Anzaldúa on this path by *completing a series of assignments that each represent a stage on the path to conocimiento.*

What is an autohistoria-teoría is the first question we usually receive from students. We refer to Anzaldúa (2002), who says, "You struggle each day to know the world you live in, to come to grips with the problems of life" (p. 540). So, we say that this assignment is meant to help students understand that struggle, to reclaim that struggle as their own, and to see the paths set before them. The second question typically is, how will we do that? So, we explain that the autohistoria-teoría is a fusion of fact and fantasy, poetry and prose, theory and memoir. Historia stands for history, the story of the self as well as the story of the culture, and auto refers to the self. Therefore, an autohistoria deals with memoir writing, autobiography, and fiction simultaneously. It's autobiographical in nature, but fictionalized. After some introspection, we ask writers to fill in forgotten details with fictive elements or adopt metaphors as a way to convey meaning about their lived experiences. The second part of the autohistoria, the teoría, asks writers to theorize aspects about those lived experiences. We ask that writers theorize these experiences as a way to provide some form of understanding in their world or as a way to come into consciousness about a particular moment or situation. This is the kind of writing that we ask our students to perform. Is it different? Yes! Is it scary? Absolutely! It's the first stage on the path to conocimiento.

In this assignment, we ask students to correlate lived experiences with the stages on the path to conocimiento. There are seven stages: 1) el arrebato . . . rupture, fragmentation . . . an ending, a beginning (a moment that shook you up); 2) nepantla . . . torn between ways (a moment you struggled with due to conflicting perspectives); 3) the Coatlicue state . . . desconocimiento and the cost of knowing (a time of fear and self-loathing); 4) the call . . . el compromiso . . . the crossing and conversion (a moment of clarity and commitment); 5) putting Coyolxauhqui together . . . new personal and collective 'stories' (the moment you put yourself back together—reimagined a new identity); 6) the blow up . . . a clash of realities (a time when your new identity fails the reality test); 7) shifting realities . . . acting out the vision or spiritual activism (shifting perspectives and doing something about it). We refer to Anzaldúa (2002), who reminds us that this journey requires that "you encounter your shadow side and confront what you've programmed yourself (and have been programmed by your cultures) to avoid (desconocer), to confront the traits and habits distorting how you see reality and inhibiting the full use of your facultades" (p. 540).

We explain that this journey requires then not only different ways of writing, but also different forms of writing that help us to reclaim some part of our identities. The autohistoria is a "genre of writing about one's personal and collective history using fictive elements," says Anzaldúa (2002), "a sort of fictionalized autobiography or memoir," and an autohistoria-teoría is "a personal essay that theorizes" (p. 578). So, we ask our students to write about each stage and to adopt at least three different genres throughout the essay. Mixing genres helps students connect with various stages on the path in a way that may be rhetorically appropriate for a particular experience. As a mode of inquire, this assignment asks students to theorize lived experiences, and that process, in and of itself, becomes an opportunity for students to reclaim any part of themselves that may have been lost due to assimilation or acculturation.

In the United States, Latinxs struggle with the erasure of their ethnicities and histories, especially in educational spaces (Haney-López, 1997; García & Castro, 2011; San Miguel, 2013). The most recent effort took place in Arizona, where the state passed an ethnic study ban in public schools to dismantle a popular Mexican-American studies program (Elnagar, 2013; Jensen, 2013; Wanberg, 2013).[11] Recently, U.S. District Judge A. Wallace Tashima blocked the ban because he found the law "was enacted and enforced, not for a legitimate educational purpose, but for an invidious discriminatory racial purpose" (qtd. in Tang, 2017, par. 4). To counter these erasures, Pérez (1999) calls for a return to an individual's own historical examination. Self-examination processes as modes of inquiry help awaken not only a historical consciousness but also race and ethnic consciousness that may expose cultural trauma. Such trauma can cause discomfort for those who try to deny that that damage exists, but the exposure can also help heal when individuals find ways to respond to the trauma of others. Psychologist Lillian Comas-Díaz (2006) argues that ethnic psychology (i.e., *cuentos, dichos,* and spirituality) serves as a cultural affirmation and resilient practice in Latinx psychotherapy. An ethnic psychology recognizes the cultural lived experiences within the Latinx community. Chicanx feminist Edén E. Torres (2003) says that exposing what she calls a "lived theory" allows people of color to "develop various methods for actualizing [a] desire for change" (p. 3). When persons of color discover meaning in a lived theory, Torres (2003) suggests, they reveal surprisingly inherent survival abilities in that a lived theory extends beyond the individual to include also the collective experiences of the community. Tied to our historic experiences as culture is the trauma that has been "accumulated in our collective psyche through racism, sexism, and classism, as well as other forms of oppression" (Torres, 2003, p. 17):

> Part of the reason this history has continued to take its toll on our communities . . . has little to do with individual will or strength. Our people have proven over and over again that we have the desire and the tenacity to not only survive, but to become whole (or self-actualized) and to actively resist oppression. Despite our attempted annihilation . . . we have continued to fight—to struggle against repression. But we cannot ignore our wounds, for they too affect the nature of our survival and the quality of our lives. (Torres, 2003, p. 18)

We use the *autohistoria-teoría* assignment as a vehicle for students, especially Latinx students, to engage a historical consciousness, to make inquiries about their bodies situated in places. Our hope is that through such introspection students reclaim what has been lost as racial and ethnic forms of consciousness awaken. Our purpose is meaningful, because we, like Anzaldúa (2002), believe that "writing is an archetypal journey home to the self, un proceso de crear puentes (bridges) to the next phase, next place, next culture, next reality," and she maintains that writing establishes a way of "rebuilding yourself, composing a story that more accurately expresses your new identity" (p. 574). Now, Anzaldúa is speaking specifically about what the act of writing offers *nepantleras*, who like us are activists forging bonds across spaces with bridges. But, nevertheless, her notions about writing are relevant when it comes to marginalized students, who must similarly seek to forge bonds across academic spaces too. These students are bordered writers, like us, who struggle with acts of writing as means to forge a bond in either a personal or academic space. To help us forge that bond, we find that we have to use our imagination often.

2. Reimagination: Awakening the Flesh for Ethnic Inquiry

> I write the myths in me, the myths I am, the myths I want to become. . . . Escribo con la tinta de mi sangre.
>
> —Anzaldúa, "Tlilli, Tlapalli"

The second rhetorical tool we draw from Chicanx feminist thought is reimagination, actions to reimagine identities by discursive practices. Reimagination aids processes of awakening the flesh for self or ethnic inquiry, for if we are to write our own myths, then we need to reimagine who we are to become. When we first entered higher education, we imagined the possibilities of an education and what that education could provide, but the barriers we faced (e.g., our time in remedial and/or developmental writing) limited our possibilities to see ourselves as writers or scholars, but only as failures who struggled to speak and write as academics (Scholes, 1998; Bartholomae, 1985). So, we had to learn how to reimagine the possibilities yet again. "Without imagination," says Anzaldúa (2015), "transformation would not be possible" (p. 44). Reimagining who we were in such environments led us to transform our identities and to reinvent our experiences in higher education. *Somos Chicanx! We are our language!* Anzaldúa (2015) explains that imagination "opens the road to both personal and societal change—transformation of self, consciousness, community, culture, society" (p. 44). Therefore, we adopt reimagination as a rhetorical tool that can serve students, especially Latinx students who need to reimagine their situatedness. As a tool, reimagination can serve as a mode of inquiry that aids in awakening, bringing into consciousness, epistemologies of the flesh, which include "those of the body, dreams, institutions, as well as senses other than the five physical senses" (Anzaldúa, 2015, p. 44).

Our ability to reimagine for ourselves epistemologies, we believe, contributed greatly to our self or ethnic inquiry as well as our discovery in the influential nature of places like home and community, but more importantly, academia. Home, school, and community contribute significantly to the development of Latinx students' epistemologies (Bernal, 2006; Epstein, 2001; Ortiz, 2004). These cultures are interconnected. It is for that reason that "culturally relevant" approaches to teaching become important because these approaches use "students' culture to help them create meaning and understand the world" (Ladson-Billings, 1992, pg. 106). To awaken the self or to reimagine the self is an embodied experience that "evolves out of the experiences of the body," according to Anzaldúa (2000, p. 98). So, we design writing assignments that place value on bodily experiences. A self-examination of those experiences aids with awakening the flesh, so to speak, for self or ethnic inquiry. Reimagination offers a space for students to reimagine their identities through acts of writing. This space can serve as a gateway to help students cross other places they find threatening, isolating, or alienating.

The Telling Our Abuela's Story Self-Examination Assignment

We often tell our students that the greatest tragedy is never truly knowing or capturing stories by the matriarchs in our lives. One of the most challenging writing assignments we require in a Composition II class, what is generally referred to as ENGL 1302 for first-year students, is the ethnographic digital narrative assign-

ment titled "Telling Our Abuela's Story." I built this project from Susan Loudermilk Garza's and Sharon Talley's event, Telling our Grandmother's Stories.[12] As a whole, this assignment is an opportunity for self-examination. The project will ask students to engage in three rhetorical moves: a personal reflection, a field study that includes an interview with a matriarchal figure in their life, and a digital narrative. The personal reflection requires an intensive self-examination and students must wrestle with their understanding of terms like feminism, sexism, sexuality, or violence. We find that they most students seem to struggle with writing about their own experiences, but often, they choose to write about a memory that is painful, shameful, or traumatic. One student, a white male, wrote about his history of sexually objectifying women. He chose to open up about his struggle with misogyny. We must stress that we never force students to move into a deeper historical examination about their flesh, but we find that when students are invited to explore their histories, they often are moved to learn more about their behaviors. This particular student eventually shared in his reflection how his mother abandoned him as a toddler, leaving him with an alcoholic and abusive father. Until then, he had never connected his anger and resentment towards his estranged mother with his history of disrespecting women. His self-examination concluded with emotional regret and shame. He realized that he did not want to become his father, and he no longer wanted to blame his mother. He eventually interviewed his great-aunt and discovered that she was quite active in her prime with feminist movements. His final digital narrative revealed an optimistic young man, whose project inspired him to learn more about how he can get involved with social movements. We align this project with a theory in the flesh because it urges students to study their own flesh for ruptures then use these ruptures to re-interpret the stories they imagined living for themselves. "For only through the pulling of the flesh," as Anzaldúa (1987/1999c) says, "can the human soul be transformed. And for images, words, stories to have this transformative power, they must arise from the human body—flesh and bone . . ." (p. 97). Through this process, we believe, students find ways to build bridges and cross borders they encounter.[13]

When it comes to literacy and literacy practices, we find Latinx bodies in the United States are notoriously bordered. For instance, Jessica M. Vasquez (2011), who writes about how educational institutions reproduce power relations and the racial hierarchy of society, acknowledges how "disastrously successful" low expectations of Mexican-Americans' achievement can be at "squelching ambition" within academic spaces (p. 178). Also, while investigating third-generation Mexican-American youth, Vasquez finds that devaluing norms have replaced segregated schooling since the *Brown v. Board of Education* ruling in 1954, such as "school tracking systems, low expectations for minority performance based on negative stereotypes, and classroom curriculum that devalues non-European American 'subjugated knowledges' " (p. 182). These attitudes toward literacy and literacy practices in the U.S. coincide with findings by Gregorio Hernandez-Zamora (2010), who writes about peoples of Mexican descent and literacy. Hernandez-Zamora claims, "Millions of descendants of the former colonized or enslaved peoples are now classified as school failures, illiterates (absolute or 'functional'), poor readers, bad writers, worse learners and slow thinkers" (p. 7). Such classifications are reminiscent of our own experiences, but fortunately not all. These classifications reflect a pervasive sociocultural and sociopolitical context over the centuries, according to Hernández-Zamora (2010):

> For five centuries Mexicans in particular have encountered European literacy and education as instruments of conquest and colonization, economic deprivation, and cultural assimilation and dislocation. And this social history of economic destruction, cultural alienation and educational segregation is inscribed in the personal histories of today's globalized Mexicans. (p. 7)

As a result, it is easy to understand why Latinx bodies are associated as occupying a representational space in border literacies. As our experiences have shown, more often than not, the social construction of Latinx identity and their language is, if not ignored, bordered in academic spaces, especially inside classrooms that involve writing (Guerra, 2004; Kells, 2002; Mejía, 2004; Villanueva, 1992). Therefore, we ask that students reflect on their identities and their experiences and to reimagine those lived spaces through acts of writing.

The Kitchen Table Assignment
   To prepare for a major social inquiry research project, we ask students to first recreate their home through a series of visual and textual art projects. One project includes a pre-writing activity titled "The Kitchen Table." For this assignment, we ask students to recreate the dining table in their home and to provide a space at the table for members of their family. We ask students to reimagine that table as a table of their own design and to make decisions

about who sits at the table in their version, and, needless to say, we find students engage this assignment creatively, providing seats at the table for God, the Devil, a deceased member of their family, abuelas, teachers, pets, etc. Our expectations are that students must define the individuals seated at the table and must indicate their significance in relation to their lives. They must also list two or three social issues that affect each individual seated at the kitchen table. "What worries abuela, and how would you list those as specific issues?" Afterwards, we ask students to spend a great deal of time cataloging these issues by either using illustrations or cut-out images. We commonly come across students that depict kitchen table with pictures of war, drugs, healthcare labels, prescription bottles, or money signs. Our goal for this activity is for students to use the kitchen table as an opportunity to frame research in a much more personal level by showcasing how that research or issues connect with figures from students' home or community. Pedagogically, this practice is a strategic and creative approach that we find aids students to reimagine their place within a home or community. Students see how personal spaces are political within their own cultural background. As a mode of inquiry, the personal becomes political when students are much more likely to engage in meaningful research and to engage in personally invested exploratory writing over social issues that truly matter to them. To engage culturally relevant issues, as this assignment demonstrates, is to ask students to awaken parts of their flesh for self or ethnic inquiry.

What the kitchen table assignment shows is how writing involves the production of spaces. There is an act of spatialization that takes place in the act of writing, where writing not only causes something to occupy space, but also places that something into a specific context. It is for that reason that writing is interactive with an environment, interpretive in its production, and situated by varying context-specificities.[14] This point of view aligns with post-process notions about writing, and as such, we consider acts of writing as interactive in that acts of writing respond to a complex matrix of activity systems within varying ecologies, ecologies of discourse in particular. Because "writing itself is spatial," as Nedra Reynolds (1998) recognizes, "we cannot very well conceive of writing in ways other than spatial" (p. 14). So, the kitchen table serves as our spatial metaphor for writing to take place, and this act of writing engenders a spatial body that constitutes a *distinctive place-identity*, "meaningful aspects of identity linked to places felt" (Hinojosa, 2016, p. 103). This act of writing will engage a student in an "activity through which a person is continually engaged with a variety of socially constituted systems" (Cooper, 1986, p. 367). Thus, the act of writing becomes "an act of being" that emerges in relation to place and the writing, in and of itself, becomes an artifact that potentially shapes "ways of being together" with and in such a place (Yagelski, 2011, p. 4). This ecological orientation of writing helps us to reimagine the composition classroom as that place "where(ever) the student is carrying out the practices of writing," as Johnathon Mauk (2003) suggests (p. 385), as well as that place where the larger purpose of writing for writers, as Robert P. Yagelski (2011) asserts, is "to *be* in the world in a more reflective, self-aware, and . . . altruistic way" (emphasis in original, p. 159). The goal in designing assignments, like the kitchen table or our *abuela's* stories, is to produce writing that is directed beyond the "limited scope of classroom assignments to address larger, public audiences" (Dobrin & Weisser, 2002, p. 58).

Conclusion

We shared our lived experiences in *testimonio-like reflections*, describing encounters with HSIs and pedagogical practices implemented in first-year composition classrooms. *Maybe our rhetorical moves show how discourses interrupt one another in academic spaces. Maybe our moves indicate alternative literacy practices. Or, maybe it simply shows that we think and read differently.* We spoke as writers, as students, as practitioners, and as scholars. Our tongues called up a linguistic polyvocality to reflect our sense of borderedness and to demonstrate the complexity of our identities. These were the discursive spaces we created as bordered writers to reveal our ethnicities and to enable our bordered brown bodies to articulate our Chicanx thought. We presented how Chicanx thought may offer practitioners rhetorical tools; tools as modes of inquiry. The first tool was reclamation, actions to reclaim bodies and their histories by discursive practices. The second tool was reimagination, actions to reimagine identities by discursive practices. Enacted together, these tools will aid first-year students in composition classrooms, especially in classrooms situated along the U.S.–Mexico border, to develop a historical consciousness that awakens their ethnic consciousness for political inquiry and their flesh for self or ethnic inquiry. We would argue that politically cognizant and self-aware individuals are more likely to recognize actions and discourses that do harm to their bodies, identities, ethnicities, or histories.

In higher education, racist and discriminatory discourses prevail to this day. Amie A. Macdonald and Susan Sánchez-Casal (2009) point out that people of color still have limited access to higher education, and persons of color who do gain access must still confront "racial bias at all levels of institution life, in particular in the form of exclusive Eurocentric curriculum, lack of equal access to educational resources, and overt and implicit racism in the classroom and on campus" (p. 2). To varying degrees, our lived experiences reflect these confrontations. But, that is not to say that all institutions of higher education limit access or harbor racial bias to persons of color. *There is hope!* Institutions of higher learning, HSIs in particular, are on a path to serve better Latinx or underserved students of color. Practitioners who contributed to this collection are evidence of that hopeful outlook. Looking back, we credit our fellow practitioners for *serving* us well at Texas A&M University–Corpus Christi, an HSI located in south Texas. It was there our now colleagues enacted lessons learned on how to serve Latinx students before Michelle Hall Kells outlined them in *Teaching Writing with Latino/a Students* back in 2007. Based on our experiences, we find that they served as our "advocates of literacy and language awareness," as our "cultural mediators," and as our mentors, promoting us along our journeys as "new scholars into PhD programs, job placements, publication opportunities, and tenured positions" (p. ix). We are who we say we are today because of such service and guidance and because of this lived experience. *Somos Chicanx! Adelante!*

Notes

1. There are numerous court cases that address inequalities in education for people of color, especially for Mexican Americans, such as *Brown v. the Board of Education of Topeka, Kansas* (1954); *Cisneros v. Corpus Christi Independent School District* (1970); *Rodríguez v. San Antonio Independent School District* (1973); *Edgewood Independent School District v. Kirby* (1989); *LULAC v. Richards* known as "The South Texas Initiative" in 1987 and later renamed *Richards v. LULAC* (1993); *Grutter v. Bollinger* (2003).

2. Some writers use the @ sign as a nonsexist signifier. However, we would like to point out how a sexist signification persists with the @ sign. As a script, the *oversized* masculine character (o) encircles the *smaller* feminine character (a) completely. In our view, this visual representation perpetuates both male dominance over females and the gender inequalities that exist between the sexes.

3. Brian V. Street publishes extensively on theoretical and applied perspectives in literacy and literacy practices, and Lisa Delpit identifies and describes a "culture of power" when it comes to literacy. She details five aspects of such power beginning with classrooms, where issues of "power are enacted." She then goes on to claim that there are "codes or rules for participating in power." Moreover, these rules are "a reflection of the rules of the culture of those who have power." Delpit asserts, "If you are not already a participant in the culture of power, being told explicitly the rules of that

culture makes acquiring power easier." And finally, she maintains that "[t]hose with power are frequently least aware of—or least willing to acknowledge—its existence" while "[t]hose with less power are often most aware of its existence" (pp. 24–26).

4. ¿De Donde? by Mary Gallagher was Hinojosa's first major production where he played an immigration lawyer and a coyoté crossing migrant workers across the border.

5. Published originally in Notes from the Second Year: Women's Liberation in 1970 by editors Shulamith Firestone and Anne Koedt, "The Personal is Political" is a paper by Carol Hanisch, who referred to "political" in the broadest sense of the word to suggest relationships with power.

6. In their work, Medina and Posadas (2012) refer to Teresa J. Guess, who wrote "The Social Construction of Whiteness: Racism by Intent, Racism by Consequence."

7. James Paul Gee (1987/1999), in "What is Literacy?" defines "a discourse" as a "socially accepted association among ways of using language, of thinking, and of acting that can be used to identify oneself as a member of a socially meaningful group or 'social network'" (p. 29).

8. Chicano historian Rodolfo Acuña (1988) claims that in practice "the treaty was ignored and during the nineteenth century most Mexicans in the United States were considered as a class apart from the dominant race" (p. 20).

9. Refer to "Now let us shift . . . the path of conocimiento . . . inner work, public acts" by Anzaldúa (2002).

10. Refer to "The 1,001-piece nights of Gloria Anzaldúa: Autohistoria-teoría at Florida Atlantic University" by Neile (2005).

11. On May 11, 2010, the state of Arizona passed House Bill 2281 to ban ethnic studies programs in K-12 public schools.

12. For more information, read "Telling Our Grandmothers Stories: Teaching and Celebrating the History of the Women of Our Lives" by Susan Loudermilk Garza and Sharon Talley (2005) in the Journal of the Association for Research on Mothering.

13. Refer to "Now let us shift . . . the path of conocimiento . . . inner work, public acts" by Gloria Anzaldúa (2002) in This Bridge We Call Home: Radical Visions for Transformation edited by Gloria E. Anzaldúa and Analouise Keating.

14. Lee-Ann M. Kastman Breuch (2002) outlines three post-process assumptions about writing: writing is public, writing is interpretive, and writing is situated.

References

Acuña, R. (1988). Occupied America: A history of Chicanos. 3rd ed. New York: Harper Collins.

Adger, C. T. (1997). Issues and implications of English dialects for teaching English as a second language. Alexandria, VA: Teachers of English to Speakers of Other Languages.

Alarcón, N. (2002). Anzaldúa's Frontera: Inscribing Gynetics. In A. J. Aldama & N. H. Quiñonez (Eds.), Decolonial voices: Chicana and Chicano cultural studies in the 21st century (pp. 113–126). Bloomington: Indiana University Press.

Alcoff, L. M. (2006). *Visible identities: Race, gender, and the self.* New York: Oxford University Press, Inc.

Anzaldúa, G. (1987/1999a). *Borderlands/la frontera: The new mestiza.* San Francisco: Aunt Lute Books.

Anzaldúa, G. (1987/1999b). La conciencia de las mestiza: Towards a new consciousness. In *Borderlands/la frontera: The new mestiza* (2nd ed., pp. 87–97). San Francisco: Aunt Lute Books.

Anzaldúa, G. (1987/1999c). Tlilli, tlapalli: The path of the red and black ink. In *Borderlands/la frontera: The new mestiza* (2nd ed., pp. 87–97). San Francisco: Aunt Lute Books.

Anzaldúa, G. (2000). *Interviews: Entrevistas.* (A. Keating, Ed.). New York: Routledge.

Anzaldúa, G. (2002). Now let us shift . . . the path of conocimiento . . . inner work, public acts. In A. Keating & G. Anzaldúa (Eds.), *This bridge we call home: Radical visions for transformation* (pp. 540–576). New York: Routledge Press.

Anzaldúa, G. (2009). The new mestiza nation: A multicultural movement. In A. Keating (Ed.), *The Gloria Anzaldúa reader* (pp. 203–216). Durham, NC: Duke University Press.

Anzaldúa, G. (2015). *Light in the dark/luz en lo oscuro: Rewriting identity, spirituality, reality.* (A. Keating, Ed.). Durham, NC: Duke University Press.

Arreola, D. D. (2002). *Tejano south Texas: A Mexican American cultural province.* Austin: University of Texas Press.

Babino, A., & Stewart, M. A. (2016). "I like English better:" Latino dual language students' investments in Spanish, English, and bilingualism. *Journal of Latinos and Education, 16*(1), 18–29.

Bartholomae, D. (1985). Inventing the University. In V. Villanueva (Ed.), *Cross-Talk in Comp Theory: A Reader* (623–653). 2nd ed. Urbana: NCTE, 2003.

Bernal, D. D. (1998). Using a Chicana feminist epistemology in educational research. *Harvard Review, 68*(4), 555–583.

Bernal, D. D. (2006). Learning and living pedagogies of the home: The mestiza consciousness of Chicana students. In D. D. Bernal, C. A. Elenes, F. E. Godinez, & S. Villenas (Eds.), *Chicana/Latina education in everyday life: Feminista perspectives on pedagogy and epistemology* (pp. 113–132). Albany: State University of New York Press.

Blair, C. (1999). Contemporary U.S. memorial sites as exemplars of rhetoric's materiality. In J. Selzer & S. Crowley (Eds.), *Rhetorical bodies* (pp.15–57). Madison: University of Wisconsin Press.

Brady, M. P. (2002). *Extinct lands, temporal geographies: Chicana literature and the urgency of space.* Durham, NC: Duke University Press.

Brown v. Board of Education of Topeka, Kansas, 347 U.S. 483; 74 S. Ct. 686; 98 L. Ed. 873 (Supreme Court of the United States 1954).

Cisneros v. Corpus Christi Independent School District, 324 F.S.D. Texas. 599 (1970).

Carmichael, J., Edwards, R., Miller, K., & Smith, J. (2007). Researching literacy for learning in the vocational curriculum. In M. Osborne, M. Houston, & N. Toman (Eds.), *The pedagogy of lifelong learning: Understanding effective teaching and learning in diverse contexts* (pp. 79–89). London: Routledge.

Comas-Díaz, L. (2001). Hispanics, Latinos, or Americanos: The evolution of identity. *Cultural Diversity and Ethnic Minority Psychology, 7*(2), 115–120.

Comas-Díaz, L. (2006). Latino healing: The integration of ethnic psychology into psychotherapy. *Psychotherapy: Theory, Research, Practice, Training, 43*(4), 436–453.

Contreras, F. E., & Bensimon, E. M. (2005, November). *An equity-based accountability framework for Hispanic Serving Institutions.* Paper presented at the meeting of the Association for the Study of Higher Education, Philadelphia, PA.

Cooper, M. M. (1986). The ecology of writing. *College English, 48*(4), 364–375.

Delpit, L. (1995). *Other people's children: Cultural conflict in the classroom.* New York: The New Press.

Dobrin, S. I., & Weisser, C. R. (2002). *Natural discourse: Toward ecocomposition.* New York: State University of New York Press.

Edgewood Independent School District v. Kirby, 777 S.W.2d. Texas 391 (1989).

Elnagar, H. (2013). *Arizona's ethnic studies ban, "othering," and the rhetoric of color-blindness* (Order No. 1543968). Available from ProQuest Dissertations & Theses Global. (1433074999). Retrieved from https://manowar.tamucc.edu

Epstein, J. L. (2001). Building bridges of home, school, and community: The importance of design. *Journal of Education for Students Placed at Risk, 6*(1–2), 161–168.

Flores, L. A. (1996). Creating discursive space through a rhetoric of difference: Chicana feminists craft a homeland. *Quarterly Journal of Speech, 82,* 142–156.

García, A. M. (Ed.). (1997). *Chicana feminist thought: The basic historical writings.* New York: Routledge.

García, M. T., & Castro, S. (2011). Blowout!: Sal Castro and the Chicano struggle for educational justice. Chapel Hill: The University of North Carolina Press.

Garza, S. L., & Talley, S. (2005). Telling our grandmothers' stories: Teaching and celebrating the history of the women in our lives. *Journal of the Association for Research on Mothering, 7*(2), 125–132.

Gee, J. P. (2006). What is literacy. In P. Vandenberg, S. Hum, & J. Clary-Lemon (Eds.), *Relations, locations, positions: Composition theory for writing teachers* (pp. 29–39). Urbana, IL: National Council of Teachers of English. (Original work published in 1987.)

González, N. (2001). *I am my language: Discourses of women and children in the borderlands.* Tucson: University of Arizona Press.

Grutter v. Bollinger, 539. U.S. 306 (2003).

Guerra, J. C. (2004). Emerging representations, situated literacies, and the practice of transcultural repositioning. In M. H. Kells, V. Balester, & V. Villanueva (Eds.), *Latino/a discourses: on language, identity, and literacy education* (pp. 7–23). Portsmouth, NH: Boynton/Cook.

Guess, T. J. (2006). The social construction of whiteness: Racism by intent, racism by consequence. *Critical Sociology, 32*(4), 649–673.

Haney-López, I. F. (1997). Race, ethnicity, erasure: The salience of race to LatCrit Theory. *California Law Review, 85*(5), 1143–1211.

Hernandez-Zamora, G. (2010). *Decolonizing literacy: Mexican lives in the era of global capitalism.* Bristol, UK: Multilingual Matters.

Hinojosa, Y. I. (2016). Localizing the body for practitioners in writing studies. In D. R. Perez, L. M. Mercado-Lopéz, & S. Saldívar-Hull (Eds.), *El mundo zurdo 5: Selected works from the meetings of the society for the study of Gloria Anzaldúa* (pp. 101–110). San Francisco, CA: Aunt Lute Books.

Hinojosa, Y. I., & Zepeda, C. (2018). The Coyolxauhqui imperative in developing comunidad-situated writing curricula at Hispanic-Serving Institutions. In S. A. Ramírez, L. M. Mercado-López, & S. Saldívar-Hull (Eds.), *El mundo zurdo 6: Selected works form the meeting of the society for the study of Gloria Anzaldúa* (pp. 57–71). San Francisco, CA: Aunt Lute Books.

Hyun, E. (2006). Transforming instruction into pedagogy through curriculum negotiation. *Journal of Curriculum and Pedagogy, 3*(1), 136–164.

Jensen, B. (2013). Chapter six: Race erased? Arizona's ban on ethnic studies. *Counterpoints.* 445, 81–100.

Kastman-Breuch, L. M. (2002). Post-process "pedagogy": a philosophical exercise. *JAC, 22*(1), 119–150.

Kells, M. H. (2002). Linguistic contact zones in the college writing classroom: an examination of ethnolinguistic identity and language attitudes. *Written Communication, 19*(1), 5–42.

Kells, M. H. (2007). Foreword: Lessons Learned at Hispanic-Serving Institutions. In C. Kirklighter, D. Cárdenas, & S. W. Murphy (Eds.), *Teaching writing with Latino/a Students: Lessons Learned at Hispanic-Serving Institutions* (pp. vii–xiv). Albany: State University of New York Press.

Kirklighter, C., Cárdenas, D., & Murphy, S. W. (Eds.). (2007). *Teaching writing with Latino/a students: Lessons learned at Hispanic-serving Institutions.* New York: State University of New York Press.

Ladson-Billings, G. (1992). Culturally relevant teaching: the key to making multicultural education work. In C. A. Grant (Ed.), *Research and multi-cultural education: From the margins to the mainstream* (pp. 102–118). London: The Falmer Press.

Lane, J. E., & Brown, M. C. (2003). Looking backward to see ahead: Implications for research, policy, and practice. *New Directions in Institutional Research, 118,* 105–111.

Luke, A. (2000). "Critical literacy in Australia: A matter of context and standpoint." *Journal of Adolescent & Adult Literacy, 43*(5), 448–461.

Macdonald, A. A., &. Sánchez-Casal, S. (2009). Introduction [Introduction]. In Sánchez-Casal, S., & Macdonald, A. A. (Eds.), *Identity in Education* (pp. 2–6). New York: Palgrave Macmillan.

Martínez, O. J. (1994). *Border people: Life and society in the U.S.-Mexico borderlands.* Tucson: The University of Arizona Press.

Massey, D. (1994). *Space, place, and gender.* Minneapolis: University of Minnesota Press.

Massey, D. (2005). *For space.* London: Sage.

Mauk, J. (2003). "Location, location, location: The 'real' (e)states of being, writing, and thinking in composition." *College English, 65*(4), 368–388.

Medina, C. A., & Posadas, C. E. (2012). Hispanic student experiences at a Hispanic-Serving Institution: Strong voices, key message. *Journal of Latinos and Education, 11*(3), 182–188.

Mejía, J. (2004). Bridging rhetoric and composition studies with Chicano and Chicana studies: A turn to critical pedagogy. In M. H. Kells, V. Balester, & V. Villanueva (Eds.), *Latino/a Discourses: On Language, Identity and Literacy Education* (pp. 40–56). Portsmouth, NH: Boynton/Cook.

Mendez Newman, B. (2007). Teaching writing at Hispanic-Serving Institutions. In C. Kirklighter, D. Cárdenas, & S. W. Murphy (Eds.), *Teaching writing with Latino/a students: Lessons learned at Hispanic-serving Institutions* (pp. 17–35). Albany: State University of New York Press.

Murakami-Ramalho, E., Núñez, A., & Cuero, K. K. (2010). Latin@ advocacy in the hyphen: faculty identity and commitment in a Hispanic-Serving Institution. *International Journal of Qualitative Studies in Education, 23*(6), 699–717.

Neile, C. S. (2005). The 1,001-piece nights of Gloria Anzaldúa: Autohistoria-teoría at Florida Atlantic University. In A. Keating (Ed.), *Entre mundos/among worlds: New perspectives on Gloria Anzaldúa* (pp. 17–27). New York: Palgrave Macmillan.

Oboler, S. (1995). *Ethnic labels, Latino lives: Identity and the politics of (re)presentation in the United States.* Minneapolis: University of Minnesota Press.

Ortiz, A. M. (2004). Promoting the success of Latino students: A call to action. *New Directions for Student Services, 2004*(105), 89–97.

Owens, K. H. (2018). In Lak'ech, The Chicano clap, and fear: A partial rhetorical autopsy of Tucson's now-illegal ethnic studies classes. *College English, 80*(3), 247–270.

Padilla, F. M. (1985). *Latino ethnic consciousness: The case of Mexican Americans and Puerto Ricans in Chicago.* Notre Dame, IN: University of Norte Dame Press.

Palmer, P. J. (1998). *The courage to teach: Exploring the inner landscape of a teacher's life.* San Francisco, CA: Jossey-Bass.

Pérez, E. (1999). *The Decolonial Imaginary.* Bloomington: Indiana University Press.

Rendón, L. I. (1994). Validating culturally diverse students: Toward a new model of learning and student development. *Innovative Higher Education, 19*(1), 33–51.

Rendón, L. I. (2009). *Sentipensante (sensing/thinking) pedagogy: Educating for wholeness, social justice and liberation.* Sterling, VA: Stylus Pub.

Rendón, L. I., Nora, A., & Kanagala, V. (2014). *Ventajas/Assets y conocimientos/knowledge: Leveraging Latin@ strengths to foster student success.* San Antonio, TX: Center for Research and Policy in Education, The University of Texas at San Antonio.

Reynolds, N. (1998). "Composition's imagined geographies: the politics of space in the frontier, city, and cyberspace." *College Composition and Communication, 50*(1), 12–35.

Richards v. LULAC, 868 S.W.2d 306 (Supreme Court of Texas 1993).

Rodríguez v. San Antonio Independent School District 411 U.S. 1; 93 S. Ct. 1278; 36 L. Ed. 2d 16 (Supreme Court of the United States 1973).

Ruecker, T. (2015). *Transiciones: Pathways of Latinas and Latinos writing in high school and college.* Logan: Utah State University Press.

San Miguel Jr., G. (2013). *Chicana/o struggles for education: Activism in the community* (1st ed.). College Station: Texas A&M University Press.

Sandoval, C. (2000). *Methodology of the oppressed.* Minneapolis, MN: University of Minnesota Press.

Scholes, R. (1998). *The Rise and Fall of English*. New Haven, CT: Yale University Press.

Selzer, J. (1999). Habeas corpus: An introduction [Introduction]. In J. Selzer & S. Crowley (Eds.), *Rhetorical bodies* (pp. 3–15). Madison: University of Wisconsin Press.

Shapiro, S. B. (1999). *Pedagogy and the politics of the body: A critical praxis*. New York: Garland Publishing, Inc.

Street, B. V. (1985). *Literacy in theory and practice*. New York: Cambridge University Press.

Tang, T. (2017). Judge blocks Arizona ethnic studies ban he found was racist. *U.S. News & World Report*. U.S. News & World Report, 28 Dec., 7:25 p.m., www. usnews.com/news/best-states/arizona/articles/2017-12-28/judge-blocks-ban-on-ethnic-studies-in-tucson-school-district.

Tileagă, C. (2006). Discourse, dominance and power relations: Inequality as a social and interactional object. *Ethnicity, 6*(4), 476–497.

Torres, E. E. (2003). *Chicana without apology: The new Chicana cultural studies*. New York: Routledge University Press.

Ullman, C. (2005). Globalization on the border: reimagining economies, identities, and schooling in El Paso. In T. L. McCarty (Ed.), *Language, literacy, and power in schooling* (pp. 241–261). Mahwah, NJ: Lawrence Erlbaum.

Vasquez, J. M. (2011). *Mexican Americans across generations: Immigrant families, racial realities*. New York: New York University Press.

Villanueva, V. (1992). *Bootstraps: From an American academic of color*. Urbana, IL: National Council of Teachers of English.

Volk, D., & Angelova, M. (2007). Language ideology and the mediation of language choice in peer interaction in a dual-language first grade. *Journal of Language, Identity & Education, 6*(3), 177–199.

Wanberg, K. (2013). Pedagogy against the state: The ban on ethnic studies in Arizona. *Journal of Pedagogy, 4*(1), 15–35.

Wheeler, R., & Thomas, J. (2013). And still the children suffer: the dilemma of standard English, social justice, and social access. *JAC, 33*(1–2), 363–396.

Yagelski, R. P. (2011). *Writing as a way of being: Writing instruction, nonduality, and the crisis of sustainability*. New York: Hampton.

Chapter 5

Familismo Teaching

A Pedagogy for Promoting Student Motivation and College Success

Yemin Sánchez, Nicole Nicholson, Marcela Hebbard

Despite the remarkable gains with an increase of 114% in the number of bachelor's degrees awarded to Latinx in higher education in the last decade (from 94,644 in 2004 to 202,412 in 2014), nationwide college graduation reporting remains a challenge for this group (Musu-Gillette et al., 2017). In 2015, according to the Institute of Education Sciences (IES) and National Center for Education Statistics, Latinx still ranked lower (37%) than Whites (42%) in the percentage of their respective college-age populations enrolled in a degree-granting institution (Musu-Gillette et al., 2017). In four-year institutions, the NCES also reported 54 percent of Latinx students complete college in a rather extensive six-year period. Nationwide, four-year college completion for Latinx is 30% versus 44% for Whites. Despite graduating the most Latinx students and being among the largest Hispanic-Serving Institutions in the United States, the University of Texas Rio Grande Valley (UTRGV, our home institution) has inherited the challenge of retaining students and improving graduation success within the standard four-year period. Compared to the national statistics, on December 2015, UTRGV Strategic Analysis & Institutional Reporting (SAIR) informed only 21% of its first-time, full-time freshmen cohorts graduated within the four-year timeframe.

These statistics and other complex realities of many Latinx students attending Hispanic-Serving Institutions (HSIs) such as their socioeconomic conditions, their misunderstood language abilities, and cultural traits often lead to deficit views. Labels such as "at-risk" or "academically underprepared" place direct or indirect blame on students (or their families) without acknowledging the institution's own limitations when they fail to provide equitable college opportunities for all students (Rios-Aguilar & Kiyama, 2012). At UTRGV, with a student population of almost 90 percent Latinx students (UTRGV SAIR, 2017), we are mindful of these challenges, and improving graduation success within the standard four-year period has become one of our priorities.

In "The Rhetorician as an Agent for Social Change," Ellen Cushman (1996) urges us to see ourselves beyond the traditional writing instructor and break down barriers. As First-Year Writing (FYW) instructors, we have accepted this challenge by addressing the needs our students holistically and by viewing them *sin fronteras* or without borders in an academic borderland which often marginalizes their ways of being, their linguistic repertoires, and their multicultural backgrounds. Thus, our priority centers on developing culturally sustaining pedagogies that improve Latinx students' learning experience, motivation and retention (Paris & Alim, 2017; Gay, 2015; Ladson-Billings, 1995). We must not assume all students have had the same lived experiences, quality of education, and opportunities because this will only continue to perpetuate the assumption that their differences in skill performances and cultural capital are congruent to cognitive deficiencies.

In this chapter, we propose *Familismo Teaching* as a pedagogy for helping Latinx students cross the cultural borders of their home environments into the spaces of higher education. We anticipate this pedagogy will allow more equitable and meaningful FYW experiences where students feel empowered and motivated to thrive in a context which feels more familial and less threatening. This chapter is divided as follows: First, we describe different factors affecting Latinx students in higher education particularly in our region. We then provide insights on what instructors can do to support Latinx students in FYW courses. Finally, we explain the origins and traits of *Familismo Teaching* and how it can be implemented in FYW classrooms, and we offer our reflections which invite further research.

Factors Affecting Latinx Students in Higher Education

Knowing our students is crucial not only to better serve them, but also for developing effective curricular plans and pedagogical interventions. Robert P. Yagelski (2000) warns that not knowing our students and their "local situations" limits opportunities for learners and creates alienating and oppressive environments; however, we must be cautious not to see differences of language and cultural capital as deficit (Araiza, Cárdenas Jr., & Loudermilk Garza, 2007); instead we must learn to recognize their value and view them as assets in our classrooms (Paris & Alim, 2017).

In the light of these principles, Yemin conducted action research in her FYW courses. She conducted a thorough needs assessment according to Brown (1995) to understand why in these courses, despite sharing the same cultural heritage as her students, there was a disconnect: a disconnect from her students and her lessons, and a disconnect from the overall academic practices. She wanted to know why many of her students would simply "disappear" from her classes despite her preparedness and efforts to deliver meaningful lessons. It was necessary to understand what led to these conditions and to trace both differences and commonalities among these students to intervene effectively.

The situation and the language-needs assessments revealed students displayed a variety of rich linguistic repertoires and of complex lived home and academic experiences. Each student held captivating life stories that they conveyed in unique ways, often translanguaging or utilizing their full linguistic repertoires, which simultaneously merged their home and academic languages (Garcia, Johnson, & Seltzer, 2017). They often spoke of their psychological and physiological constraints. For many, it was the first time they experienced new social roles and responsibilities. They had new jobs and new sentimental relationships and they had to manage new budgets and schedules. They had less family supervision and scarce academic support. Some did not know how to address an unplanned pregnancy. They felt lost. We have witnessed their constraints in the form of rapid weight loss or weight gain, bald spots, tiredness in their eyes, and absentmindedness during class.

This assessment corroborates previous research which states large numbers of Latinx students in four-year institutions may feel disoriented, displaced, and anxious, especially if they are first-generation students or those coming from families where neither parent had more than a high-school education. Under such conditions these students might leave college by the end of their first year (Pascarella, Pierson, Wolniak, & Terenzini, 2004). At UTRGV, over 60% of the students are first-generation students (UTRGV SAIR, 2017).

Furthermore, the assessment also revealed how geographical conditions impact our students. Many students confronted unpredictable and dangerous commutes from Mexico into the United States or lacked transportation from their remote *colonias* to campus, which affected their attendance. This has also been noted by other researchers in different contexts (Mendez Newman, & García, this volume; Ruecker, 2014). Being one of the poorest areas in the country, many students face critical socioeconomic and educational challenges. Under these conditions, students become one of the "hardest to serve" (Arias, 1986; Fields, 1988; Oakes, Rogers, Silver, Valladares, Terriquez, McDonough, Renée, & Lipton, 2006; Gándara & Contreras, 2009).

However, the most significant finding was the impact of *familismo*. The cultural trait was most salient among Latinx students and in many ways reaffirmed their identity more than their language. *Familismo* is a multi-disciplinary term widely researched mainly in sociology, anthropology, and psychology. The term can be traced back to the 1950s when it was introduced as "familism," a universal concept referring to strong feelings for the family with emphasis on mutual support, desire to promote the family goals, and the coexistence of the group (Bardis, 1959).

For Latinx communities, *familismo* is the strongest core cultural value (Villarreal, Blozis, & Widaman, 2005) because the family has always served as a tool for survival and coexistence, particularly during harsh social conditions such as poverty, inequality, and racial discrimination (Behnke et al., 2008). Latinx communities have developed the unique capability of supporting each other during difficult circumstances, mainly through their system of familial cultural values and behaviors.

Scholars within cultural change theory emphasize that family support provides psychological comfort; consequently, since it is expected that the family will be the primary source of instrumental and emotional support, there is a desire to maintain strong family ties (Halgunseth, Ispa, & Rudy, 2006). Research conducted by Okagaki and Frensch (1998) found Latinx students (94% from Mexican descent; 50% immigrant) valued motivation and social skills more than cognitive skills and gave priority to socioemotional characteristics more than to academic achievement.

Familismo is understood as a multifaceted construct with attitudinal and behavioral manifestations (Keefe, 1984). In education, it can foster both positive and negative effects. *Attitudinal familismo* refers to feelings of "loyalty, solidarity, and reciprocity" among family members and is comprised of four main components (Lugo Steidel & Contreras, 2003):

1. Desire for familial interconnectedness or maintaining strong family ties.

2. Belief that family comes before the individual's needs and desires.

3. Belief in family reciprocity or mutual benefit in exchanging assets or services.

4. Belief in familial honor and loyalty.

Behavioral familismo refers to the behaviors that reflect these beliefs, such as childrearing, taking care of an ill family member, living near or visiting kin, or providing support for close family and friends (Calzada, Tamis-LeMonda, & Yoshikawa, 2012). At UTRGV, behavioral *familismo* was manifested in the form of constant absences due to the students' needs or desires to support their family in labors such as babysitting for a young sibling, taking care of an elderly family member, or helping out with the family business.

Although attitudinal *familismo* has been observed to be a means of motivation to excel in education for the sake of the family (Esparza & Sánchez, 2008; La Roche & Shriberg, 2004), research also suggests it may negatively impact students' education as we observed previously. Behavioral *familismo* frequently draws the student away from academic practices and environments as students will often join the workforce to provide financial stability for the family. This typically has a negative impact in the student's college attainment since the student's time and energy is often placed on the demands of the job. In addition, this will often cause external and internal conflicts for the student, as they may doubt the need to fulfill their academic or personal goals in order to meet the family needs (Mendez Newman, 2007) and sometimes choose to withdraw completely from college (Velez, 1989). *Familismo* resides in complex borderlands as it coexists between interactions of traditional Latinx culture and contemporary mainstream cultures (Calzada, Tamis-LeMonda, & Yoshikawa, 2012). This constant flux of crossings between these two contexts is hard to navigate, particularly for First Generation Students.

For Latinx students, the family nucleus is broad. It often expands beyond the immediate family to include close relatives and even friends. They get support from these social structures and from their family and home funds of knowledge (Moll et al., 1992). This historically and culturally accumulated set of knowledge, skills, and resources is essential for individual functioning and well-being (Halgunseth et al., 2006). Funds of knowledge also serve as a type of "cultural glue" which sustains relationships between the group beyond the nuclear household (Velez-Ibanez & Greenberg, 2005). To make learning more relevant, experts in education suggest incorporating funds of knowledge into the curriculum, yet they argue that not many know how to transform students' funds of knowledge into effective pedagogical practices (Rios-Aguilar et al., 2011). Following, we explore additional considerations for contemporary pedagogy development and we offer a brief analysis of how *Familismo Teaching* resembles in many ways the principles rooted in some well-established pedagogies.

How Can FYW Instructors support Latinx Students?

We can begin by recognizing the need for more culturally sustaining pedagogies. H. Samy Alim and Django Paris (2017) stress the importance of cultural pluralism for our society and for replicating that pluralism in our classrooms. Instead of assimilation to the academic, White, middle-class, dominant norms, they call for "cultural dexterity." As we know, HSIs were not initially established to serve the educational needs of Latinx students. HSIs began as predominantly White institutions and later became HSIs because they were located close to growing Latinx communities or had an enroll-ment of at least 25% of Latinx students (Hurtado & Ruiz Alvarado, 2015). This reality explains why pedagogies in many composition classrooms at HSIs have been rooted in what Matsuda (2006) calls "the myth of linguistic homogeneity," or the prevalent, unquestioned acceptance of the dominant image of composition students as "native speakers" of Standard English. Thus, we must take action, cross borders, and promote innovative pedagogies by drawing from our students' rich mixture of experiences, languages, and cultural attributes.

We must recognize that different factors, not necessarily academic, also affect students' achievement. Therefore, preparing faculty to work with our increasingly diverse population is crucial, especially at bordered institu-tions where the homogenized U.S. curricular models are no longer effective (Brunk-Chavez, et al., 2015). Instructors should know students are not only physically bordered, but also face ideological constructed borders of language and performativity (Mendez Newman & García, this volume).

Because the FYW classroom is "potentially one of the most student-centered, social sites in students' early academic experience, it could figure prominently in the HSI student's decision to persist or dropout, to cross the threshold or to retreat from the institution" (Mendez Newman, 2007, p. 23). This creates challenging social responsibilities for FYW instructors as they may be contributing, unknowingly and unintentionally, to the oppressing cycle against the most vulnerable groups, denying them access and opportunity.

We are by no means suggesting our colleagues working with Latinx students lack dedication or expertise in the teaching of writing. Rather, our contention is that many may not yet be familiar with the traits and conditions of this group, or they may not be comfortable implementing non-traditional, culturally oriented pedagogies. Therefore, we deem necessary a reconceptualiza-tion of our practice and to be more open and accepting of culturally relevant and responsive pedagogies (*Familismo Teaching* included).

Among such pedagogies is Gloria Ladson-Billings's (1995) Culturally Relevant Pedagogy (CRP) and Geneva Gay's (2010, 2015) Culturally Respon-sive Teaching (CRT). The first one, a "pedagogy of opposition," calls us to use the students' cultures, texts, languages, and ways of being as central and foundational components for successful teaching (see also Hinojosa and de León-Zepeda, this volume). The second emphasizes the need to sustain the heritages, experiences, and perspectives of ethnic groups to better serve students. CRT invites us to recognize that students' achievement extends beyond the academic spectrum and to be cognizant of the "power of caring" because our beliefs will mirror our behaviors in the classroom. Although Ladson-Billings's (1995) and Gay's (2010, 2015) pedagogies were created to meet mostly the needs of African-American children, these are globally applicable and benefiting for any ethnic group.

Familismo Teaching embraces these principles and, just like Gay, we believe teaching is both epistemological and methodological and that diverse cultures can become vehicles for teaching academic knowledge and skills, as well as for enhancing students' personal, social, cultural, and civic development. However, *Familismo Teaching* distinguishes itself from these pedagogies as it emphasizes heavily on *how* the content is delivered. It focuses on creating a multicultural space which encourages students to simultaneously cross over the borders of their home environment into the mainstream academic spaces and vice versa, providing students with opportunities for *transculturing* and for sustaining their ways of being by creating more pleasant educational experiences.

Theoretical Framework and Main Components

Familismo Teaching was designed and developed by Yemin Sánchez in 2015. It is an asset pedagogy that fully embraces the attitudinal and behavioral attributes of *familismo*. As stated previously, Latinx are known to hold robust socioemotional competencies (Reese, Jensen, & Ramirez, 2014) such as those displayed in Latinx families, and which are greatly influenced by their values and practices (Calzada, Tamis-LeMonda, & Yoshikawa, 2012). Thus, it was logical to propose intervention measures that would resemble these sociocultural traits. One of these measures is the implementation of *class families*. These are small teams that serve as the main channel of student interaction and learning throughout the course.

The Latinx funds of knowledge are used to bring a family support system into the learning environment, one which will serve as a positive "pull-in factor" to enhance students' motivation throughout their challenging academic experience. This family support system developed throughout the course is expected to balance the "pull-out factor" often resulting from the demands of the home and family. Rooted in Vygotsky's (1978) theory of learning and important elements of social constructivism (Adams, 2007), the *class families* will serve to develop content knowledge and skills while simultaneously enhancing their most precious sociocultural structure, the family. As a family, students will share academic and personal experiences, goals, stressors, and so forth. This will result in the building of strong family ties, reciprocity, and interconnectedness. The constant mutual support within the *class families* should provide strong motivation when dealing with the scholarly rigors.

This approach challenges previous claims stating the "home family pull-out factor" cannot be outdone by the pull of the educational responsibilities (Mendez Newman, 2007). If indeed the home family pull-out factor cannot be surpassed, Latinx students will always be at a disadvantage. But what about creating a similar force within the classroom that helps students balance the interest and commitment they give to their home with the commitment and interest needed to achieve academically? This is what *Familismo Teaching* tries to do. This approach does not "undo" the attitudinal and behavioral features of the home family; instead, it incorporates all aspects of *familismo* in the classroom. *Class families* will help ease the feelings of alienation or detachment from the academic experiences and increase motivation through the social supportive experiences they create. This mechanism is anticipated to boost retention in our FYW classrooms.

To further enhance students' learning and academic experiences, it was necessary to reduce their stressors (those discussed in the initial needs assessment). For this, *Familismo Teaching* relies on a second component: the *holistic conferences*. These student-teacher interactions are used not only for developing cognition, but also for strengthening other elements of human nature. Drawing from the Rogerian Humanism theory of learning which aligns in many ways with Fink's (2003) Taxonomy of Significant Learning, these conferences are designed for students to enhance their sociocognitive and psychological (emotional/affective) dimensions. In addition, these are designed to promote student metacognitive awareness of their learning processes or actions which yield or hinder academic success. During the *holistic conferences*, the instructor is expected to orient students about scholarly practices and to provide individualized support throughout the course. The instructor should be resourceful, assertive, and nurturing throughout these interactions. Figure 5.1 offers an overview of the essential components of *Familismo Teaching*: Class *families* and strategic *holistic conferences*.

Implementing Familismo Teaching *in the FYW Classroom*

We now discuss how *Familismo Teaching* can be applied in the FYW classroom.

FORMING CLASS FAMILIES

We first suggest forming teams of about 4 to 5 students. These teams or *class families* will develop powerful interconnectedness, support, and cohesion if they share common traits. In our experiences, successful *class families* are

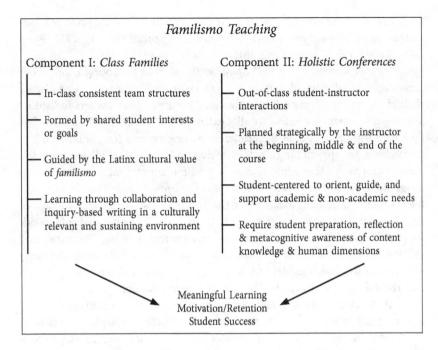

Figure 5.1. Description of main components and general goal.

those typically formed based on similar goals or interests like majors or disciplinary inclinations.

The formation of *class families* has to be strong from the beginning and maintained throughout the course. Unlike many classrooms where collaborative groups are formed ad hoc based on seating habits or changing class projects, the *class families* in *Familismo Teaching* are stable throughout the whole semester. To foster strong and long-lasting foundations, the instructor must provide initial recommendations (orally or written in the syllabus) for how to maintain their *class family*. This can be done by touching base on aspects of *familismo* like reciprocity, respect, loyalty, and mutual support.

We recommend technological support for enhancing communication among the *families*; therefore, exchanging personal profiles and contact information at the beginning of the course will be fundamental. *Families* can use social networks such as Messenger, WhatsApp, Slack, Yammer, or the like as a resource for relating important content information, for asking questions, or for seeking informing about missing assignments when they are absent. We have found students embrace their *families* quite readily and make them their own, not only by giving them unique family names, but also by their tendency of communicating with their class families in their preferred languages. Thus, valuing our students' languages is crucial (CCCC, 1974; Baca, 2007; Canagarajah, 2006; Lang, this volume).

Further strengthening of the *families* throughout the course comes from meaningful inquiry-based writing projects where students develop and discuss their ideas as the project evolves. Although there are instances where individual learning assessment is needed, we allot extensive collaboration within their *class families* during all stages of the academic writing process (i.e., brainstorming, researching, interpreting information, giving and receiving feedback, etc.). We wish to emphasize that while many composition courses include some group assignments, *Familismo Teaching* advocates for a *family* collaboration among a team which will remain together for the entire course. A major advantage of forming *families* is that the team will begin to form its own social framework supported by each member's previous and current writing, linguistic, and cultural experiences. These conditions support Thomas and Thomas's (1989) idea of cohesive and consistent student writing groups, which encourages trust and risk-taking over time, thus benefiting writing development.

To develop cohesion among family members we also encourage developing informal interpersonal interactions. Occasionally, we allocate class time for students to share ideas or experiences about current issues, news, personal "fun facts," or the like. These non-content related topics often motivate students as their presence changes the rigid atmosphere of the class to a more familial environment. Everyone, including the instructor, shares something. This *Family Time* is allocated once a week for 3 to 5 minutes.

Focusing on developing interpersonal relationships among members of the *class families* fosters motivation in Latinx students as their physical, emotional, and educational wellbeing have been observed to increase when familial structures and exchanges of cultural values are in place (Bird et al., 2001; Dumka et al., 1997). In addition, cooperative learning will yield higher achievement and retention (Shrum & Glisan, 2010). We have experienced multiple benefits by integrating *class families* into our courses. The main ones include higher levels of student motivation and an intricate *class family* interconnection which oftentimes yields retention.

IMPLEMENTING HOLISTIC CONFERENCES

Conferencing is a common practice in many composition classes since it is generally accepted that individualized instruction and writing-process feedback is more effective than group-based instruction (Fisher & Murray, 1971; Murray, 1979; Carnicelli, 1980). However, the *holistic conferences* offered in *Familismo Teaching* expand beyond the scope of most traditional conferences.

We offer logistical advice for how to conduct these effectively. First, instructors must set expectations regarding these conferences from the beginning, preferably in the syllabus. The *holistic conferences* are scheduled strategically at the beginning, middle, and end of the course, and each conference is designed to meet different student needs; therefore, these vary in objectives, tasks for students, and length of time. In addition, students must be informed about the point value each session will carry. Since these conferences require anticipated student preparation (often involving previous reading, researching, and reflective writing which increases in difficulty and skill level after each conference), we recommend the first conference should have less point value than the final one. These conferences should take place in the instructor's office or at any place where orientation about location or educational practices might be needed. Instructors must allocate a time that will not conflict with their daily schedules; perhaps considering the cancellation of one or two class sessions would be suited to accommodate all students (this is highly suggested particularly for the third conference, which is more intense and time-consuming).

At first glance, these conferences could easily be dismissed as the usual office hour visits required by some instructors, but that would be an underestimation of their actual intent and value. What sets *holistic conferences* in *Familismo Teaching* apart from other forms of conferencing are the following characteristics:

1. They attend students' needs holistically by addressing all aspects of the human condition, not only cognitive (i.e. sociocultural, psychological, physiological, etc.).

2. They require previous preparation through critical reading, reflection, and metacognitive practices.

3. Scheduling is strategically disseminated throughout the semester to cover different goals (i.e., to orient, inform, reduce stress, assess, provide individualized academic intervention, etc.).

The following is a detailed explanation of these conferences and of their goals and objectives.

First Holistic Conference

The *first holistic conference* is meant to orient Latinx students about the scholarly practices of higher education (raising inquiries, seeking for professional assistance, researching, networking or developing professional social interactions, etc.). We schedule this meeting early in the semester (week 2 or 3) to establish these expectations promptly. This 2- or 3-minute intervention is intended to counterbalance Crosnoe's (2005) observations that male students from less-advantaged families are generally "low-achieving" in terms of grade average and are "weakly oriented" about the scholarly environment as opposed to their non-Latinx counterparts. This first conference is also offered in response to the initial needs assessment where Latinx students were observed to have different cultural views for "office hours." For female students "seeking for help" during this time was congruent with "*causando molestias*," or bothering the instructor, and for the males it was perceived as a weakness or a threat to their "*machista*" pride. Thus, requiring *holistic conferences* orients students' views by allowing them to recognize this valuable and resourceful academic practice and encourages them to employ it more often. In keeping with the second main characteristic of the *holistic conferences*, students are required to prepare before the conference by reading a text such as the syllabus or any other course reading and to raise inquiries about these texts. At the time of their conference, these inquiries will be answered briefly in meaningful one-on-one conversations.

SECOND HOLISTIC CONFERENCE

The *second holistic conference* takes place at mid-semester. It serves as a "temperature-check" of the student's class progress. The instructor provides feedback on specific project(s), but students are also invited to have non-academic talks, again allowing acknowledgment of the whole individual. For this conference, we ask the student to prepare a reflective narrative about the learned content up to that date and an analysis of their perceived strengths and weaknesses in a current project in our course.

The conference then begins with the student's thoughts and concerns, thus allowing the student to set the agenda and take a more active role in this and following conversations (Murray, 1979; Madigan, 1988; Newkirk, 1989). These initial turns of the conversation are crucial for setting the tone for student participation in this environment, especially for second-language students (Ewert, 2009). Asking students to come to the conference prepared to actively negotiate the text at hand sets the stage for a more meaningful exercise in self-assessment (Beach, 1989). It also helps them take more responsibility for their own writing revisions sooner. In addition, we ask students to include in their written reflection a description of a "non-academic" experience they are currently facing and which they feel comfortable sharing. Students often share personal situations affecting them such as an illness, a family problem, or a troubling relationship. We ask students to articulate how that situation impacts their academic performance and together the student and instructor construct solutions to reduce the student's tensions. Thus, this *second holistic conference* (which lasts between 5 to 8 minutes) is offered as a type of "therapeutic session" or "emotionally supportive space" as recommended by Reese, Jensen, and Ramirez (2014). The strategic timing of this conference (week 6 or 7 of the semester) often allows for timely intervention or for prevention of student withdrawal.

THIRD HOLISTIC CONFERENCE

Finally, the *third holistic conference* is scheduled toward the end of the semester (week 12 or 13). It is focused primarily on providing feedback for revision of final products (i.e., final research papers or other projects). Again, we ask students to prepare for the meeting, identifying the strengths and weaknesses of their products, once more allowing students to take ownership over the direction of the conference. This final meeting (about 20 to 30 minutes) can also be an opportunity for a *class family* conference. The small group writing conference fits seamlessly into the Rogerian model and allows for a more dynamic feedback process (Thomas & Thomas, 1989). The objectives of this conference are for the most part academic. However, since a previous personalized and trusting relationship has already been established between instructor and student; those students in need of holistic (non-academic) support will often request it.

We would like to note that considering the student holistically in the context of HSIs will often mean being aware of our students' individual linguistic backgrounds. The range of linguistic repertoires present in our classes could not possibly be addressed completely in whole-group instruction, yet it is an opportunity to acknowledge and embrace them in every *holistic conference*. These conferences are particularly important for ESL students who often perceive our written feedback as vague and hard to understand, rarely resulting in significant revisions (Zamel, 1985). But, when face-to-face conferencing techniques are used, these can be adjusted sensitively to work within each student's zone of proximal development (ZPD) (Vygotsky, 1978) for language growth (Patthey-Chavez & Ferris, 1997). In addition, when ESL students are actively engaged in the negotiation of meaning of their texts, they are more likely to make substantive revisions (Goldstein & Conrad, 1990). We have found that one-on-one conferences allow us to relieve the anxiety many of our multilingual students express about their control of the language. We are also able to gently reassure and redirect them to the deeper elements of rhetorical writing and organization, rather than on the sometimes debilitating grammatical and sentence structure focus they bring.

Since the *first holistic conference* at the beginning of the semester, students should have established a personalized relationship with their instructor, which according to Harris (1986) allows time to 'get acquainted.' This is important as it demonstrates to students how invested we are in them as individuals and that we are interested in who they are, in their ways of being, and in what they have to say. These human interactions will gradually build a relationship of trust between student and instructor and will be reinforced with consistency and practice throughout the course. We would like to highlight how these *holistic conferences* allow students to talk to us about topics that are usually less frequent or absent in traditional, formal academic settings. And, while we do not pretend to take the role of social workers, counselors, or therapists, this approach provides the opportunity for us to acknowledge their struggles and orient them in the right direction when university support might be needed. Most importantly, it is an opportunity to make appropriate student-specific instructional plans and make timely informed decisions to ensure their academic success.

The nature and sequence of these individualized conferences allow students to become more comfortable with different scholarly practices. *Familismo Teaching* implements these required *holistic conferences* as key elements for sustaining healthy relationships and pleasant academic experiences, which will simultaneously inform about the student's quality of learning regarding content and human development. As Mendez Newman and García (this volume) note, these one-on-one interactions with instructors can make a considerable impact on our students' levels of confidence in their voices and writerly inclinations, resulting in significant gains of the students' academic and personal well-being. *Holistic conferences* are also beneficial for instructors as they can use the information obtained through them to assess and modify instructional planning.

Our Reflections as Scholars and Instructors of *Familismo Teaching*

Even though all three of us have seen the positive effects of *Familismo Teaching* in our classrooms, we primarily share Nicole's experiences with this approach since, despite her experience working at other HSIs with different student populations, she still encountered difficulties when transitioning to UTRGV. When Nicole first started teaching at this institution, she was discouraged by the retention rates, which were lower than she had ever experienced. When she heard about *Familismo Teaching*, she was immediately interested and began implementing it the following semester. In the semesters that have followed, similar to Yemin's experiences, she noticed an increase in retention as well as in the cohesion and overall positive tone of the classroom. She has noticed how *Familismo Teaching* helps develop a safer environment for sharing ideas, for giving and receiving feedback, and for communicating in diverse ways. Additionally, she has noted how the learning develops in a more "caring" space as envisioned by Hinojosa and de León Zepeda (this volume). Initially, Nicole was skeptical about the nature of the *holistic conferences*, as these differ from the traditional writing conferences. However, she quickly saw how stronger relationships of trust developed and that they were established sooner than with her former conferencing techniques which typically happened nearing the end of the course.

More than once since the implementation of *Familismo Teaching*, colleagues have commented on the nature of our conferencing approach, emphasizing how our conversations are focused, individualized, and in many ways inviting. For the most part, our students feel recognized not only as producers of texts in "distant" academic languages, but also as human beings with tangible complex lives. They feel oriented and safer in unfamiliar academic borderlands. This is a direct result of our efforts to show our esteem for their holistic human worth and their individual academic potential. Preliminary observations of student reflections resulting from an ongoing study on *Familismo Teaching*, highlights *holistic conferences* as an important resource for reducing academic stress and fostering retention even in non-Latinx students. For example, Komal, a Hindu Indian female explained, the "honest, resourceful, and caring" interactions with her instructor Yemin was what allowed her to keep motivated and to succeed in that challenging yet rewarding course.

In addition, students consistently report their *class families* made a significant difference in their academic experience, highlighting how much they enjoyed the class because of these structures while also emphasizing on their social and cognitive growth. Memorably, Nicole recalls that on the last day of class in a recent semester, two students thanked her for the course design, confessing they would skip other classes, but never English and that if it weren't for their *family* they wouldn't have stuck with the course. They didn't want to let each other down.

Some questions regarding the long-term effects of *Familismo Teaching* on the overall academic performance and student retention will be the subject of future research, questions such as: How does this approach contribute to the academic development of non-Latinx students or of students whose racial or ethnic backgrounds value more individualism? How might this pedagogy work in different contexts such as emerging HSIs rather than high-percentage HSIs? Could this pedagogy be used to cross cultural differences and unite heavily divided racial and ethnic groups?

Developing pedagogies like *Familismo Teaching* represents multiple challenges particularly for novice instructors or those new to HSIs as it requires knowledge and experience in multiple realms. It often calls for action research which is demanding and time-consuming. Mendez Newman (2007) suggests adopting a cultural focus in the development of pedagogy or curriculum, requires instructors to make "extraordinary efforts." In part, this is because not only we will need content knowledge, but also knowledge about our institution and our students' needs beyond the academic realms. Millward et al. (2007) argue that no graduate course has prepared us for how to teach Latinx students, and, to learn how, we would most likely have to take additional courses in different disciplines like sociolinguistics, psychology, pedagogy, ESL, Spanish, etc. In the foreword from *Teaching Writing with Latino/a Students: Lessons Learned at Hispanic-serving Institutions* (2007), Michelle Hall Kells suggests that if we want to be successful composition instructors at HSIs, we do not necessarily have to be Latinx. Instead, we need to develop "transformative pedagogies" such as in *Familismo Teaching*, which draw on multiple disciplines as Severino (2009) recommends. This task is challenging, but not impossible.

Our observations about our students' retention and academic performance after the implementation of *Familismo Teaching* indicate positive gains for Latinx students as well as other minority groups (including White students in our context). The main components of *Familismo Teaching* (*class families* and *holistic conferences*) have produced indicators of increased motivation and in some cases are described by students as reasons for retention. *Familismo Teaching* among Latinx students has effectively balanced the push-pull factors of the borderlands between the school-life and the home-life. We encourage instructors new to HSIs or those from different ethnic backgrounds to consider *Familismo Teaching* as a way to meet students halfway in the complicated crossings of teaching and learning. We have heard frustration in the voices of colleagues when their classes of 25 students are reduced to only 6 students. For these or more experienced instructors who still sense something is missing in their practice, these efforts may bring valuable dividends.

No one pedagogy will fully satisfy the needs all students, of every instructor, or every institution; however, intentional adoptions from a culturally responsive and relevant pedagogy such as *Familismo Teaching* will indeed promote great differences in the academic experiences of our students. The ethical responsibility we hold and our willingness to create new pedagogies to provide high quality education, social justice, and access for all students regardless of their abilities, their skills, or their cultural capital will make significant contributions for paying off what Ladson-Billings describes as our longtime "overdue academic debt."

References

Alim, H. S., & Paris, D. (2017). What is culturally sustaining pedagogy and why does it matter? In D. Paris & H. S. Alim (Eds.), *Culturally sustaining pedagogies: Teaching and learning for justice in a changing world* (pp. 1–24). New York, NY: Teachers College Press.

Adams, P. (2007). Exploring social constructivism: theories and practicalities. *Education, 34*(3), 243–257.

Araiza, I., Cárdenas Jr., H., & Loudermilk Garza, S. (2007). Literate practices/language practices: What do we really know about our students? In C. Kirklighter, D. Cárdenas, & S. W. Murphy (Eds), *Teaching writing with Latino/a students: Lessons learned at Hispanic-Serving Institutions* (pp. 87–97). Albany: SUNY Press.

Arias, M. B. (1986). The context of education for Hispanic students: An overview. *American Journal of Education, 95*(1), 26–57.

Baca, I. (2007). It is all in the attitude—The language attitude. In C. Kirklighter, D. Cárdenas, & S. W. Murphy (Eds.), *Teaching writing with Latino/a students: Lessons learned at Hispanic-Serving Institutions* (pp. 145–168). Albany, NY: SUNY Press.

Bardis, P. D. (1959). A Familism Scale. *Marriage and Family Living, 21*, 340–341.

Beach, R. (1989). Showing students how to assess: Demonstrating techniques for response in the writing conference. In C. M. Anson (Ed.), *Writing and response: Theory, practice, and research* (pp. 127–148). Urbana, IL: National Council of Teachers of English.

Behnke, A. O., MacDermid, S. M., Coltrane, S. L., Parke, R. D., Duffy, S., & Widaman, K. F. (2008). Family cohesion in the lives of Mexican American and European American parents. *Journal of Marriage and Family Relations, 70*(4), 1045–1059.

Bird, H. R., Canino, G. J., Davies, M., Zhang, H., Ramirez, R., & Lahey, B. B. (2001). Prevalence and correlates of antisocial behaviors among three ethnic groups. *Journal of Abnormal Child Psychology, 29*, 465–478.

Brown, J. D. (1995). *The elements of language curriculum: A systematic approach to program development*. Boston: Heinle, Cengage Learning.

Brunk-Chavez, B., Mangelsdorf, K., Wojahn, P., Urzua-Beltran, A., Montoya, O., Thatcher, B., & Valentine, K. (2015). Exploring the contexts of US-Mexican border writing programs. In D. St. Martins (Ed.), *Transnational writing program administrators* (pp. 138–159). Boulder, CO: University Press of Colorado.

Carnicelli, T. A. (1980). The writing conference: A one-to-one conversation. In T. R. Donovan & B. W. McClelland (Eds.), *Eight approaches to teaching composition* (101–131). Urbana, IL: National Council of Teachers of English.

Calzada, E. J., Tamis-LeMonda, C. S., & Yoshikawa, H. (2012). Familismo in Mexican and Dominican families from low-income, urban communities. *Journal of Family Issues, 34*(12), 1696–1724.

Canagarajah, S. (2006). Toward a writing pedagogy of shuttling between languages: Learning from multilingual writers. *College English, 68*(6), 589–604.

Cushman, E. (1996). The rhetorician as an agent of social change. *College Composition and Communication, 17*(1), 7–28.

Conference on College Composition & Communication (CCCC). (1974). Students' Right to Their Own Language. Retrieved from http://www.ncte.org/library/NCTEFiles/Groups/CCCC/NewSRTOL.pdf

Crosnoe, R. (2005). The diverse experiences of Hispanic students in the American educational system. *Sociological Forum, 20*(4), 561–588.

Dumka, L. E., Roosa, M. W., & Jackson, K. M. (1997). Risk, conflict, mothers' parenting, and children's adjustment in low-income, Mexican immigrant, and Mexican American families. *Journal of Marriage and the Family, 59*, 309–323.

Ewert, D. E. (2009). L2 writing conferences: Investigating teacher talk. *Journal of Second Language Writing, 18*, 251–269.

Esparza, P., & Sánchez, B. (2008). The role of attitudinal familism in academic outcomes: A study of urban, Latino high school seniors. *Cultural Diversity & Ethnic Minority Psychology, 14*, 193–200.

Fisher, L. A., & Murray, D. M. (1971). Perhaps the professor should cut class. Paper presented at the Annual Meeting of the National Council of Teachers of English, Las Vegas, NV.

Fields, C. (1988). The Hispanic pipeline: Narrow, leaking, needing repair. *Change, 20*(3), 20–27.

Fink, L. D. (2003). *Creating significant learning experiences: An integrated approach to designing college courses.* San Francisco: Jossey-Bass.

Gándara, P., & Contreras, F. (2009). *The Latino educational crisis: The consequences of failed social policies.* Cambridge, MA: Harvard University Press.

García, O., Johnson, S. I., & Seltzer, K. (2017). *The translanguaging classroom: Leveraging student bilingualism for learning.* Philadelphia, PA: Caslon.

Gay, G. (2010). *Culturally responsive teaching: Theory, research, and practice* (2nd ed.). New York: Teachers College Press.

Gay, G. (2015). The what, why, and now of culturally responsive teaching: International mandates, challenges, and opportunities. *Multicultural Education Review 7*(3), 123–139.

Goldstein, L. M., & Conrad, S. M. (1990). Student input and negotiation of meaning in ESL writing conferences. *TESOL Quarterly, 24*(3), 443–460.

Halgunseth, L. C., Ispa, J. M., & Rudy, D. (2006). Parental control in Latino families: An integrated review of the literature. *Child Development, 77*(5), 1282–1297.

Harris, M. (1986). *Teaching one-to-one: The writing conference.* Urbana, IL: National Council of Teachers of English.

Hurtado, S., & Ruiz Alvarado, A. (2015). Realizing the potential of Hispanic-Serving Institutions. In A. Núñez, S. Hurtado, & E. Calderón Galdeano (Eds.), *Hispanic-Serving Institutions: Advancing research and transformative practice* (pp. 1–14). New York: Routledge.

Kells, M. H. (2007). Foreword: Lessons learned at Hispanic-Serving Institutions. In C. Kirklighter, D. Cárdenas, & S. W. Murphy (Eds.). *Teaching writing with Latino/a students: Lessons learned at Hispanic-Serving Institutions.* Albany, NY: State University of New York Press.

Keefe, S. E. (1984). Real and ideal extended familism among Mexican Americans and Anglo Americans: On the meaning of close family ties. *Human Organization, 43,* 65–69.

Ladson-Billings, G. (1995). Toward a theory of culturally relevant pedagogy. *American Educational Research Journal, 32*(3), 465–491.

La Roche, M. J., & Shriberg, D. (2004). High stakes exams and Latino students: Toward a culturally sensitive education for Latino children in the United States. *Journal of Educational and Psychological Consultation, 15,* 205–223.

Lugo, Steidel A. G., & Contreras, J. M. (2003). A new familism scale for use with Latino populations. *Hispanic Journal of Behavioral Sciences, 25,* 312–330.

Madigan, C. (1988). Applying Donald Murray's "responsive teaching." *College Composition and Communication, 39*(1), 74–77.

Matsuda, P. K. (2006). The myth of linguistic homogeneity in U.S. college composition. *College English, 68*(6), 637–651.

Mendez Newman, B. (2007). Teaching writing at Hispanic-Serving Institutions. In C. Kirklighter, S. Wolff Murphy, & D. Cárdenas (Eds.), *Teaching writing with Latino/a students: Lessons learned as Hispanic-Serving Institutions* (pp. 17–36), Albany, NY: State University of New York Press.

Millward, J., Starkey, S., & Starkey, D. (2007). Teaching English in a California two-year Hispanic-Serving Institution: Complexities, challenges, programs, and practices. In C. Kirklighter, D. Cárdenas, & S. W. Murphy (Eds.), *Teaching writing with Latino/a students: Lessons learned at Hispanic-serving institutions* (pp. 37–59). Albany, NY: State University of New York Press.

Moll, L. C., Amanti, C., Neff, D., & Gonzalez, N. (1992). Funds of knowledge for teaching: Using a qualitative approach to connect homes and classrooms. *Theory Into Practice, 31*(2), 132–141.

Murray, D. M. (1979). The listening eye: Reflections on the writing conference. *College English, 41*(1), 13–18.

Musu-Gillette, L., de Brey, C., McFarland, J., Hussar, W., Sonneberg, W., & Wilkinson-Flicker, S. (2017). *Status and trends in the education of racial and ethnic groups 2017* [NCES 2017-051]. U.S. Department of Education, National Center for Education Statistics. Washington, DC. Retrieved from http://nces.ed.gov/pub search

Newkirk, T. (1989). The first five minutes: Setting the agenda in a writing conference. In C. M. Anson (Ed.), *Writing and response: Theory, practice, and research* (pp. 317–331). Urbana, IL: National Council of Teachers of English.

Oakes, J., Rogers, J., Silver, D., Valladares, S., Terriquez, V., McDonough, P., Renée, M., & Lipton, M. (2006). Removing the roadblocks: Fair college opportunities for all California students. *UC All Campus Consortium for Research on Diversity and UCLA.* Los Angeles: Institute for Democracy, Education, and Access.

Okagaki, L., & Frensch, P. A. (1998). Parenting and children's school achievement: A multiethnic perspective. *American Education Research Journal, 35*(1), 123–144.

Paris, D. & Alim, H. S. Eds. (2017). Culturally sustaining pedagogies: Teaching and learning for justice in a changing world. New York: Teachers College Press.

Pascarella, E. T., Pierson, C. T., Wolniak, G. C., & Terenzini, P. T. (2004). First-generation college students additional evidence on college experiences and outcomes. *The Journal of Higher Education, 75*(3), 249–284.

Patthey-Chavez, G. G., & Ferris, D. R. (1997). Writing conferences and the weaving of multi-voiced texts in college composition. *Research in the Teaching of English, 31*(1), 51–90.

Reese, L., Jensen, B., & Ramirez, D. (2014). Emotionally supportive classroom contexts for young Latino children in rural California. *The Elementary School Journal, 114*(4), 501–526.

Ríos-Aguilar, C., & Kiyama, J. M. (2012). Funds of knowledge: An approach to studying Latina(o) students' transition to college. *Journal of Latinos and Education, 11*, 2–16.

Rios-Aguilar, C., Kiyama, J. M., Gravitt, M., & Moll, L. (2011). Funds of knowledge for the poor and forms of capital for the rich? A capital approach to examining funds of knowledge. *Theory and Research in Education 9*(2), 163–184.

Ruecker, T. (2014). Here they do this, there they do that: Latinas/Latinos writing across institutions. *College Composition Communication, 66*(1), 91–116.

Severino, C. (2009). "We are not all the same": Latino students, Hispanic Serving Institutions, and the need to reform rhetoric and composition. *College Composition and Communication, 60*(4), 137–145.

Shrum, J. L., & Glisan, E. W. (2010). *Teacher's handbook contextualized language instruction.* Boston: Beth Kramer.

Thomas, D., & Thomas, G. (1989). The use of Rogerian reflection in small-group writing conferences. In C.M. Anson (Ed.), *Writing and response: Theory, practice, and research* (pp. 114–126). Urbana, IL: National Council of Teachers of English.

University of Texas Rio Grande Valley Office of Strategic Analysis and Institutional Reporting SAIR). (2017). Data and Reports. In Institutional Summary 2016–2017. Retrieved from http://www.utrgv.edu/sair/_files/documents/instsummary2016.pdf

Vélez-Ibáñez, C., & Greenberg, J. (2005). Formation and transformation of funds of knowledge. In L. Gonzalez, C. Moll, & A. C, *Funds of knowledge: Theorizing practices in households, communities, and classrooms* (pp. 47–70). Mahwah, NJ: Erlbaum.

Velez, W. (1989). High school attrition among Hispanic and non-Hispanic white youths. *Sociology of Education, 62*, 119–133.

Villarreal, R., Blozis, S., & Widaman, K. (2005). Factorial invariance of a pan-Hispanic familism scale. *Hispanic Journal of Behavioral Sciences, 27*, 409–425.

Vygotsky, L. S. (1978). *Mind in society: The development of higher psychological processes.* Cambridge, MA: Harvard University Press.

Yagelski, R. P. (2000). *Literacy matters: Writing and reading the social self.* New York, NY: Teachers College Press.

Zamel, V. (1985). Responding to student writing. *TESOL Quarterly, 19*(1), 79–101.

Chapter 6

Teaching with Bordered Writers

Reconstructing Narratives of Difference, Mobility, and Translingualism

Beatrice Mendez Newman and Romeo García

The almost 2,000-mile border spanning from Brownsville, Texas, to San Diego, California, has created spaces of languaging hybridity and geo-negotiations that challenge traditional explanations of linguistic and performative crossings. Within that longer border, there is the Lower Rio Grande Valley (LRGV), our site of study, a region edged by both an almost 100-mile geopolitical border and internal checkpoints that run parallel 70 miles north of the border. Reflecting a symphony of linguistic and bodily performativity, the narratives, writing, and practices of students at a Hispanic-Serving Institution (HSI) in the LRGV provide opportunities to explore the linguistic crossings and positionings created by bordered writers. *Bordered writing* presents both a construct for abstract considerations about translingualism but also a lived reality of mobility in the context of languaging on the U.S.–Mexico border. *Bordered writers* are bordered writers not because they live and write in a bordered region, but because they have constructed spaces of linguistic and bodily performativity shaped by realities of literal and constructed place. What those spaces of linguistic and bodily possibility look like is under-researched.[1]

At the outset, we offer a contextualization of *bordered writers/bordered writing* beyond extant, traditional discussions of bilingualism, which we find limiting. In academic spaces, bilingualism has traditionally been cast as a special circumstance in which speakers of L1 are guided toward acquisition of L2 in order to participate meaningfully and completely in social, political, and economic possibilities. Elementary and public schools devote significant resources to bilingual programs that are variously labeled dual-language programs, sheltered programs, ESL, ELL, and a variety of other labels including the pejorative Limited English Proficiency (LEP). At the core of these programs is the goal to engender in the speaker competence and proficiency in L2. Politically, this goal results both in inclusion and exclusion. Students are placed in these programs on the basis of a non-English home language and/or performance on state-approved language tests. Students who come from English-Only homes are never subjected to questions about language competence. Furthermore, language support programs in public schools are operationalized in ways that other-ize bilingual students: they are segregated into language development classes or are pulled out for special language instruction. Such traditional approaches to bilingualism unfortunately promote the impression that speaking multiple languages is a deficiency that must be corrected through academic intervention.

We acknowledge the shift in attitudes about dual or multilingualism as researchers, scholars, and educators have embraced the term *translingualism*. For those of us who live and work on the border, though, translingualism is a way of life. *Translingualism* is the ability to draw on linguistic systems, mindsets, rhetorics, logics, intellectualizing, and practicalities from two or more languages to achieve the speaker's communicative goals (Garcia & Kleyn, 2016; Mendez Newman, 2017; Allard, 2017). Translingualism is marked by crossings and borrowings rather than by the boundaries, distinctions, and alternatives established by traditional ESL approaches where the goal is to achieve mastery of the target language (with the subtext that the original language is deficient, wrong, or insufficient). Translingualism begins to explore higher iterations of linguistic dexterity in which language crossovers reflect spatial crossings, linguistic innovation, and reconstructions of the spaces we embody through our constructed discourses. Still, missing in current research is the direct connection between the movement and mobility of the body and language together—and that is what we showcase through our explorations of bordered writing.

In the academic spaces of the expansive 2,000-mile border between Mexico and the United States, translingualism is manifested as *bordered writing*. The academic institutions along this border reflect the realities of the communities in which they thrive: students at border institutions are predominantly Hispanic, and while not all borderlands students are bilingual, the vast majority are. The term "border" is pivotal because *border* suggests both boundaries and crossings, both limitations and possibilities. A "border" is an actual physical location, the crossing of which changes the sense of place and ways of interacting with physical and constructed space (Cresswell, 2013, p. 113). Crossing a border promotes a sense of inclusiveness acquired by actual and imagined crossings—but it also creates a sense of tentative participation in the dominant discourses of the crossed-into space. Our discussion of bordered writers explores the ways spatial positionings in academic and social settings illuminate the rich realities of bordered languaging and the concomitant pedagogies that celebrate bordered writing. In examining the writing of bordered writers, we necessarily assess the way embodiment of space shapes discourses of translanguaging. Through our narratives of bordered writers, we hope to highlight translinguistic behaviors, choices, expressions, and affect that operationalize translingualism as means and agency toward inclusion.

Translingualism and Difference

A translingual orientation to linguistic multiplicity has been praised for its focus on difference, but its theoretical focus overlooks potential pedagogical application. While much effort has been expended on exploring translingualism as an alternative to monolinguistic ideology, little scholarship exists to explain the particularities of linguality, difference, and bordered writing. Translingual scholars focus on how language is an "emergent" and "in-process activity" of becoming, wherein difference is both the "locus" of meaning and the "norm of language in-practice" (Horner et al., 2011; Canagarajah, 2013a/2013b; Lu & Horner, 2013; Leonard & Nowacek, 2016; Canagarajah, 2016). An expression of "emergence" and "becoming" breaks from the view that language-use is merely a by-product of conventions and norms—or in the context of bilingualism, the result of conscious choices among language alternatives. Seeing language as "emergent" and "becoming" edifies language as "subject to variation and change" in the co-construction (and re-construction) of meaning-making (Horner et al., 2011). The implication that language extends beyond a "right" and into something used and co-created illuminates performativity wherein language-users accommodate, revise, and/or transform meaning from daily interactions and encounters (Lu & Horner, 2012; Canagarajah, 2013a). Infusing the elements of performativity and deliberative choice in language use reflects a multi-modal politics of being and becoming in space and time. Language embodies not just linguistic utterance but active intent, which includes positioning ourselves in specific locales and within targeted discourses. Our study of bordered writing is scaffolded on the centrality of spaciality as a catalyst for linguistic and bodily performance.

Unfortunately, when discussions of translingualism are couched in theoretical musings, the realities of lived linguistic difference and dexterity are overshadowed by hypotheticals about egalitarian difference. Discussions of translingualism unfounded in real writers' experiences expose the potential of excess and normalization of difference (Matsuda, 2013). The argument that "[w]e are always translingual" is growingly a concern (Bawarshi, 2016). As Keith Gilyard's response to translingualism warns, the "linguistic everyperson" gives the impression of sameness of difference. What can ensue is the flattening of language difference or erasure of historical and unresolved struggles involved in meaning-making practices and knowledge productions (Gilyard, 2016). The realities of bordered writing manifested in our border institution spaces engender a mindfulness of difference, which begins in observations of the dialectics between nexus of practice and the particularities of everyday life. One stark reality of bordered languaging is that bordered writers are always and realistically translingual; thus, attending to the nuances of translanguaging of bordered writers enables us to move beyond Gilyard's warning and to avoid the elision of true linguistic difference with intellectualized difference. Furthermore, bordered writing is necessarily reflective of the mindset that conflates space and expression: on the border, we talk of *la frontera, el otro lado, ni de aquí ni de allá.* The border is both an ever-present reality and a liminal symbol of spatial difference and separation but also a platform for linguistic nuance in the practices of translingualism.

Current discussions of translingualism foster confusion and misrepresentation of true linguistic crossing. Translingualism is *not* code switching, is *not* error, is *not* interlanguage, is *not* code meshing. We venture to propose that translingualism represents an unconscious appropriation of possibilities, structures, systems, and rhetorics. Code switching seems to be the most drawn-upon false equivalence for translanguaging, but consider that when individuals code switch, they do so in linguistically "comfortable" spaces, among other individuals who recognize the intentional crossings and literally think nothing of the crossing because they understand the two systems and value the enhanced expression enabled through conscious code switching. However, that same code switching would be a marker of deficiency or incompetence in a monolingual space—unless that individual is so secure in his/her status that the code switching becomes an even more pronounced declaration of linguistic difference (as in the somewhat aggressive code switching we see in the writing of Junot Diaz).

For speakers of multiple languages who live in dualities of culture, language, and experience, translingualism is a robust rhetorical process that reflects intentionality and innovation in-and-between human subjects and sites, spaces, objects, time, place, and other realities that impact understandings of experience. We need to establish that translingualism cannot and should not be romanticized as a trope for attention or self-conscious declaration of linguistic and cultural difference. Translingualism is a genuine melding of systems, purposes, and spaces to empower authentic communicative intent.

So, what does translingualism in bordered writing look like, sound like? Let's examine this excerpt from a first-year writer:

> I was there sitting on the second desk next to the window and one voice in the background was trying to get in the middle of my thoughts, but as a child; the sound of the first Mexican War was not a rival against my favorite T.V. show, sponge bob. Those prosy words and the heavy voice belonged to Mrs. G., a History teacher from A. Elementary school, in Mexico.

This doesn't "sound" like English prose because of the integration of Spanish structures. A speaker of Spanish would "hear" the cadences of Spanish fluidly and innovatively blended into English syntactic and semantic systems. Prescriptively, we can say this writer has made errors, or we can descriptively celebrate the understanding evoked by the phrase "prosy words and heavy voice." A true understanding of "heavy" in this construction relies on the knowledge that *pesado/a* in Spanish metaphorically conveys an agency/agent of oppression or visceral aversion (in Spanish, the term *tiene sangre pesada* [he/she has "heavy blood"] marks that individual as being unpleasant, hard to like, someone to avoid). Literally, there is no word in English that would encapsulate so powerful an assessment of the writer's view of the teacher in this passage as the phrase "heavy voice." It is not a false cognate or mistranslation or second language error; it is a gem of translanguaging.

For translingual writers in border sites, the awareness of the possibilities afforded by linguistic spaces challenges traditional views of linguistic multiplicity. The historical expectation of monolinguistic homogeneity created a mainstream/non-mainstream binary, whereby those marked as different in language-use evidenced their own deficiency (and deviancy) and need for assimilation. Yet, in re-thinking language differences and agency, translingualism invites explorations beyond the resistance/subversion paradigm, wherein students are "put in the unenviable position of seeming to have to choose between either submitting to demands for conformity . . . or, on the other, resisting such demands" (Lu & Horner, 2013, p. 584). Translingualism expands considerations of linguistic diversity to encompass theories of structuration (Giddens, 1979), sedimentation of language and meso-political action (Pennycook, 2010), and agencies, proposing a spatial-temporal framework to observe how language practices emerge and engage in processes of becoming. In the context of deliberative spatial positionings and "being-in-the-space" as a way of combining location, landscape, and meaning (Cresswell, 2013), we suggest a necessary consideration of geo-positioning as a concomitant factor in the translanguaging we see in bordered writing. We suggest a retrospective consideration of monolinguistic ideology as a contrasting platform for the complexity of translinguistic positioning: bordered writers are not merely acquiring a second language; they are, more expansively, recalibrating themselves as participants in two or more social, political, practical, economic, and geographic discourses enabled through mobility. Translingualism, thus, moves bordered languaging toward spatially constructed difference as the norm of language use and of all language acts, in and with power, power manifested in deliberative, innovative reconstructions of space.

At the site of our study, the geographic border between the U.S. and Mexico is in some cases only a few miles away. One campus is literally across the street from the border; another campus is only about 20 miles from the border. Comings and goings are fluid, easy, frequent. Bilingualism is a social, economic, and political necessity: service workers frequently speak only Spanish, clerks in stores frequently speak only Spanish, and bilingual employees are prized. A spatiotemporal framework of difference in translingual conversations must begin at the scale of human practice, the everyday, because it is observable. A nexus of practice, according to Ron and Suzie Wong Scollon (2004), emerges from a historical sense of "body" and place where, in a particular place and time, social practice is recognizable, creating an "ecosystem" of discourse and action that can lead to change. Our observation of bordered writers writing and learning in our classroom spaces allows us to consider whether macro "social structures" constrain human agency and practice and to explore how human agency and practice give way to "structural properties" through participation (Pred, 1987). Bordered writing, at the core a manifestation of translingualism, appropriates language as a dynamic process of structuration (Lu & Horner, 2012), extending to meaning-making practices and application of knowledge productions through action (Giddens, 1981; Cresswell, 2004). In practice, bordered writing is generated and produced from within micro- and macro-level structural properties by cultural claims and expressions of everyday life (Pred, 1987; Pink, 2012). Bordered writers construct their stories and academic products from the macro position of dual embodiment in two cultures, two languages, and two mindsets. At the micro level, this duality is reconfigured as a positioning in the real space of immediacy, the space of a classroom, a social venue, a job, or other spatial manifestation. This duality suggests constant positioning, constant mobility across real and liminal borders.

The fragile and irreducible entanglements of movement, representation, and practice bring into focus contexts for movement and product of movement. When we consider how bordered writers cross real borders while crafting linguistic hybridity, movement is "rarely just movement," because it "carries with it the burden of meaning" (Cresswell, 2006). A *politics of mobility* begins to capture the essence of our argument that students, like language, are not "still" (Cresswell, 2010). A focus on movement and mobility—the "contexts for movement" and "product of movement"—draws attention to the relationship between time and space as "performed" rather than "preformed." All mobility involves the body as an "affective vehicle," which not only evidences how "places are about relationships, about the placing of peoples, materials, images," but also about the "systems of difference that they perform" (Sheller & Urry, 2006, p. 214). Therefore, space and place, like language, both are imagined and created from the locality and immediacy of practice (Pennycook, 2010). The significance of students relocalizing in classrooms, therefore, is paramount as it suggests the potential for classrooms, for compositions, to be "changed" or transformed as students rewrite culture, subjectivity, and language. Pedagogical practices in bordered-writing spaces should promote possibilities, celebrate innovation, and value hybridity. Thus, we propose an *¡ándale!* approach to pedagogy that celebrates "intrusions" of Spanish as gems of authenticity and linguistic authority.

The multi-valenced Spanish term *¡ándale!* can mean, on one hand, the imperative "go!" or "walk!" but more interestingly an affirming idiom: "way to go!" or "you got it!" or perhaps even "awesome!" *¡Ándale!* simultaneously conveys encouragement and possibility. We believe *¡ándale!* moments can be fostered through revised pedagogies that focus on bordered writers' trajectories toward positioning themselves in spaces that transcend linguistic and cultural boundaries.

The Space of Bordered Writing: Stories from the Lower Rio Grande Valley

In our stories of bordered writers,[2] we privilege the view of a unified linguistic system over the traditional view that linguistic production is driven by performance in one or another system. Ever present in bordered writing is the remarkable dexterity of movement between linguistic duality that is in the view of some linguists not duality but construction of a unified single system from the differences of two systems (Garcia & Kleyn, 2016, p. 10). Thus, we adapt terms such as "hybridity," "innovation," and "crossings" to explore linguistic nuances in bordered writing and to highlight the ways and means that location can be recreated into spaces for "being-in-space" (Cresswell, 2013). Living and functioning in the spaces of translingualism, bordered writers bring to the classroom a confluence of linguistic and historical experience that allows them to reshape genres, recreate discursive spaces, and validate linguistic innovation.

Hybridity as Normalcy

In a macro sense, it is easy to classify bordered writers as ESL writers because of their obvious linguistic and cultural familiarity with two languages. Traditional ESL scenarios, which cast linguistic mobility as a trek away from one language (L1) toward mastery of another (L2), blur the micro spaces of immediacy that realistically and materially impact bordered writers' constructions of translingualism. The complexity in which language construction is generated or reproduced in border sites reflects a confluence of macro experience, which tends to generalize, and micro experience, which relies on material immediacy as a tool toward linguistic agency.

The spaces of institutionalized learning trigger linguistic discord as bordered writers realize that leaning toward conformity (shaped by macro expectations) threatens the normalcy of linguistic negotiation (which reflects micro experience). Alondra, a bordered writer in an upper division English class, explains it almost as a multi-modal process in which L1 and L2 blend instead of functioning as opposite poles:

> I have a hard time putting my thoughts in writing. I believe that it has something to do with my bilingualism. Sometimes, I feel that a word can only be expressed in Spanish and cannot translate in English. What I am trying to say, often gets lost in translation. I also find that when I am writing in English, I am thrown off by listening to my family speak in Spanish in the other room. I used to think of Spanish and English as a switch. I could either be on Spanish or English. But the switch metaphor no longer applies to me. I may be writing in English but I am thinking in Spanish or a combination of the two. My mind is made up of a jumble of Spanish and English.

Alondra's "jumble" is an expression of the hybridity that characterizes bordered writing. "Jumble" suggests linguistic confusion; the reality, however, is that this jumble results from the bordered writer's struggle between conformity to linguistic expectations and freedom to explore and appropriate language as a means of seizing individual agency. Alondra's words—*bilingualism, translate, translation, switch, combination, jumble*—strongly point to the historicality of the stigma of linguistic difference.

Alondra's explanation invokes the mainstream/non-mainstream dichotomy which positions translingual writers as linguistic others with below par competencies in L2. The problem with applying traditional ESL constructs in the context of bordered writing is that, for the apprentice writer, error equals mistake. Alondra's comment points to the limitations imposed by novice/expert and entering/assimilation binaries: we see an abdication of agency in meaning-making practices because of her expressed inability to "switch" between L1 and L2. True analysis of bordered writing involves replacing the error-as-evidence of-trajectory-toward-L2 model with individualized attention to the hybridity that the bordered writer is constructing. True analysis, moreover, should account for how students relocate their linguistic and literate practice in the classroom, in lieu of assimilating, and consequently re-imagine language-use. Alondra's "jumble" operationalizes the blending of linguistic systems into a hybridity that affords her linguistic flexibility that allows her to position herself in the discourse of bordered writing.

Alondra's self-awareness of her linguistic crossing counters romanticized notions of translingualism as a manifestation of code switching, code meshing, or simple transference. Alondra *positions* herself in a trans-space between her family language which she can hear in the next room and the academic exigencies which she has to address in the space of her school-based experience. This duality of positioning vividly reflects the lived reality of bordered writers: they must forge a space of authentic linguistic experience every time they venture into discursive inclusivity.

As a bordered writer in an advanced, upper division English class, Alondra has reached the stage where she can ruminate and reflect on her linguistic prowess, but for younger writers, the journey toward linguistic resilience is fraught with negotiations of space and personal agency. As a first-year writer, Rico illuminates the need to look beyond surface features to discover the ways bordered writers seize authority as they embody learning spaces. Rico's history highlights the intersections of mobility, performativity, and resistance to linguistic conformity:

> Even though I was born in the U.S., for family issues my mother had to move back to Mexico where I was raised and where I learned my first language, Spanish. I grew up and went to school in Mexico until 5th grade when I got ran over and I had to come back to the U.S. for treatment and surgery and starting going to school in Alamo where I study from 6 to 12 grade. Learning English with the introduction of the STAAR test [mandated standardized exam in Texas] was not easy, I had to rush and learn it fast before the test and do it to it I couldn't understand it nor speak it well leading to the reason why English wasn't my favorite subject and why I was scare of doing and showing my essay to others.

Learning English, for Rico, in this scenario, is not a personal goal; it is, instead, a means to master a mandated exam, but the externally imposed need to learn English "fast" so he can pass a test that stifles individual agency. Thus, he brings to his college learning spaces a sense of otherness as a speaker of English and a subtle resistance to using English as a way of blending in.

In the space of the classroom, Rico emphasized his difference by creating a class-based group in which Spanish was the language of collaborative networking, and during class discussions, when the instructor called on Rico, he always answered "*Mande?*" In typical, Spanish discourse, "*mande*" is an imperative functioning as a sign of respect. When a child responds, "*mande*" to an adult, the semantic sense is "tell me what to do," but as a speech act, it signals a receptiveness to participate politely and willingly in spatial interaction: "I'm here ready to do what you need me to do." Nonetheless, in the context of an English class at an American institution, Rico's insistence on using "*mande?*" to enter the space of the class discussion points to a historicality of difference. In a bordered community, "*mande*" is a cultural trope that embodies realities of discursive relationships and placements. By introducing "*mande*" into the classroom community, Rico has recreated the classroom space to pull professor and student writer into the space of rich cultural practice. Rico's "jumble" is operationalized in the way he positions himself in the space of classroom interactions in order to be a full participant in class discourse. "*Mande*" prolifically represents both agency and resistance, both of which Rico carried over into his writing.

In Rico's writing, this difference and resistance were manifested as a propensity to approach every assignment as a story. This sample, from an early draft of an essay exploring a significant educational accomplishment, illustrates how Rico enters the space of academic writing not through traditional expository routes, but through a reconstructed dialogue that fuses the "point" of the essay with his lived experience with minimal attention to how the writing may confuse the reader:

> "Felix with Mrs. Gutierrez," I heard from the distance while I was reviewing my choices for my senior classes. "Felix, take a seat please and provide me your student information." Mrs. Gutierrez said. After finishing all your math and sciences before senior year, I can choose more electives to enjoy the last year more and stress less while working on my college decisions. . . . I would like to have Band, Pharmacy Tech, Food Science, and BIM I please. 'sorry, all your choices work except for food science, due to the times of each class, the only class that fits your schedule is at the time left is Introduction to Education." After all, it was my only choice as I thought 'Oh well, it doesn't sound bad but doesn't sound fun."

Rico's choice for his essay was an analysis of earning a substitute teaching certificate, but he recasts the academic task as an opportunity to somewhat dissociatively recreate a scene in which temporal exigency intersects with agency: "it was my only choice" reflects Rico's desire to tell a story by historicizing experience while positioning himself as the true constructor of the experience and eventual outcome. But the emphasis on story deflects Rico's attention from the "preformed" expectations for academic analysis.

During a state of the class session, Rico said he didn't know how to start his essay. The professor knew that Rico had ended his current draft with a discussion of the day he got his certificate. The professor said, "If I were writing your essay, I would start with something like *On May xx, 2016, I earned my substitute teaching certificate. I had worked with a class of fifth graders for x weeks and. . . .*" Rico's eyes widened, and he smiled, and he nodded. In a few minutes, he had sketched out a possible intro. These excerpts show how he eventually transformed experience into an engaging analysis of self-discovery:

> [The introduction] May 27, 2016—"Good morning students, please take out a sheet of paper and something to write with" I said as I started a 2nd grade class for the day, finally as a certified substitute teacher, something I never thought to be if it wasn't to a class of 5th graders that thought me how fun and lovely being a teacher could be. . . . The experience left by the program made me a greater person, through hard work and dedication, the meaning of my certification as a substitute teacher is something words can not describe.
>
> [The conclusion] Not a long time has passed since I achieved this wonderful document that changed my mind and myself . . . and gave me the strengths to not give up; well I usually doubt myself on almost everything I try, even knowing what I'm capable of; but it thought me to not be captured by this negative feeling. It is scary to try something new, something strange, mysterious, but giving it a try won't harm you; in fact I can tell you that it is best to let your adventurous self out, and get captured by the unknown.

Rico's writing represents performativity reflective of his positioning in the space of a classroom where he embraced his difference, inserted his linguistic history into the class discourse, and eventually reworked a rambling story into a coherent, hybrid narrative in which the cultural tradition of storytelling allows the writer to take ownership of an academic writing task.

Olivia, an upper division student, further illustrates how hybridity promotes social action and agency. Her childhood memoir about a terrifying storm experience allows her to explore the centrality of her family's *rancho* in her history. At the core of this mud-puddle scene is a confluence of spatial and linguistic positioning:

> I dug my fingers into the walls of mud and threw handfuls at RJ and Vanessa. After a long and intense game of lets-see-how-filthy-we-can-get transpired we climbed out of the ditch just in time for my grandma to catch us. *"Wercos fregados!"* She yelled as she opened the *manguera* and began washing us off. *"Que estaban pensando,"* Ama said as she rubbed my cheeks purple while scrubbing off the dirt. "I fell," I sputtered. Ama chuckled, unimpressed at my attempt to lie. *"Mira a sus hijos Roberto!"* She called to my father who was now making his way toward us with a grin on his face. *"Déjalos Ama, son niños,"* he replied. My father understood how the mud bath liberated us. . . . He picked up my sister in one arm and I in the other and carried us home while my little brother trotted behind us. I looked back at our little pond and said goodbye to the gift the storm left my siblings and I.

Olivia's writing could be simplistically labeled a "textbook example" of code switching, but there appears to be an integral cross-linguistic merging in her discourse. To replace the Spanish words with English expressions would defy equivalency: the meaning she is trying to create would be lost because the rhythm, the linguistic tonality, the authenticity of the memoir would be diminished. This intentionality of discourse choices is absent from analysis of code switching and code meshing. In writing about her essay, Olivia explained that she wanted to show "the innocence of childhood and how a healthy environment created by my family and the ranch is the foundation of who I am as a person." Olivia's translingualism opened up meaning-making practices that reflected her border orientation: to have told her story in 100% English would have deflated the evocative power of the scenes.

The writings of Alondra, Rico, and Olivia reveal the complexities in which modality and linguality emerge together, as well as the fact that experience is what undergirds the "being with" and "doing" aspects of language and embodiments. Their linguistic hybridity is an indication of the decontextualization process involved in language-use, and the recontextualization of language-use, which calls attention to action and agency in space and time. The hybrid practices of bordered writers showcase the potential for modifying language and the emergent aspect of language in action, of language as being, of language as doing.

Resisting the Deficit Model

In the best pedagogical spaces, hybridity should be celebrated as an indication of full-fledged claiming of space and agency. However, because linguistic modification can easily be dismissed as aberration or error, bordered writers almost always arrive in our college classrooms with histories of perceived linguistic deficiency. Despite the ESL tradition that error is an indicator of linguistic risk-taking, error is a signifier of difference; error is a marker; error is a "mistake." Bordered writers bring to classroom spaces the baggage of error because errors are easy to point out but difficult to explain. Persistence of the deficit model precludes full understanding of bordered writers' linguistic dexterity, but a spatially oriented view of bordered writing catapults error into realms of translingual innovation.

Efrain's story illustrates how the historicality of the deficit view can be reconfigured through linguistically informed pedagogy. For the first few weeks of his first-year writing class, Efrain was a perfunctory participant during in-class activities. His demeanor—little eye contact with group members, tense posture at the table, and almost no conversation with group members—suggested self-imposed distancing from the classroom community. In whole class discussions, he joined in only when the instructor invited him to offer a comment. On the eve of the major draft due date, he sent the following email message to his professor:

> I'm really having trouble understanding your work and how to turn in your assignments. I try to use [all the instructions], but I still don't understand it and I'm afraid to ask you question in class cause last time I asked you a question you made me feel dumb in front of the class. I'm sorry but English is my weakest subject, but I'm still trying my best to get that A.

Efrain's message reveals a duality in his embodiment of classroom space. On one hand, there's the suggestion of resistance in the use of second person *your/you* to cast the instructor in the role of controller of the space. There is more overt resistance in the accusation that "you made me feel dumb," clearly embracing the role of victim with the instructor as oppressor. But, in the end, he exposes his sense of difference and deficiency in this space with his apologetic revelation that English is his weakest subject, but he's aiming for an A.

Efrain's message reveals his efforts to position himself spatially and temporally in the bordered landscape. Eventually, the writing he produced in response to the task referenced in his email shows how he transforms perceived deficiency into linguistic agency. The writing task called for an analysis of how a significant educational event changed his view of himself as a learner. This was Efrain's first paragraph from the draft he brought to class:

> "*Pasa. . . . Disparar. . . .* Goal"!!! Those were the words that I grew up with. I was just about 3 or 4 years old when I saw my first soccer game on television. I remember seeing my dad at the couch seeing the game. He was so into the game that he was jumping up and down and yell "*Dale . . . no manches.*" So I go to him and sat down next to him and copied every single face expressions/moves that he would make. He noticed what I was doing, he smiled and said "*Ay mi nino como te querio.*" Then a few days pass, I was at the living room and saw that my father walked it with a soccer ball in his hand "*Mijo, quieres jugar conmigo*"? That's how I fell in love with a sport called soccer.

In a class conference, the instructor praised Efrain for using Spanish phrases to create authenticity. However, Efrain's effort was stifled by his confusion over the writing task; he wanted to write about playing soccer in middle school, but he had written two pages without ever even mentioning that he played organized sports in school. The instructor guided Efrain to focus on the holistic aspects of the story he was telling, urging him to describe "the worst game" which he had mentioned in one of the paragraphs and later in the draft the game in which "we played soccer in a way that we never played before." Efrain responded viscerally: his body relaxed, the tenseness in his face turned into a smile, and he thanked the instructor for her help. He had written notes and arrows all over his draft as the instructor worked with him in the conference. The instructor's mentorship served as the catalyst for Efrain's conflation of space, temporality, and agency. In the end, his essay demonstrates that the story of *futbol* in his life becomes an opportunity for discovery of his embodiment of academic space:

> Soccer has been part of my life for the past 17 years and counting. It really help me in life in an emotional, physical, and educational way. When I was still a child, I was a really big troublemaker. I was the kid that would yell and make the teacher's life miserable. I was in the office on a daily basis and never cared about my grades, but soccer helped learn to behave and boosted up my grades. It was my medicine for behaving well. Today *Futbol* is still with me. Even though I didn't get a scholarship to play, I spend most of my time at the Urec playing the sport that I love. No

matter where I'm at, what I'm doing, or where I'm going, soccer will forever be with me.

Efrain's story of writing agency shows the intensity of pedagogical effort necessary to pull bordered writers out of the deficiency model into realms of confidence, into an affective realm of negotiating academic space and time. The instructor partnered with Efrain; she helped him craft a coherent story; she showed him how to be excited about his writing, even though Efrain had to persist through numerous drafts, revisionings, and conferences to get to the point where he could say, "Im proud to accomplish this essay because I'm sure I did great." The story of Efrain shows the need to validate and celebrate our bordered writers' efforts as a strategy to counter the otherization, insecurity, and conflict promoted by the deficit model. This *futbol* essay enabled Efrain to configure and reconfigure scenes of writing with his everyday life (relocalization), expanding his ability to see how he can indeed appropriate his linguistic hybridity to reconstruct and negotiate genres in academic spaces.

Cross Border Mobility: The Myth of Assimilation

A salient aspect of the culture of bordered writing is the way that border crossings materially and symbolically reconfigure relocalization to challenge the myth of assimilation. The historical narrative about immigrant populations promotes the expectation that entry into a new land leads to a full embrace of new language and culture with the concomitant designation of the native language and culture as secondary. Our bordered writers, however, demonstrate through their negotiation of multiple languages and cultures that traditional assimilation is *not* the primary goal. For many of our bordered writers, crossing the U.S.–Mexico border is a reality that powerfully informs their construction of linguistic, social, personal, and political spaces.

Whereas students like Rico came to the United States when their families immigrated, other students emigrate on their own, at surprisingly young ages. At 13 years old, Abrienda left Mexico without her parents' blessing to relocate herself with relatives living in the U.S. so that she could attend school here. This excerpt, however, suggests that she initially resisted learning English, one of the hallmarks of assimilation:

> I tried my best to achieve the goal of having that [Certified Nurses Assistant] pin and make my parents proud also change the bad perspective they had of me. Wishing for that pin, made me more independent I was working so hard for something I wanted, this

time mom and dad weren't there for me. I focused so much at
school, because of that pin! Everything was changing, my grades,
my self-esteem, now going to school was fun, because of the CNA
class, then I started speaking more English because my classmates
didn't know Spanish and in a "nursing class," you have to do team
work which required me to speak. After almost 4 years I started
speaking English because my grades on that class depended of
having the pin. Finally after preparing for one year, I took the test,
I was scared and nervous, there were 25 skills I needed to know
by memory and more than 100 medical words that I needed to
know. I prayed God to help me pass the test, I wanted to make
my parents proud, I wanted to show all those bullies that I was
intelligent, that it didn't matter from where I was, or my language;
I wanted to show everyone that my sacrificed was worth it.

Abrienda's story brings into question the myth of assimilation by showcasing
the influence of space and place on linguistic performativity. Abrienda struggles
to learn English not to become an American but to fulfill a goal that would
allow her to reconstruct her relationship with her parents. When Abrienda
relocates herself across the border, the classroom space allows her to recast
the crossing as a venture in which language acquisition triggers personal
fulfillment and social repositioning. When she writes "it didn't matter where
I was, or my language," Abrienda affirms the role of mobility in triggering
reconstruction of self through language.

Miguel, who fits the definition of "dreamer," tells a different story of
mobility. In his essay, "Past *el rio*," he presents scenes of his family crossing
the river in inner tubes, trekking across a *monte* of mesquite trees, diving
to the ground when their steps get too loud and his father orders "*al piso!*,"
arriving at a safe house where his father hands over "a roll of green" to an old
woman, and finally being picked up by his uncle who transports the family
to safety and a new home. Miguel's memoir focuses on the reconstruction
of self in the new land as he learns English. But as he excelled in school, he
realized the peril of being an undocumented immigrant, without "numbers
assigned to [his] name." When he wins recognition, it exposes the vulnerability he and his family live with:

The most difficult part of my achievements was not earning
the recognition rather making the decision to take the risk. My
hesitation stemmed from the awareness of my vulnerability. Fear
was always present in my mind . . . in every competition and
every mile before the Falfurrias checkpoint [50 miles north of

the LRGV where a sign boasts how many illegal immigrants have been "caught" to date each year]. I believed that if I was "found out" my family would follow. It felt like a decision between my family's security and my own aspirations. I felt guilty and selfish for jeopardizing the rest of my family.

Miguel presents his story of border crossing in increments of mobility and reconstruction reflected in his subheadings: "*Al piso!*," "*Siempre positivo*," "*Vamos parra 'ribba*," and "*Al fin*." He ends with his graduation from high school which marks a new crossing:

> In that instance, I reminisced in my family's journey—from the moment we boarded the bus in San Luis to the moment we sank into the muddy bank, to the meal and bed provided by the old woman. To the few months with our Tios, the lonely lunches and first English words, to the moment I realized I could not attend the college I dreamed of and was accepted, to the moment I received an acceptance letter from my local University. To the moment my parents told me how proud they were. *Al fin*, I had done it. I had made the best of the opportunity given to me. I was on my way to a career, not just a job, that would allow me to provide for my family.

Miguel and Abrienda are young immigrants in a land where they have seized agency and reconstructed the mobility narrative of assimilation. Crossing the border allows these young people to remake themselves as participants in mainstream America, but with a core of difference reflected in the historicality of relocation. In the end, the distinctive Spanish cadences of their writing reflect their construction of a framework where history informs their positioning in the micro and macro discourses of their new land.

¡ándale!—The Role of Linguistic Mentoring in Bordered Writing

The stories of Alondra, Rico, Efrian, Abrienda, and Miguel represent both micro and macro positionings in bordered writing. Their narratives illustrate realities of *being-in-translingual-spaces*, where personal agency is juxtaposed with larger issues of linguistic, political, economic, and academic positionings. But, positionings are real and personal. Eduardo, another first-year writer, pushes the narratives of these writers a step further to explain the resilience that marks the journeys of bordered writers in academic spaces. Reflecting on his first-year writing experience, Eduardo conflates his success as a writer with the instructor's pedagogical practices:

> This is the second time I take 1301 and the difference in teachers is really a big factor in the ends result. Last time I took it the teacher didn't explaind nor conferenced with us. I got an F. but now with all the help of . . . the professor I am confident I can write a great essay I can be proud of. Now I like writing and I look forward to teach what I learned from this class to other people.

Eduardo's assessment of his first-year writing (re)-experience emphasizes the need for an edifying pedagogy where the instructor is a mentor and the writer an apprentice. Talking in person to the instructor, Eduardo explained that the first instructor had marked his writing deficiencies but had never explained how to move forward. Working with bordered writers pushes us to pedagogical boundaries where a single step can intentionally or inadvertently quash voice, intention, motivation, and inclination in a writer. Deborah Brandt's extensive discussion of literacy in America (2001; 2009) connects literacy to the contact zone construct (Pratt, 1991), where literacy sponsors provide (or withhold) access to tools and practices that promote individual adaptations of traditional literacy practices, where students then decontextualize meaning, negotiate norms and practices, and reinterpret meaning through practices of production. The stories we've shared of our bordered writers point to the exigencies of looking beyond the immediate response to space and time toward the recognition of the role of translingualism in recreating self and possibility. As we work with bordered writers, we can adapt Brandt's reminder that "literacy takes its shape from the interests of its sponsors" (2009, p. 27). In our work with bordered writers, we must recognize the need to foster the trust that enables writers to share stories of crossings, discovery, growth, and repositioning. We must craft pedagogical spaces that enable bordered writers to discover their possibilities and potentialities as writers, operationalized by practices that foster trust and risk-taking. In our stories of our bordered writers, we have tried to showcase some core pedagogical practices:

1. We must provide time and space for considered, reflective, gratifying writing. If this means cutting back on the number of writing tasks assigned, then that's what should be done. Writing, even for experts, requires vast amounts of thinking, planning, redoing, rewriting, tossing out, restarts, and consultations with other writers. Bordered writers are, first, apprentices in language learning and, secondly, apprentices in

writing. Thus, we need to adjust writing schedules to ensure that the complexities of these two tasks are afforded ample time for supportive sponsorship to occur such as is illustrated through the stories of Efrain and Rico where mentorship reduces the stigma of difference and deficiency.

2. Our pedagogy needs to offer assurance that authenticity is the heart of effective writing. We need to look beyond the mainstream/non-mainstream dichotomy toward linguistic reconstruction. We should consider the holistic aspects of the writing: the authenticity, the engagement with topics that matter, the coherence that reflects rhetorical intent, the drive to tell one's story, and the confidence that instructor feedback is intended as guidance toward efficacy not as an indicator of deficiency.

3. We must celebrate translingual hybridity. We must consider the exceptionality of writers who can draw on two or more linguistic data banks and cultural referencings to create authentic writing. It is tough enough to write from a mono-lingual perspective; writing that springs from multilinguistic ways of thinking and experiencing should be recognized as an amazing, enviable accomplishment.

Safeguarding Spaces of Linguistic Negotiation

Working with bordered writers has enabled us to construct a space of lin-guistic mentorship grounded in our *¡ándale!* approach with the overlay of the *¿mande?* mindset. If *¿mande?* signals an appeal for direction, *¡ándale!* affirms the instructional positioning of guidance, support, and expectancy.

We want to forge spaces of linguistic bravery and assertiveness.

Imagine a classroom scene at our border institution where students are in a break-out session for collaborative work on a project based on analysis of characters in a school movie.

[At one table]: *Como se escribe . . . ?*

[Naming the letters in Spanish, another student at the table spells out the character Badriyah's name.] *Be| a| de| erre| e| a.*

[First student] *Thank you.*

[Second student] *De nada.*

[At the middle of the room]: *Mándame, tenemos que hacer every-thing, mam?*

[At another table]: *Badriyah era.* . . . [The student pauses and asks aloud] *Como se dice?*

[Group members respond] *of the majority.*

[The student says to herself and others, processing in English and Spanish the student writes in the notebook a sentence in English with side notes in Spanish] *Como que no—la mayoria.*

In this classroom, the "everyday" of the classroom was filled with teachable and pedagogical moments as students moved with facility and assurance between discourses, spaces, intentionalities, and possibilities. "*Como se dice?*" captures the confluence of spatial, temporal, and linguistic borderings toward discovery of new spaces of individual empowerment and authority. The use of language here, the movement of language, the claimed trust in a space that supports translanguaging captures the essence of bordered writing. This scene epitomizes the way that bordered writers transform difference into inclusivity, transform the seemingly stable spaces and fixed temporalities of the classrooms into a site of productions of space and time. We must be capacious in our ways of accounting for difference, then, because it is irreducible, yet catalytic. We must be open to this possibility.

We end with an appeal for attention to possibilities and potentialities clarified through bordered writing experiences. Our narratives are a beginning in much-needed research and discourses about how culture, space, mobility, and linguistic recreation shape the experience and practice of bordered writers. Our stories of bordered writers affirm how language and bodies on the move enable agency constructed from difference, which once acknowledged and valued, illuminates how students are makers of place, shapers of subjectivities, and engineers of negotiated linguistic and literate practices. Bordered writers and their mentors shape the boundaries of translanguaging, claiming expansions of expression and facilitating convivial, collaborative construction of understanding that sees difference not as aberration but as meaning-formation. Fleshing out the constellations of movements, representations, and practices as exhibited through linguistic and bodily performativity constitutes our "work" as researchers of composition and rhetoric.

Notes

1. We acknowledge the differences between space and place as articulated by scholars such as Tim Cresswell. But, for the purpose of this essay, space and place will be used interchangeably unless specified otherwise.

2. In all of the bordered writing samples showcased here, the writer's original language has been preserved with no alterations in spelling, syntax, or punctuation.

References

Allard, E. C. (2017). Re-examining teacher translanguaging: An ecological perspective. *Bilingual Research Journal, 40*(2), 116-130, DOI: 10.1080/15235882.2017.1306597

Bawarshi, A. (2016). Beyond the genre fixation: A translingual perspective on genre. *College English, 78*(3), 243–249.

Brandt, D. (2001). *Literacy in American lives.* New York: Cambridge University Press.

Brandt, D. (2009). *Literacy and learning: Reflections on writing, reading, and society.* San Francisco, CA: Jossey-Bass.

Canagarajah, S. (2013a). Negotiating translingual literacy: An enactment. *Research in the Teaching of English, 48*(1), 40–67.

Canagarajah, S. (2013b). *Translingual practice: Global Englishes and cosmopolitan relations.* New York: Routledge.

Canagarajah, S. (2016). Translingual writing and teacher development in composition. *College English, 78*(3), 265–273.

Cresswell, T. (2004). *Place: A short introduction.* Oxford, UK: Blackwell.

Cresswell, T. (2006). *On the move: Mobility in the modern Western world.* New York: Routledge.

Cresswell, T. (2010). Towards a politics of mobility. *Environment and Planning D: Society and Space, 28*, 17–31.

Cresswell, T. (2013). *Geographic thought: A critical introduction.* West Sussex, UK: Wiley-Blackwell.

Garcia, O., & Kleyn, T. (2016). Translanguaging theory in education. In O. Garcia & T. Kleyn (Eds.), *Translanguaging with Multilingual students: Learning from classroom moments* (pp. 9–33). New York: Routledge.

Giddens, A. (1979). *Central problems in social theory: Action, structure and contradiction in social analysis.* Berkeley: University of California Press.

Giddens, A. (1981). *A contemporary critique of historical materialism.* Vol. 1. *Power, property, and the state.* London: Macmillan.

Gilyard, K. (2016). The rhetoric of translingualism. *College English, 78*(3), 284–289.

Horner, B., Lu, M., Royster, J. J., & Trimbur, J. (2011). Opinion: Language difference in writing: Toward a translingual approach. *College English, 73*(3), 303–321.

Leonard, R. L., & Nowacek, R. (2016). Transfer and translingualism. *College English, 78*(3), 258–264.

Lu, M., & Horner, B. (2012). Translingual literacy and matters of agency. *The Work Paper Series on Negotiating Differences in Language and Literacy*, 1–36.

Lu. M., & Horner, B. (2013). Translingual literacy, language difference, and matters of agency. *College English, 75*(6), 582–607.

Matsuda, P. K. (2013). It's the Wild West out there: A new linguistic frontier in U.S. college composition. In Canagarajah, S. (Ed.), *Literacy as translingual practice: Between communities and classrooms* (pp. 128–138). New York: Routledge.

Mendez Newman, B. (2017). Tutoring translingual writers: The logistics of error and ingenuity. Forthcoming. *Praxis: A Writing Center Journal, 14*(3), 5–9. Retrieved from http://www.praxisuwe.com.

Pennycook, A. (2010). *Language as a local practice*. London, UK: Routledge.

Pink. S. (2012). *Situating everyday life: Practices and places*. Thousand Oaks, CA: SAGE.

Pratt, M. L. (1991). Arts of the contact zone. *Profession, 91*, 33–40.

Pred, A. (1987). Place as historically contingent process: Structuration and the time-geography of becoming places. *Annals of the Association of American Geographers, 72*(1), 279–297.

Sheller, M., & Urry, J. (2006). The new mobilities paradigm. *Environment and Planning A, 38*(2), 207–226.

Scollon, R., & Scollon, S. W. (2004). *Nexus analysis: Discourse and the emerging internet*. New York: Routledge.

Testimonio 3

Inhabiting the Border

Heather Lang

In the fall of 2010, I began my teaching career as a graduate instructor at New Mexico State University, a Hispanic-Serving Institution in Las Cruces, New Mexico. Nestled in the Mesilla valley near the Texas and México borders, the NMSU student population was 47% Hispanic, a statistic that was also reflected in my own class. A newly minted alumna of the same institution, I was nervous but so excited to be at the front of my very own classroom. Steeped with enthusiasm, prepared by a week-long orientation, and emboldened by my background in journalism and women's studies, I was wide-eyed and wondering at the enormous responsibility given to me: I would teach students to write.

It was not long before I realized I was in over my head. The classroom presented me with questions I could not answer and problems I could not solve. I had been gifted (by the luck of registration) with a wonderful group of students, and I had as much to learn from them as they might learn from me. When I reflect on this class, I remember a non-traditional student taking classes while fighting cancer; an army brat who spoke fluent German, but struggled with reading and writing in English; an engineering student who advocated for wind energy to support the New Mexican economy and electric structure. There were many amazing stories in that classroom. But when I think back about the experience that taught me the most about my role in the classroom, I always come back to Valeria.

Valeria was an excellent student. Quiet, but always willing to contribute, respectful of others' work and beliefs, and genuinely interested in the work of the class. She commuted to Las Cruces from Ciudad Juárez, México, to complete her classwork, and frequently shared her experiences living and participating in communities on both sides of the border. As part of our course work, I asked students to write an 8-page argumentative essay about a local issue; Valeria proposed a paper on the ongoing gang wars in her home-town. At the time, Juárez was the focus of local, national, and international headlines as the city and its citizens spiraled into chaos as a result of drug and weapons trafficking and gang wars. The ongoing tragedy and violence in Juárez seemed to target no one and everyone, all at once. I was enthusiastic about Valeria's topic because I thought it would help her classmates and me begin to understand the situation in Juárez more thoroughly. Too, it was an important local and transnational topic. I approved the topic without a second thought. But I didn't, at the time, realize the personal significance this project would have for Valeria or me.

Though the topic was certainly important, it proved to be somewhat dif-ficult to pursue from a practical standpoint. Namely, the assignment required peer-reviewed sources, which could include books or journal articles. As she was working on her project, Valeria was concerned that she might not be able to meet these requirements. The problem, she told me, was that she wanted to argue that both the United States and Mexican governments shared the blame for the eruptions of violence, but there were very few English-speaking scholars who addressed the violence at all. To address this, Valeria focused her research on works written by Spanish-speaking, mostly Mexican, writ-ers. She asked my permission to use those sources to meet the requirement, rather than trying to force-fit sources written by English-speaking, or Ameri-can, writers. I mulled it over and decided this was reasonable enough but requested that Valeria use only those sources for which she was also able to provide a translation because I was concerned that my own language barrier would prevent me from supporting Valeria as she drafted the project and thus compromise my ability to assess the final draft. Valeria agreed that translation was a reasonable requirement, and she continued drafting.

Valeria's essay, "Whose Fault is it Anyway?" was, and remains, one of the most engaging pieces of writing I have ever read. It is not a technically perfect essay—it includes a few fragments, drop quotes, misplaced punctua-tion or misformatted titles—but it carries the ethos of an expert. It addresses the development of several cartels, and the ways in which U.S. and Mexican governments contributed to their development and resultant war. The essay also provides some reasonable suggestions for how the U.S. government might make up for its share in the violence. But most moving is when Valeria shares her personal experiences with the violence. Hauntingly, she writes:

> This war has had many consequences, my family and I have lived
> in Ciudad Juárez all our lives and we had never felt fear the way we

feel it now. At first it was said things happened only to the people that were involved with the cartels, truth is that the people from the cartels abuse citizens with fear, and take advantage, whether you are involved or not. (Ocana, 2012, p. 61)

Valeria's personal experience is tucked into the middle of the essay, inextricably a part of her argument, but not the central focus. Her focus remains on action as she invokes her colleagues at NMSU as potential agents of change, and continues to demand that the U.S. government take responsibility for its actions. For example, Valeria shares the story of the assassination of her friend Eder Diaz, an American citizen and a student at the University of Texas–El Paso, and laments the lack of response from American leaders and citizens to the unjust deaths of Mexican and American citizens alike. In closing, Valeria renders this personal story political by refocusing on her charge: "I urge my classmates, and fellow students at NMSU to prepare to confront this war, for it is in our hands to have a better world in the future" (Ocana, 2012, p. 61).

I was blown away by Valeria's passion, depth, and fortitude in drafting this essay, and began to anxiously await her final project: a presentation that would share her argument with the class. I squirmed a little in my seat as another student presented his argument in favor of the U.S.–México border wall, and chewed my pen as Valeria prepared to give her presentation. Though the class was made up of a little less than half Hispanic students, I wasn't sure how the class would accept Valeria's accusations of the U.S. government and its citizens, nor did I know what they would make of her call to action for the United States to collaborate with México to end the violence. After spending the better part of the semester working with students on argument papers, I had a pretty good understanding of the political climate into which Valeria would be sharing her message. I didn't know how to protect her, or if I needed to, so I sat quietly and waited.

For her presentation, Valeria focused on what had been a small portion of her essay. Almost in passing, she wrote, ". . . my family and I adopted a mission to demand, fight, and work day-to-day for peace in our town, for it is our duty as citizens of Ciudad Juárez" (Ocana, 2012, p. 61). In continuing that mission, Valeria used her presentation to introduce her classmates to *Amor Por Juárez*, an organization aimed at fostering goodwill in Juárez by encouraging the development of the arts. As with her essay, Valeria spoke with authority, sharing background on the organization, its purpose, and her family's experience working with *Amor Por Juárez*, and she implored her classmates to think toward the development of more advocacy organizations and more solutions. In closing her presentation, Valeria passed out bookmarks and bracelets to invite her classmates to be part of the movement she was helping to build. Students seemed receptive and interested, and many of them indicated that they had not known about the violence in Juárez, despite our university's proximity to the city. In the end, Valeria didn't need my protection. She had what she needed—a platform on which to share her message.

At the end of the 2010–2011 academic year, having taught another great group of students, but never forgetting the effect of "Whose Fault is it Anyway?" I encouraged Valeria to submit her final essay to the NMSU English Department's essay competition. I was delighted when Valeria's work won second place. At the departmental awards ceremony, Valeria introduced me to her parents, and we enjoyed snacks and took turns praising Valeria's hard work. As a result of her placing in the contest, "Whose Fault is it Anyway?" was published in *Paideia 14*, the textbook used by all freshman composition classes at NMSU. And thus, her platform was expanded.

In working with Valeria, I encountered the border in a way I never had before. Gloria Anzaldúa (1987), in her foundational work *Borderlands/ La Frontera*, argues that:

> Borders are set up to define the places that are safe and unsafe, to distinguish *us* from *them*. A border is a dividing line, a narrow strip along a steep edge. A borderland is a vague and undetermined place created by the emotional residue of an unnatural boundary. It is in a constant state of transition. (25)

In many ways, the experiences I shared with Valeria reflect this loaded un/ safe place in both literal and figurative ways. Valeria's essay and lived experience, literally, took place on the border—the U.S.–México border—and in a particularly contested part of that border. The violence in Juárez has long been fueled by false binaries, U.S./México, cartel/citizen, innocent/guilty, and so on. Valeria's essay does a lot of work to undo those binaries, demonstrating that the residents of the border, Mexican and American, are in equal danger and share responsibility in resolving the cartel violence. Moreover, in her presentation and her published essay, Valeria refuses a one-sided, that-side-of-the-fence solution to the drug wars. She represents a division of blame as unnatural and demonstrates that events on one side of the border initiate a ripple effect on the other. Instead of recognizing a division, Valeria insists on symbiosis. In figuratively representing the border, Valeria brought the border with her into the classroom by sharing her experience with a class of predominantly American citizens. Through her presentation, by her mere presence as a Mexican student in an American classroom, she muddied the waters of what it means to be a U.S. citizen or a Mexican citizen. In Valeria's view, we are all implicated. The border is not 40 miles south, but wherever we are, when we have the ability and the responsibility to take action.

My role in all of this is ancillary at best. I provided the space in which Valeria could construct her border, but little more than that. I believe I made the right choice in allowing Valeria to use texts written in Spanish, but now I wonder if requesting a translation of the works further contributed to the border between Valeria and me. It did, after all, create a distinction between us and them—me, the English-speaking audience, and, her, the Spanish-speaking writer. I made this request not to protect the integrity of the work, but to protect my own position as the authority figure in the classroom. My request for translation preserved the monolingual nature of the assignment and privileged the English-speaking members of the classroom, and assumed that my expertise was more central to the project than was Valeria's. And perhaps worse, the act of translation placed the burden on Valeria, alone, to traverse the chasm between two cultures and two languages.

The answer to the unease, I believe, lies in Anzaldúa's *mestiza* consciousness, an alternative identity that is not grounded in binary oppositions, but is fluid, hybrid, and always changing. In making the case for this identity, Anzaldúa, like Valeria, draws on the history and violence of the border, which she argues is an artificial and always violent distinction. She discusses the fracture of self that occurs when Western/Masculine ways of knowing devalue non-logocentric, or otherwise Othered ways of knowing and positions language use as central to that fracturing of the self. In exploring the relationship between language and identity, Anzaldúa (1987) reasons that "we internalize how our language has been used against us by the dominant culture, [so] we use our language differences against each other" (80). In other words, the repression of home languages in classrooms, and in other institutions (including family), weaponizes, rather than celebrates, linguistic and cultural difference. In this frame, difference is characterized as weakness, which may keep people from fully accepting themselves and continues to marginalize non-English speakers.

I did my best to circumvent this negative frame, and I believe that allowing Valeria to use Spanish-written sources was an opportunity to validate her home language; I hope she felt a sense of pride and belonging in doing so. Yet, perhaps instead of norming Valeria's Spanish to the English of the classroom, I could have encouraged her to write bilingually, so we might more fully enact and challenge the borders already at play in her writing, and in our classroom, affirming her linguistic difference. As Anzaldúa (1987) writes, "until I am free to write bilingually and to switch codes without having always to translate, while I still have to speak English or Spanish when I would rather speak Spanglish, and as long as I have to accommodate the English speakers rather than having them accommodate me, my tongue will be illegitimate" (81). If I had it all to do again, I would not ask for Valeria to accommodate me as an English speaker. Instead, I would encourage Valeria to not only cite Spanish-written sources, but to use them in whichever language she felt was most appropriate. Doing so would decentralize my role as "expert" and allow me to situate her as the expert. I might have joined her in the mestiza performance by renegotiating my own language uses and preferences and negotiating the two languages and cultures myself. In doing so, I might have met Valeria at the border and made meaning alongside her.

In the time that has passed since my experiences with Valeria, I have felt very strongly about encouraging students to write with and about scholars who compose in students' home languages and to write with and in the languages and dialects they choose. This is aligned with scholarship in composition that encourages the development of and engagement with scholarship written by and about people of color (Villaneuva, 1999), a line of argument I would extend to our students and their reading and writing as well. This kind of integration does not make for neat or tidy teaching practice. It makes for blended practices which begin to dismantle a variety of borders.

To begin this work, we must invite the mestiza consciousness into our classrooms whenever possible. Per Anzaldúa (1987), this means allowing the writer her own freedom of voice, her own agency to switch amongst identities, languages, and knowledges, as she will, and per Villanueva (1999), this means encouraging students (and our colleagues) to read works by and interesting to scholars of color, and thus encouraging our students to do the same. This invitation, which can be issued simply through the inclusion of writers who write in Spanglish and through formal and informal writing assignments that make room for blended languages, is a valuable opportunity to invite students (and ourselves) the opportunity to dismantle binaries, explore history and trauma, and imagine our own contributions to both. Additionally, instructors must renounce the role of linguistic gatekeeper by abandoning the notion of what we "allow" students to compose. If, as instructors, we extend an invitation to the mestiza, we should not congratulate ourselves for "allowing" students, as I did, to read and write bilingually or in their home languages. "Allowing" denotes gatekeeping and maintains the instructor as the centralized author-ity. Instead, we should encourage students to use the linguistic tools most appropriate to their message, audience, and purpose as they see fit. We should not limit class focus to American research and scholarly conversation, and we should encourage all students to investigate transnational and personally relevant topics. In doing so, we invite the mestiza into the classroom, and we might meet students at the border to make meaning alongside of them, and to support them as they shift amongst identities as they choose, and not as they are silenced into one or another by the dictates of the university.

This invitation is not without its complications. In some ways, the blending of border cultures, practices, and roles disrupts the usual work of the classroom. This invitation asks us to reconsider the kinds of support we offer to students and to find the balance between interventions that help students shape their messages and provide access to a platform from which students can share their messages. Likewise, assessment must be reconfigured to emphasize transcultural meaning-making, rather than logic-driven or grammatically perfected arguments. This kind of meaning may be difficult to quantify and may require instructors to do their own translation work, which can be tricky and time-consuming. While there are no simple solutions to these concerns, these adjustments present a worthwhile challenge, and if we promote diversity in reading and writing—if we live and make meaning on the border—we may ultimately find that authority and assessment become less worrisome. Instead, we may shift our focus to the making and sharing of meaning across perceived boundaries, the *sharing* of responsibility, language, and meaning across many personal, cultural, and linguistic boundaries. We might embrace the untranslatable, then un-assessable, the conflicting, and the shifting. U.S. citizens may finally "admit that Mexico is your double, that she exists in the shadow of this country, that we are irrevocably tied to her. . . . And finally, tell us what you need from us" (Anzaldúa, 1987, p. 108). In other words, we may join each other at the border.

References

Anzaldúa, G. (1987). *Borderlands/La frontera: The new mestiza*. (4th ed.). San Francisco, CA: Aunt Lute Press.

Ocana, V. (2012). Whose fault is it anyway? *Paideai, 14*, pp. 59–65.

Villanueva, V. (1999). On the rhetoric and precedents of racism. *College Composition and Communication, 50*(4), 645–661.

PART III

PROFESSIONAL AND TECHNICAL WRITING

Chapter 7

Hispanic-Serving Institution as Programmatic Invention

Identifying Learning Objectives for HSI Writing Programs

KENDALL LEON AND AYDÉ ENRÍQUEZ-LOYA

In fall 2014, California State University, Chico, a midsized campus in Northern California, was designated as a Hispanic-Serving Institution (HSI). Since that moment, CSU, Chico, has developed campus-wide initiatives to redesign the institution to reflect and enact this new institutional identity. In 2015, only 4% of faculty identified as Latino/Hispanic (CSU Office of Diversity and Inclusion, 2015). Stemming from the HSI designation, along with a 2016 Diversity Action plan identified objective, the campus has worked to actively hire faculty to support and reflect the changing institution in terms of their demographic makeup, as well as with their teaching and research interests (CSU Office of Diversity and Inclusion, 2016). It was with this aim that in 2016 we were hired to be the first Assistant Professors of Latinx/Chicanx rhetorics in the English Department. Drawing from our past experiences as first-generation Chicanx students and faculty at both HSI and non-HSI campuses, we know that when students and faculty of color step into new spaces—especially in spaces during transformative moments when culture, identity, and difference are recognized—our bodies are placed on the front lines. We bring this awareness, as new faculty in an English Department that still has a predominately White student body, as we know how critical it is to build programs that centralize and legitimize the experiences of students typically marginalized in institutions.

While the numbers of Latinx[1] students are increasing, this change is slowly felt as the English department classrooms, and the greater Chico area, are predominantly White.[2] In other words, while the demographics are changing, Latinx students are still venturing into spaces where they might still feel alone. In this way, these Latinx students are also placed at the front lines. The task then turns to us as Latinx/Chicanx faculty. How are we putting ourselves on the front lines as well? How are we challenging these spaces? Regardless of our own ethnic background, how are we changing our classes to be conducive to engage the difficult conversations we desperately need? Equally important, how are we changing our programs so that all our students know that they are welcomed, supported, encouraged, and that they are the primary audience we have in mind for our curriculum?

As we see it, a major component of our hiring responsibility is to help design a writing program that integrates and builds on HSI as institutional identity. As noted in studies on HSI campuses, HSI, a relatively new institutional designation, was created to incite change, "on the theory that a critical mass of individuals from a group—in this case Latinos—influences organizational change at institutions of higher education to address this mass" (Santiago, 2008, p. 8). Therefore, an intent in creating the HSI designation was for the identity to be productive and inventional. As a nation, we are undoubtedly experiencing a demographic shift where the "Hispanic" demographic growth is four times the rate of the nation's growth rate, with a projected Hispanic population exceeding 30% by 2050. In California specifically, Latinos/as are the largest ethnic group. As a result, our educational institutions have shifted as well—not just in terms of the people that inhabit these spaces, but also in terms of the institution's rhetorical practices and processes, which include program design and evaluation.[3] We aim to ensure that the changing student demographic is intertwined not only in program and curriculum naming, but in the very foundation of our writing program. At the same time, we reinforce the importance of locale when discussing HSIs. While the institutional demographics create connections between the campuses represented in this collection, our differences, and the differences in our student populations, are equally important to recognize as we build this body of research on HSI writing programs. And yet, we can begin to identify and articulate shared practices.

Building from scholarship in Cultural Studies and Professional and Technical Writing (PTW), in this chapter we outline the approach we will take to design a writing program, which involves curriculum that examines identity and culture.[4] In drawing on this scholarship, we suggest an approach grounded in "invention as articulation" in the specific locale (Sun, 2009), and identify three learning objectives that we argue, can be extended on a programmatic and curricular level at HSIs. From this approach, we provide an example of HSI as invention in one Technical Writing (TW) course that we plan to extend to our future program as well.

Situating the Institution

Before we discuss our program design, we need to localize our institution. Despite the fact that, as of 2015 there are 435 HSI institutions in the United States, with that number anticipated to grow with a changing demographic, there is very little research in Rhetoric and Composition on teaching and research at, or from, HSIs. Aside from the scholarship in the groundbreaking edited collection *Teaching Writing with Latino/a Students*, "Hispanic-Serving Institutions (HSIs) are among the most underserved and under recognized sites for teaching, research, and educational activism" (Kells, 2007, p. viii). More recently, Rendón, Nora, and Kanagala (2014) studied the challenges of the college experience for Latin@ students at HSIs. They argue that recognizing and utilizing students' individual and cultural epistemological frameworks must be considered assets that can help them more successfully transition into college life (Mendez et al., 2015). In PTW more specifically, Matveeva's (2015) research surveying HSI PTW programs' websites and catalogue descriptions of curricula, offers a broad view of the types of programs currently offered, as well as generalized strategies for engaging Latinx students with PTW curriculum. In this collection, Gonzales's chapter provides us with a rich and local case study of teaching a technical writing class on the border. More importantly, through her case study, Gonzales demonstrates the resources our Latinx students bring that enrich the practice and theory of PTW. However, being underserved means that HSIs as institutions have yet to be fully researched as affinity spaces within and from their own diverse locales and programs. Many HSIs are located in urban areas. Even within our own large state system that includes 20 Cal State campuses that are HSIs, and 159 HSIs statewide, there are substantial differences between campuses in terms of their institutional ethos and student body.

CSU, Chico, has about 17,000 students, with 1,200 of that number representing graduate students. Around one-third of incoming students are transfer students. Approximately 96% of the student population is from the state, with most students coming from surrounding counties. The university is well known for its efforts in sustainability and environmental initiatives, and for civic engagement. The campus is located in a part of the state that is rural and primarily agricultural. Although the campus is not in a geographic "border region," the writers we teach in our classes and the institution itself experience different kind of borders: one between rural and urban, Southern California and Northern California, and between the university and the community. Many of the students we have had in our classes thus far have expressed a border that develops when they step outside of their home communities that may read as very dissimilar from the space of this particular university. As a result, several of our students have shared with us feeling anxious about stepping out of the comfort of their home communities in Southern California, which read as diverse to them, and into this new region where cultural diversity is unrepresented. While approximately 20% of the city population is not White, this makeup is geographically segregated in particular neighborhoods, and also not equally reflected in city leadership or community-based organizations. Kendall remembers growing up in Chico, living in low-income housing in one of these segregated neighborhoods. She recalls feeling as though the university was in another city, even though the campus was less than two miles away from her childhood home. At that time, the university's presence did not positively impact her disenfranchised community.

As we know, identifying gaps and fissures makes institutional change realizable and a rhetorical act (Porter et al., 2000). Fortunately, our current university is actively addressing these disconnects and gaps: gaps between community and institutions, gaps between home and curriculum, and gaps between student and faculty demographics. They have been actively addressing a representation gap in the current faculty: in the last year alone, the incoming faculty cohort included many Latinx identified members. In this way a rhetorical moment for invention and reinvention arises when a university is designated a "Hispanic-Serving Institution" as campus work to take up that identity in its policies and practices. While the designation reflects a 25% Hispanic undergraduate student population, it also demonstrates a university's commitment to supporting these students with associative federal funds for student support. Becoming an HSI and inhabiting that institutional identity is therefore an opportune time for program design (and redesign) that centralizes "Hispanic" and/or Latinx students across the curriculum. Most notably at CSU, Chico, there are campus wide initiatives and hiring practices, as was the case with our positions, which have resulted in changes in the campus community. It is not just that there are in general visibly more students of color on campus, and in our classes (even in the English Department!). The feel and ethos of the campus reflects a commitment to centralizing these students and their experiences to the driving force in the institutional design. For example, as part of this initiative, our campus started a semester long faculty learning community that serves a dual function. To start, faculty members are integrated into a focus group to help think through and develop their own pedagogies. Then, as the focus group serves as a generative space where the learning community members are articulating, and by association, building what it means to be an HSI. Likewise, although we have just begun serving in our new positions, we are actively considering how to centralize HSI in our writing courses, and working to build a new Rhetoric and Writing major. However, there are very few models in our disciplinary field for designing writing programs at HSIs.[5]

Localization as Program Design for HSIs

In Rhetoric and Composition, teacher-scholars have shared their processes and findings from building curriculum and coursework that connects with their student populations (Perryman-Clark, 2013; Inoue & Poe, 2012; Fox, 1992). In doing so, these scholars have demonstrated the programmatic learning objectives, and increased access, afforded by these culturally attuned pedagogies. More research is needed that connects general writing program design within the locale of HSIs. Teachers and administrators have acknowledged the potential for design methodologies grounded within the local institutional context to be a powerful "mechanism for institutional change," as moments for invention are identified and acted upon (Hocks, Lopez, & Grabill, 2000). As institutions are identified and designated HSIs, they have the potential to reinvent these spaces through the articulation of that cultural identity.

To consider inventing HSI programs in a way that integrates the participants of the spaces, along with the particular cultural contexts, and universalized best practices, we turn to the work of Professional and Technical Writing (PTW) scholar Huatong Sun's work on localization. Huatong Sun (2009) analyzes the way that mobile communications use and practice is integrated and adapted within a cultural context. In her case, she examines the interplay between mobile technologies (that are designed for particular globalized usages), with individual users and the ways these users adapt these universally designed technologies as part of identity work within local contexts. We draw a parallel from her comparative case studies of mobile users within different locales to adapting generalized best practices of HSIs and PTW curricular design, as an interplay with the identity of HSIs, and the local contexts of these institutions.

Using this model of localization enables what Sun identifies as *invention through articulation*. Articulation describes the process in which groups appropriate and recombine social practices and processes for their own use (see Hall et al., 1996). Although Sun's article focuses on mobile technologies, her discussion of *locale* and localization as it relates to articulation is a useful framework in which to consider HSI program design invention because it asks us to consider design from the standpoint of the multiple and layered interactions that constitute *locale*. Specifically, Sun describes the theoretical conversations on the affordances of moving from space (the physical surround) versus place (the social interactions of a space) as a unit of analysis for design and points out the limits of either focus. Instead, Sun draws from Giddens's (1984) emphasis on *locale* over *place* to highlight "human agency in constituting contexts of interaction" that remains grounded still in the physical and cultural surround (p. 247). Considering HSIs, and HSI writing programs specifically, in this way invites us to consider not just the space of the HSIs, or place as defined as just the inhabitants in the space, but rather, the dynamic between the two, and the experiences of that dynamic, as integral to the design considerations.

Locale also includes subjective experience and experiential knowledge-making of individuals and groups and the encounters these groups have within a particular space. In Sun's article she describes localization as the adaptation and customization of IT products and services to a locale with a distinctive culture. For us, we argue that localization for HSI writing program design involves taking HSI and PTW best practices and localizing them to fit into our institution's local cultural context and its users (the learners in these spaces). It is with this framework in mind that we later propose adapting three learning objectives that align with typical PTW program principles and then are taken up and transformed through our HSI locale.

Labeling our campus as an HSI institution is an act of naming the elements that comprise the institution; and in that naming, it fosters new connotations and practices to emerge. It is in localization as articulation where our program design commitments lie: naming and renaming elements of a writing program within the framework of HSIs, and specifically with the identity of its users in mind, enables us to reclaim and productively use pedagogies and programs toward our own end. In doing so, according to Sun "as users are engaged in the work of localization, they are also doing identity work. The user localization *itself* is the articulation of a sense of identity" (p. 258, emphasis added). We suggest this approach for HSIs in particular because, while we acknowledge that labeling a campus as an HSI does not automatically enact visible or impactful institutional change for Latinx students, we argue that this naming is intentional because identity affiliations are rhetorical insofar as it produces an ethos and material things. Therefore, we are interested in looking at ways that identities—both institutional and cultural—have been taken up methodologically as inventional materials that are established through articulation.

Post-positive realist theorists, like Paula M. L. Moya (2002) and Linda M. Alcoff (2005), give us a framework for conceptualizing individual and group identities as inventional and rhetorical. Identity is rhetorical insofar as it is productive and does something. Identity can reflect our material and lived reality, structure and mediate our experiences in the world, and provide a heuristic through which we act and make decisions. It is through identity, and more specifically, cultural identity, that communities and groups are built.[6] Identity then, can be seen as material, or topoi, for invention, which is part of the process of localization. Returning to localization, Sun (2009) argues that "user localization is an articulation work of constructing the subjective experiences according to a user's lifestyle and identities. It links the instrumental aspect of the mere use process to the subjective use experience situated in a particular cultural context" (p. 258). We similarly argue that HSI is a technology that can be integrated into the "fabric" of our writing program, and the lives of its participants, as a way to "establish and maintain their identities"—in this case, as PTW students whose identities are created by and create the documents we ask them to create (Sun, 2009, p. 258).

In particular, we claim that PTW is a pivotal space where HSI as identity can be articulated on a programmatic level. The dearth of research on HSI, or identity in general, is even more apparent when we extend our scope to include PTW program design. Identity in PTW program literature has typically focused on two research avenues: translating for globalized audiences or worker/professional identity. This is an especially limiting perspective because these writing programs have traditionally been plagued by an imperialist tradition in which racialized discourses are widely disseminated yet positioned as ethically neutral. Within Technical Writing (TW), students are trained to construct documents for an artificial world that generally disregards issues regarding race, class, gender, sexuality, and disability. They are trained to write on behalf of others who often have no say or voice on the choices they make in their writing. In the pursuit of document design and formatting, in the pursuit of getting the job done, ethics step out. For example, it is commonly misperceived that TW documents are strictly utilitarian, which creates a series of problems within the classroom and perpetuates a dangerous trend in their production and distribution in diverse communities. At the same time, PTW program design is the most opportune space for articulation, and the space for HSI as identity can be used to shape its pedagogy. PTW scholars have long recognized the need for a more cultural-studies approach to the pedagogy in these classes (Haas, 2012; Katz, 1992; Scott, Longo, & Wills, 2006).

Like institutions where Latinx students may be marginalized, Scott, Longo, and Wills (2006), explain, TW as a writing practice is very much embedded within a system that deprives marginalized groups, enforcing instead a top-down knowledge base whereby those in power, those in control, are able to make the decisions for everyone below. These power relations must be questioned; they must be challenged. Furthermore, TW documents have the capacity and, as Dobrin (2002) argues, the responsibility to communicate "complex, highly detailed problems, issues, and subjects . . . that help audiences visualize and understand information so that they can make informed and ethical decisions or take appropriate and safe actions" (p. 16). At the same time, it is through such documents that affiliation-building can occur.

We can also reframe best practices for PTW as part of an HSI initiative. For instance, HSI literature suggests that building meaningful connections between campus and community is pivotal for Latinx student success and retention. In the TW classroom, connections between the classroom and community practices have to be intrinsically linked and transparent, where students are able to not only adapt and appropriately respond to in-classroom scenarios and apply this knowledge within their communities but also recognize why this is vital to both spaces. This idea must also be transferred to then thinking about the redesigning of programs for HSIs. Our programs must be accountable to its community in thinking about the type of relationship it needs to build. This is needed in order for students to recognize their own responsibility and affinity to the local community and also to understand how the program centralizes this framework within its core.

Identifying HSI Writing Program Learning Objectives

In our efforts to redesign our writing courses at CSU, Chico, we move beyond reflecting HSI in their titles. While we acknowledge that naming matters, we also know that identity work, and by extension, the work of institution building happens in day-to-day practice and participant activity. In our future courses, we plan to integrate PTW that centralizes Latinx identities and concerns and problematizes the boundaries of PTW—boundaries of expertise, of linguistic ability, of vernacular and institutions. Dismantling these boundaries, we believe is one central practice that HSIs should undertake to make space for bordered writers who may have felt arbitrary borders have caused them to feel restricted from certain places. An example of what this will look like in practice can be seen in an upcoming TW course. We treat this class as a space where we can centralize HSI in a way that is not just about content and course titles. In particular, we have identified three learning objectives from this course that can be articulated and extended as HSI writing program design principles: identifying rhetorical moments; analyzing oppressive systems; and community building and engagement. While we understand these objectives may not seem novel for PTW teachers, we argue that they take on different meaning when articulated within the HSI space.[7]

Learning Objective 1: Identifying Rhetorical Moments

Our first learning objective asks students to recognize the dynamic transformation of HSIs as contested spaces where students' multiple epistemological frameworks are fused within the rhetorical moments. Although academia has made significant changes, the colonial legacy of institutions of higher education, including HSI campuses and their surroundings, continues to negatively impact incoming students and especially problematizes the role that first-generation Latinx students can play on campus. Identifying and responding to rhetorical moments that arise within and outside of the classroom and are complicated as institutions become more diverse is especially significant given the challenges within the production and dissemination of TW documents.

When students are first confronted with the dynamic role that TW documents play in the problematic history of our nation, of our corporations, and of our institutions' everyday practices, students are often resistant and incredulous. The reasoning usually relies on the question, how can a "memo" be so dangerous? A common starting point and or initiation into this topic is a class discussion of Steven Katz's (1992) "The Ethics of Expediency: Classical Rhetoric, Technology, and the Holocaust" which starts by presenting a memo dated June 5, 1942, right before the Final Solution during World War II. The memo presents a request for needed maintenance and upgrades on vans used to transport "loads" due to overcrowding, the need for extra lighting, and to expedite the cleaning process (p. 255). The loads this memo refers to but fails to name are human beings. And the reasoning for this request includes the large number of humans that were packed into vans who would scream as the doors shut and the darkness set in, and the cleaning of the drains that would clog from bodily fluids such as blood, vomit, urine, and feces. As Katz identifies the ethical issues with the exigency of this memo, students utilize this rhetorical moment to examine the role technical documents played in the Nazi Holocaust, how these seemingly simple memos could be aiding in the deaths of millions. This recognition opens up the space for a serious investigation of technical documents through multiple rhetorical moments. Students begin to interrogate how these technical documents are used, for example, to facilitate the use of harmful pesticides in the food industry, the drawing of voting districts to favor particular parties and politicians, the articulation of ableist and racist teaching practices, and the design of laws that jeopardize communities of color.

These are serious conversations that are needed in the TW classroom so that students recognize and adequately respond to different audiences and critical issues in an efficient and professional manner. Within a newly designated

HSI, especially, confronting conversations regarding race and racist practices in our everyday lives is difficult because so much of it is ignored and or accepted.[8] Within the TW classroom, challenging the narratives about others, specifically people of color, is difficult to navigate for all students involved. However, if we want our students to identify these rhetorical moments for what they are and in order for them to produce documents and respond to their audience needs, they must be given the space, the resources, and the opportunities to engage these difficult conversations without being silenced. In doing so, students learn to identify rhetorical moments as opportunities for examination and interrogation, and also to engage real-world discourses that reflect their lives and or their own lived experiences.

Additionally, at HSIs it is critical that identifying and interrogating rhetorical moments in the classroom be extended to the local community. We must seek opportunities to question how our institutional practices are responding to community needs. For example, how does the influx of vehicles at the beginning and end of every year impact the local communities' physical, economical, and environmental resources? How are these negative impacts mediated and or lessened? How is student employment during the fiscal year impacting the local community that requires employment year-round? How is our institutional research working with, representing, and responding to the local community? How are we held accountable? The designation of an institution as a new HSI presents a dynamic rhetorical moment for everyone involved. It is critical that key practices are instituted so that these measures can grow organically with the program.

Learning Objective 2: Analyzing Oppressive Systems

Writing programs at HSIs must centralize learning about the colonial history of the spaces they inhabit as rhetorical moments. Another learning objective for HSI writing programs should include analyzing ways systemic oppression is created and enforced through technical writing, as a form of critical thinking. Once students identify rhetorical moments, they must then learn to use the tools and their abilities to unpack these moments to understand the power dynamics and mechanisms of power at play to locate spaces for intervention.

What this kind of learning looks like in practice takes shape in a TW class we offer at Chico State. In this TW class, we utilize a zombie apocalypse narrative to provide students with the inventive space to critique social systems of power. As a rhetorical trope, zombies have been widely used in popular culture to critique the ethics of a capitalistic society by directors such as George Romero and theorists such as Henry Giroux (2010). In addition, however, we argue that zombie discourses can be utilized to tease out a decolonial narrative, and within the writing classroom it can serve as a pedagogical framework that deconstructs hierarchical, systemic forms of oppressions regarding race, class, gender, sexuality, and ableism as they manifest within technical documents[9].

Within any academic setting, the ability to critique and challenge social systems of power is integral to utilizing critical thinking skills, but within an HSI, these actions have the capacity to also create and transform spaces. The use of zombies within the classroom allows diverse students to be drawn to the theme of the course, and the theorizing of zombies allows us to make significant critiques. For example, when students develop weapon manuals for the zombie apocalypse, we discuss the ethics of this process in the Alerts and Special Considerations sections. We ask students, "What are the implications of building a tool used to hurt and even kill another person?" Students typically respond, "Well, zombies are not really humans. Not anymore." From there, we utilize critical race theory to think about when minorities were considered less than human and in the way of "progress" by discussing issues having to do with, for example, the Holocaust, slavery, attempted genocide of indigenous people, forced sterilization of women of color, use of people of color on which to test deadly viruses, among many other historical events. Suddenly the questions become: When does the zombie cease to be a human? What are the implications of developing definitions of zombies as less than human especially once we recognize that the social systems of power currently in place are precisely those that led to the zombie apocalypse to begin with? Whether or not the class itself is diverse or has high rates of Latinx students, presenting these issues in this way allows us to question our history of oppression, our actions against and for each other, and our imprecise understanding of the role technical documents have played.

The discussions that the zombie apocalypse allows us to have extend our conversations far beyond race. They allow us to look at the social problems from a much broader perspective and at the intersections between concerns through an interdisciplinary approach. Since TW courses are typically designed for STEM majors, the critical discussions that this zombie course yields can make dramatic impact on a diverse body of students and also across various majors on a college campus. Students confront the fact that critical discussions on issues of oppression are not reserved for the humanities courses, but that as a society we are all implicated. We recognize, always, that our failure to address these problems will lead to our ultimate demise. Within the classroom, students have to learn to work together, engage in controversial topics while building alliances, and consistently interrogate the impact each decision-and-action will have on various communities, specifically marginalized communities. Within an HSI, these actions can be key points for transforming programs that not only centralize their focus on reading texts by writers of color, but also encourage students to see themselves as responsible and accountable to their local communities.

Learning Objective 3: Community Building and Engagement

The third learning objective tasks writing programs at HSIs to pair opportunities to challenge spaces with opportunities to build (and rebuild) communities. Community engagement is a frequent practice in writing programs as part of experiential and client-based learning. However, we articulate this practice as vital for Latinx student retention and student learning centered on producing change. While recognizing the oppressive systems within HSIs is key to interrogating the various discourses at play, working on creating a narrative that allows for the creation of alliances and community is pivotal to the overall success of the student and the program.

The TW course on the zombie apocalypse starts with a "State of the Zombie Union" analysis, where students write a status report on current social justice issues discussing how TW and writers are implicated in either perpetuating or challenging the system. Their research then is not solely on the nature of the event but also on the rhetorical construction of the event, actors, and discourse as evidenced by technical documents. This early assignment is critical, so students learn early on how TW functions and has functioned in the foundation of our nation and in our everyday constructions of society too. Students need to recognize the link between the theory they read in class and what happens in their real worlds.

By the end of the semester students work on a final team writing project to develop their "Manifesto for the Post-Apocalyptic World" in a formal report that both documents and provides the opportunity for students to theorize their understandings of the various social justice issues. The purpose of this assignment is for students to provide a narrative by which to begin to rebuild society in the aftermath of a zombie apocalypse. Having studied the issues that led to the demise of the vast majority of humanity and with the opportunity to start over, students provide the groundwork for reimagining a better future for a post-apocalyptic world, a world that will not repeat the same mistakes that destroyed our world. Through this assignment, students not only learn the dynamic and complex components of team writing and engage the decolonial pedagogy covered all semester, but also develop their own theories of resistance. The "Manifesto for the Post-Apocalyptic World" report presents a wonderful opportunity to not only scrutinize the problems communities are facing but also to articulate solutions as a group. In developing their Manifesto, they must negotiate the most efficient, ethical, and intersectional approach to rebuild a society, and consider what changes they would implement if (and when) given the task to make societal changes. In doing so, students must connect their course learning to the communities they inhabit.

Assignments like the Manifesto, and the theoretical basis for them, are essential within curricular and programmatic revisions at an HSI. The Manifesto in particular is designed in a way that the community that is interrogated and rebuilt, can be articulated as proximal, virtual, imaginary, or concrete. It is flexible enough to be taken up at HSIs like CSU, Chico, where the students may not feel connected to the surrounding city but come to our classes with an understanding and valuing of community as part of their identity. Programs must then find ways to interrogate the social justice problems within the localized area, as well as the student's home communities, in a way that blends theory, critical thinking, and action. As previously mentioned, these students are on the front lines. As educators, we must both present the knowledge they need and seek opportunities for them to build new knowledges by learning to work together and build community together.

Anticipated Challenges and Future Goals

We are currently headed into a stage of data gathering through faculty and student focus groups in our department to give space for invention through articulation—to build our locale as one where HSI is the centralized discourse and rhetoric that assembles the cells of the university. In terms of practice, we are filling roles as mentors to students on our campus to help them identify HSI in their faculty's faces, and with our shared experiences. As we move forward with designing our writing program as part of an HSI as locale, we anticipate facing challenges along the way. One such challenge involves remedying the campus/community schism. Because we know that community connections are pivotal to Latinx student retention and connecting to communities through service learning endeavors benefits writing students, we must begin the long process of building community networks and spaces in a community that has not yet been articulated as a Latinx space. In addition to utilizing writing opportunities like the Manifesto, which gives space for students to imagine the community they will rebuild, we also hope to address the limited buy-in for community engagement that students who are not from the regional area may experience, through fostering virtual service learning opportunities with Hispanic-Serving organizations. Naming and sharing best practices about how to engage students with the communities that surround our HSI campuses in ways that can be adapted to specific locales are necessary cross institutional conversations to have as we build scholarship on HSI writing programs.

As the number of HSIs increase, more and more of us writing scholars, teachers, and administrators will find ourselves teaching in these Latinx spaces. We ask you to remember that writing programs, like institutions, can and should be responsive, inventive, and reflective of the identities that constitute these spaces in both content and in form. Rethinking and redesigning pragmatic programs more responsive to the needs of a newly designated HSI does not require everyone to teach Ethnic studies. Instead, it requires us all to acknowledge that our courses and institutions do not exist within a bubble without people of color or without problems pertinent to contemporary and long-standing issues of social and community justice.

Notes

1. A note on terminology: when discussing the institution, we will use "Hispanic." When discussing people, we will use the term "Latinx" or Chicana (if self-identified).

2. According to 2010 census data, Chico is 80.8% White and 15% Hispanic or Latino (U.S. Census).

3. In 2016, San Francisco State University received HSI designation, raising the number of HSI Cal State university campuses to 20 (of the 23 Cal State campuses). As a result of this demographic and institutional shift, the CSU has adopted a system wide 2025 Graduation Initiative aimed toward increasing graduation rates for students who typically face obstacles in achieving timely graduation, and to address achievement gaps (California State University Public Affairs, 2016).

4. The CSU, Chico, English Department formerly offered a certificate in Editing and Publishing. Within that certificate program, students could take Professional and Technical Writing courses. During the budget cuts in 2008, the certificate program ended. We first offered Introduction to Technical Writing in the fall of 2017 as a lower division course. Since then, this course has been changed to an upper division course, added to the general education program, and offered every semester. In addition, we are working on building an entire curriculum for a rhetoric and writing emphasis in the major.

5. One program we have turned to as a model is the writing program at University of Texas at El Paso. Our geographic and institutional differences, however, compel us to develop a localized approach to our writing program design.

6. For instance, in Kendall's past research on the building of a Chicana feminist organization, the Comisión Femenil Mexicana Nacional, she analyzed the way that the organization's leaders reframed and rearticulated organizational practices as part of their reinvented history of Chicanidad, which enabled these mechanisms to be used to produce action. As these organizational leaders were able to utilize identity articulation as inventive and productive, we argue that we can extend this to institutional spaces as well (Leon, 2013).

7. We do not intend the focus of this article to be on Aydé's TW course. We simply draw from this course because it provides helpful instances that illustrate the learning objectives in practice.

8. For example, Pimentel and Gutierrez (2014) examine how racism is produced discursively through commercials made by General Mills Company for taco shells from Old El Paso made available through YouTube. They then also work to analyze the comments section following the commercial. The Old El Paso commercial clearly displays a racist representation and objectification of Mexican Americans, but the initial comments focus on the humor of the video. However, as individuals start to challenge the racialization and problematic nature of the commercial, other commentators are quick to discredit and silence the discussion (pp. 90–93). Pimentel and Gutierrez (2014) demonstrate that examining the commercial as a rhetorical moment allows us to see and question what moments are beyond reproach.

9. The zombie is very much a child or distant nephew of early monster films, and it is rather well documented that these films have consistently played on the fears and anxieties plaguing society, often exposing their inner demons. For example, in both versions of the *Night of the Living Dead*, George Romero's (1968) and Tom Savini's (1990), the one African-American lead character Ben is killed by the end of the film. In Romero's version it is used to speak about the violence against African Americans since Ben survives the night but is still killed by a White militia, while in Savini's re-release of the film, Ben is infected, becomes a zombie, and must be killed. So, in either version, the African-American character must be killed because leaving him as a sole survivor problematizes the discourse within its timeframe (Hardman, Streiner, & Romero, 1968; Menahem Golan & Savini, 1990).

References

Alcoff, L. M. (2005). *Visible identities: Race, gender, and the self.* Oxford: Oxford University Press.

California State University, Chico Office of Diversity and Inclusion. (2016). *To form a more inclusive community: The CSU, Chico 2011–2016 Diversity Action Plan.* Chico, CA.

California State University, Chico Office of Diversity and Inclusion. (2015). *Diversity Documents.* Diversity demographics. Chico, CA.

California State University Public Affairs Department (Sept. 12, 2016). Two additional CSU campuses become Hispanic Serving Institutions. Long Beach, CA.

Dobrin, S. (2002). A problem with writing (about) "alternative" discourses. In C. Schroeder, H. Fox, & P. Bizzell (Eds.), *ALT DIS: Alternative discourses and the academy* (pp. 45–56). Portsmouth, NH: Boynton/Cook-Heinemann.

Fox, T. (1992). Repositioning the profession: Teaching writing to African American students. *Journal of Advanced Composition, 12*(2), 291–304.

Giddens, A. (1984). *The constitution of society.* Berkeley, CA: University of California Press.

Giroux, H. (2010). *Zombie politics and culture in the age of casino capitalism.* New York: Peter Lang Publishing.

Hall, S., Morley, D., & Chen, K. H. (Eds.). (1996). *Stuart Hall: Critical dialogues in cultural studies*. London; New York: Routledge.

Haas, A. M. (2012). Race, rhetoric, and technology: A case study of decolonial technical communication theory, methodology, and pedagogy. *Journal of Business and Technical Communication, 26*(3), 277–310.

Hardman, K., & Streiner, R. (Producers), & Romero, G. (Director). (1968). *Night of the Living Dead* [Motion picture]. USA: Continental Distributing.

Hocks, M. E., Lopez, E. S., &, Grabill, J. (2000). Praxis and institutional architecture: Designing an interdisciplinary writing program. *academic.writing*. Fort Collins, CO: Colorado State University.

Inoue, A., & Poe, M. (Eds.). (2012). *Race and writing assessment*. New York: Peter Lang.

Katz, S. B. (1992). The ethic of expediency: Classical rhetoric, technology, and the Holocaust. *College English, 54*(3), 255–275.

Kells, M. H. (2007). Foreword. In C. Kirklighter, S. W. Murphy, & D. Cárdenas (Eds.), *Teaching writing with Latino/a students:* Lessons learned at Hispanic-serving institutions (pp. vvii–xiv). Albany, NY: State University of New York Press.

Leon, K. (2013). Chicanas making change: Institutional rhetoric and the Comisión Femenil Mexicana Nacional. *Reflections: Public Rhetoric, Civic Writing and Service Learning, 13*(1), 165–194.

Moya, P. M. L. (2002). *Learning from experience: Minority identities, multicultural struggles*. Berkeley, CA: University of California Press.

Matveeva, N. (2015). Teaching technical, scientific, or professional communication at Hispanic-serving institutions. *Programmatic Perspectives, 7*(1), 3–20.

Menahem, G. (Producer) & Savini, T. (Director). (1990). *Night of the Living Dead* [Motion picture]. USA: 21st Century Film Corporation.

Mendez, J. P., Bonner II, F. A., & Méndez-Negrete, J. (Eds.). (2015). *Hispanic Serving Institutions in American higher education: Their origin, and present and future challenges*. Sterling, VA: Stylus Publishing.

Perryman-Clark, S. (2013). *Afrocentric teacher research: Rethinking appropriateness and inclusion*. New York: Peter Lang.

Porter, J. E., Sullivan, P., Blythe, S., Grabill, J. T., & Miles, L. (2000). Institutional critique: A rhetorical methodology for change. *College Composition and Communication, 51*(4), 610–642.

Pimentel, O., & Gutierrez, K. (2014). Taqueros, luchadores, y los brits: U.S. racial rhetoric and its global influence. In M. F. Williams & O. Pimentel (Eds.), *Communicating race, ethnicity, and identity in technical communication* (pp. 87–99). Amityville, NY: Baywood Publishing Company, Inc.

Rendón, L. I., Nora, A., & Kanagala, V. (2014). *Ventajas/Assets y Conocimientos/ Knowledge:* Leveraging Latin@ strengths to foster student success. San Antonio, TX: Center for Research and Policy in Education, The University of Texas at San Antonio.

Santiago, D. (2008). *Modeling Hispanic serving institutions: Campus practices that work for Latino students*. Washington, DC: *Excelencia in Education*.

Scott, J. B., Longo, B., & Wills, K. V. (2006). Introduction: Why cultural studies? Expanding technical communication's critical toolbox. In Scott, J. B., Longo, B., & Wills, K. V. (Eds.), *Critical power tools: Technical communication and cultural studies* (pp.1–19). Albany, NY: State University of New York Press.

Sun, H. (2009). Toward a rhetoric of locale: Localizing mobile messaging technology in everyday life. *Journal of Technical Writing and Communication, 39*(3), 245–261.

United States Census Bureau. (2010). Retrieved from https://www.census.gov/quickfacts/fact/table/chicocitycalifornia/PST045217

Chapter 8

Teaching Technical Communication on the México/U.S. Border

A Brief Case Study

Laura Gonzales

Introduction

During my first semester as a faculty member and writing instructor at the University of Texas–El Paso (UTEP), I had the privilege of teaching an upper-level undergraduate technical writing course. Since this course served as a general elective open to all undergraduate students, there was a wide representation of majors and disciplinary interests among the 23 students enrolled in class. Students' majors included kinesiology, nursing, health sciences, mathematics, social work, and education. In addition to their varied disciplinary interests, students' linguistic and cultural backgrounds echoed those of the broader UTEP population[1]: all students in my course identified as Mexican or Mexican American, with 2 students identifying as Mexican Nationals who live in Juárez, Chihuahua, México, and commute to El Paso to attend classes at UTEP each week. Students in the class also identified as speakers of Spanishes and Englishes to various degrees and for various purposes; some stated that they preferred speaking English, while others preferred speaking in Spanish and reserved communication in English primarily to the classroom. Similar to a large portion of the borderland population, most of the students in this class stated that they constantly navigate among and mix Spanishes and Englishes depending on the context, audience, and rhetorical situation in which they are communicating.

As a bilingual, South American, immigrant Latina instructor with experience teaching technical communication in other contexts (including a recently designated Hispanic-Serving Institution in Florida and a Predominantly White Institution in the Midwest), I came into this technical communication course at UTEP excited and grateful for the opportunity to engage in discussions about technical communication with bilingual students from a wide range of disciplines and backgrounds. Because my research interests are situated at the intersections of technical communication and translation, I was particularly interested in learning more about how my students at UTEP would engage with the opportunity to create bilingual technical documents through our course assignments. These assignments included a bilingual memo providing current definitions of technical communication, a usability report of a digital platform, a community-based project where students created bilingual digital materials for a nonprofit organization that serves Latinx communities across the United States, and a multi-step collaboration with translation students at Ghent University in Belgium, where my technical communication students were asked to prepare technical documents that would be translated into Dutch by translation students.[2] Although the specifics of each assignment are beyond the scope of this chapter, it is important to note that each assignment in this course was intended to help students draw connections between technical communication and translation, allowing students to leverage their linguistic strengths by composing and submitting assignments in both (or either) Spanish and English depending on their individual approaches and rhetorical goals.

While each course assignment rendered interesting discussions about the connections between technical communication and translation, the overall experience of teaching this course helped me think about the unique positionality of teaching technical communication in this borderland context—a space where languages, cultures, and identities are constantly in motion, unconstrained (or constantly constrained) by a single identity marker or category (Noe, 2009). Although I had taught and practiced technical communication in diverse bilingual environments before—both as an instructor and as a technical translator—the unique approaches to technical communication exhibited by students in this class provided an opportunity to productively complicate my understanding of how cultural and linguistic diversity can influence and inspire technical communication pedagogies. Specifically, teaching technical communication in this context with this population of students helped me understand the importance and potential of continuing to push the field of technical communication to emphasize different layers of diversity, not only in research and practice, but also in programs, pedagogies, and professional training. In turn, as I will further demonstrate in this chapter, teaching technical communication on the border provided useful implications for the broader efforts being made to support and recognize diversity in the field of technical communication, specifically for and with Latinx student populations.

In order to illustrate how technical communication students on the México–U.S. border can inform emerging conversations about diversity in the field of technical communication, I will first provide an overview of emerging discussions highlighting the value of recognizing and sustaining Latinx student diversity in technical communication programs. Using student anecdotes, course reflections, and experiences from my course, I will then go on to explain how technical communication students on the border can help our field to intricately understand and re-conceptualize our approach to teaching and assessing technological literacy and cross-cultural communication. Finally, I will draw implications for other technical communication programs seeking to teach technical communication with culturally and linguistically diverse students, specifically those from Latinx communities.

Literature Review:
Technical Communication with and for Latinx Students

Since what has been described as the "cultural turn" in technical communication (Scott, Longo, & Willis, 2006), researchers and teachers have continued to recognize the importance of acknowledging and addressing issues of race, culture, and power in technical communication research and pedagogies (Agboka, 2013; Barnum & Li, 2006; Haas, 2012; Jones, 2016; Longo, 1998; Scott, Longo, & Wills, 2006; Savage & Mattson, 2011; Savage & Matveeva, 2011). Thanks to the important work of technical communication researchers and teachers, and to ongoing efforts by organizations such as the *CPTSC Diversity Committee*, research on technical communication pedagogies continues to advocate for increased diversity and intercultural training for technical communication students, faculty, and administrators (Jones, Savage, & Yu, 2014; Savage & Matveeva, 2011). As part of this work, emerging research emphasizes the role of technical communication in social-justice advocacy, presenting technical communication training as an opportunity for students and practitioners to enact cross-cultural competency, empathy, and dignity (Colton & Walton, 2015; Gonzales, 2017; Walton, 2016; Jones, Moore, & Walton, 2016).

While there is extensive work focused on issues of diversity and difference in technical communication more broadly, recent conversations have also focused specifically on technical communication with and for Latinx populations (Evia & Patriarca, 2012; Germaine-McDaniel, 2009; Gonzales & Turner, 2017; Johnson et al., 2008; Matveeva, 2015; Medina, 2014; Pimentel

& Balzhiser, 2012; Savage & Matveeva, 2011). This work has pushed the field of technical communication to consider how conversations about and efforts toward diversity in the field should pay close attention to differences and overlaps in categorizations of race, ethnicity, language, and culture, understanding that these identity markers cannot and should not be flattened or generalized. Rather, by pointing to the intricate differences encompassed in broad cultural categories such as those typically considered "Latinos" or "Latinx," researchers like Johnson et al. (2008), Pimentel & Balzhiser (2012), and Medina (2014) urge technical communication researchers, teachers, and practitioners, to consider how differences *within* racial and ethnic minority groups should be recognized and addressed, particularly when attempting to design and localize systems, documents, technologies, and pedagogies that can effectively engage and be shaped by marginalized populations (Agboka, 2013). This is of particular importance in Latinx communities where there are vast differences in the racial, ethnic, linguistic, and cultural practices enacted between different communities and populations that may use or identify with the term "Latinx." For instance, although they may all be identified as "Latinx" on census documents and school records, there are broad differences in Latinx populations from Central and South America and Mexican or Mexican-American student populations living in or commuting to the United States. Thus, technical communication research should continue working to "uncover manifestations of racism and 'whiteness'" that seek to flatten or whitewash difference, even in systems that were designed with or for marginalized communities (Johnson et al., 2008, p. 234 qtd. in Matveeva, 2015, p.4).

In her analysis of 240 course catalogue listings that identified undergraduate and graduate programs and certificates in technical, scientific, or professional communication programs at Hispanic-Serving Institutions, Matveeva (2015) shared four strategies for supporting Latinx students in technical and professional writing programs. These strategies include: (1) Addressing ESL issues in the classroom, (2) Adding learning modules or additional courses on diversity and workplace communication, (3) Establishing close ties with local nonprofits and businesses in order to provide students with internship and workplace experience, and (4) Identifying and teaching skills for employability. Through this discussion, Matveeva (2015) explained that "by responding to our students' needs, using their cultural and linguistic knowledge, and connecting them to and maintaining close ties with their local cultural communities, technical communication instructors can better motivate students and help them succeed in their professional lives" (p. 4).

While Matveeva (2015) provides recommendations for teaching technical communication at HSIs based on her analysis of course catalogue descriptions, Medina (2014) offers a localized example of how Latinx discursive practices can be supported in technical communication courses. Specifically, through his discussion of Latinx student engagement on Twitter, Medina (2014) concludes that Latinx technical communication students should be encouraged to enact their "ethnically marked linguistic variance" when using and creating tools and technologies (p. 64). In this way, Medina (2014) explains that technical communication teachers and researchers can continue dismantling the generalized and frequently embraced "middle-class, White, male ideal 'voice' in technical communication," making space for language variance in communication design (p. 64). Thus, as Medina (2014) demonstrates, supporting Latinx student success in technical communication requires a purposeful pedagogical shift—one that pushes technical communication instructors to focus less on helping Latinx students to assimilate into "traditional" communicative frameworks, and more on helping the field of technical communication to recognize difference as central to (rather than tangential to) successful technology and communication design (Haas, 2012; Johnson et al., 2008; Williams, 2009).

Drawing on emerging work that highlights the importance of Latinx communities to technical communication pedagogies and practice, I will now share some examples of how students in my technical communication course at UTEP engaged with issues of language and technology as they were presented in our course assignments. By putting my students' examples in conversation with emerging research about Latinx communities in technical communication, I suggest more research and engagement with technical communication on the México–U.S. borderland can provide fruitful insights into the layers and intricate differences encompassed in technical communication's understanding of and engagement with Latinidad. As Leon and Enriquez-Loya argue in their chapter within this collection, technical communication is a "pivotal space where HSI as identity can be articulated."

Neither English nor Spanish:
Accessing Language Practices on the Border

The field of technical communication has paid extensive attention to issues of language access and accessibility. Plain language and minimal design movements advocate for democratic information access, encouraging technical communicators and information designers to use "simple" or "clean" language and design methods that can be understood by publics who may not have access to discipline-specific knowledge or jargon (Steinberg, Bowen, & Duffy, 1991; Thrush, 2001). This push for plain language use in technical designs has gained added popularity in conversations about engaging with international audiences, where technical communicators emphasize the need to use simple language in order to avoid confusion for users who may speak English as an additional language (St. Amant & Sapienza, 2011). While these efforts toward language accessibility are incredibly valuable, teaching technical communication on the border helped me understand the blurred lines between "expert" and "non-expert" discourses, between "simple" and "messy" design, and between what I may have considered "mono" versus "multi" lingual, highlighting the value and importance of messiness and complexity in communication design.

For example, students in my technical communication course at UTEP were asked to partner with and design materials for a nonprofit organization that aims to serve Latinx communities.[3] When I introduced this assignment, students' first questions were not so much focused on the intricacies of the assignment itself, but rather focused on getting to know the cultural and linguistic practices of their community client. For instance, when I introduced our partnering organization as one that serves Latinx communities, one student immediately asked, "You mean Latinx like Mexican or from where?" Although I've worked with this partnering organization for several years through several different service-learning projects at various institutions, my UTEP students were the first to immediately realize that they would need to know more about the specific Latinx community that they would be representing in their materials. They knew, from the beginning, that a Mexican or Mexican-American audience would interpret materials differently than a Latinx-identified population from Central or South America or from other parts of the United States.

After learning more about the various Latinx populations that they would be representing in their client project, students in my technical communication course continued thinking about how they would handle language issues as technical communicators for this organization. While our previous discussions about translation and technical communication provided some useful framing, students in this course opted to use materials that were inherently bilingual—choosing to represent both Spanish and English in a single design, rather than designing two different documents for Spanish and English speakers. For instance, students designed information flyers for their partnering organization that placed English and Spanish phrases next to each other, arguing that "there are some things people who live in the U.S. won't understand in Spanish because they are more used to seeing these terms in English." In other words, because students in this course knew that they were creating materials to be disseminated within the U.S. for a U.S.-based organization, they knew that certain words, phrases, and idioms would not need translation, and that, in fact, translating these phrases would only create more confusion for the user. Thus, while I had originally envisioned my students translating their materials and keeping Spanish and English separate, their own experiences with technical communication on the México–U.S. border inspired them to create bilingual designs that would be useful to Latinx communities who live and work in the United States.

In a sense, my students' decisions to include both Spanish and English in their designs, and to embed visual design elements that represented broader Latinx populations increased the messiness and complexity of the language and the practices of this service-learning project. Rather than opting for simple-language and design choices that would communicate information directly, students in this course chose to represent multiple language and cultural practices in a single design. The flyers, business cards, and infographics they designed did not adhere to plain language and simple design recommendations. Instead, students enhanced the complexity of their materials by including multiple languages and multiple cultural representations across their materials. In this way, students blurred conceptualizations of expert and lay terminology, positioning neither English nor Spanish, Latinx nor Anglo identities at the center by creating designs that embraced the complexity and depth of their target audiences.

From Technical Access to Technological Innovation

In addition to helping me rethink perceived linguistic boundaries between English and Spanish, students in my technical communication course provided me an opportunity to reconsider how I approach technological access and literacy in developing technical communication pedagogies. Rather than determining students' expertise with technology based on my own assumptions about what constitutes technological literacy, I was able to see how students' previous experiences and histories shaped their orientation toward learning and manipulating new digital platforms.

During the first couple of weeks in the semester, I sent my technical communication students a link to a Google doc and asked them to use this document to sign up for individual conferences with me. After noticing that no students had signed up on my Google doc, in the following class session, I asked students if something kept them from accessing the document. Several students commented that they didn't sign up for conferences not because they couldn't view or edit the document I had shared with them, but rather because they "didn't know how to save" their information on the Google doc platform. At this point, I realized that when I sent students' instructions, I made assumptions about their previous engagement to and access with Google docs, assuming that students had used Google docs before and that they would know that their edits to the document are saved automatically.

Initially, I was inclined to generalize this Google doc example into a broader assumption about my students' technological literacy, thinking that since students did not have previous experiences and training with a simple platform like Google docs, they may not have much experience with more complex software. However, as the course progressed, and as students continued working on their assignments, I quickly learned that my assumptions about students' technological literacy were flawed and oversimplified.

In one of our course assignments, students were asked to provide a usability report for a digital platform of their choice. As part of this assignment, students would need to understand and engage with the intricacies, affordances, and limitations of their chosen digital platform, crafting a review of the interface navigation that might be useful to other users in the course. During this assignment, I was able to see how students engaged with numerous digital platforms in their daily activities. These platforms ranged from common social media apps like Facebook and Twitter to other messaging platforms that would allow them to engage with users outside of the United States. For example, several students in the course reviewed Whatsapp, a free messaging application that allows for fast and reliable international texting, voice, and video calls. In their usability reports, students mentioned that they use Whatsapp to communicate quickly with family members in both El Paso and Juárez, and that they liked how the Whatsapp platform allows them to create and maintain specific group messaging clusters. Unlike iMessage or other U.S.-centered platforms, students explained that Whatsapp was an easy way for families to form group messages, regardless of their cell phone providers, phone plans, and physical location.

In addition to intricate messaging apps, students in my course exhibited a willingness and ability to learn new software and technologies to complete their course assignments. For example, during our client-based service learning project, where students were asked to design materials for a nonprofit organization, several students chose to explore a new digital platform that they had not had experiences with before. For instance, one student used this assignment as an opportunity to teach herself Adobe Photoshop and InDesign, claiming that she had been meaning to learn these platforms but had not had the time to devote to practice with them. Similarly, several students in this class decided to create online profiles for their community partner, experimenting with web design through new platforms like Weebly and Squarespace. While these students explained that they hadn't created websites before this class, they were more than open to the opportunity of working with a new platform, and even expressed gratitude for the chance to learn to use a new digital tool. In the end, I learned that although students in my technical communication course at UTEP may not have had previous access to what may be deemed "traditional" digital tools like Google docs, their readiness and willingness to experiment with new technologies resulted in various moments of technological innovation and creativity. Indeed, the materials that students designed for their community partners in this course were some of the most creative and localized I've witnessed across all my technical communication courses. Students' willingness to engage with new platforms, and their interest in learning intricate details about their client audiences, positioned them to develop nuanced technological literacies that I could have easily overlooked under my initial assumptions.

Implications:
Why Study Technical Communication Pedagogies on the Border?

Although emerging work in technical communication with and for Latinx communities, such as Matveeva's (2015) study, provide some introduction into the possibilities for Latinx technical communication, based on the brief examples and experiences of teaching this technical communication course at UTEP, I'd like to offer the following implications for further consideration, particularly as technical communication researchers and teachers continue developing frameworks for engagement with Latinx communities in other contexts.

1. Latinx Students Bring Relevant Work-Related Experiences to Technical Communication

As I witnessed students engaging with new digital platforms in my course, I quickly learned that students' orientation to learning new technologies was often related to their previous experiences as professionals. While my example with Google docs illustrated some limitations that students may have had in their previous access to educational technologies, students in this course were also willing to learn and manipulate new digital platforms to accomplish their work. This included learning new design software (e.g., Adobe Illustrator and Photoshop), as well as using their rhetorical skills to tailor designs for local communities. Through our conversations, I learned that most of my students, as is the case in other commuter campuses and Hispanic-Serving Institutions, held jobs outside of the university, where they also had to learn and engage with new and previously unfamiliar technologies. Thus, students came into my technical communication course with previous experience in technical communication, experience that they gained as they adapted to new technologies in workplace contexts. In this way, when faced with a new client project in my classroom, students already understood how to find the best resources available to communicate their ideas, and how to tailor information to meet the needs of diverse users.

2. Latinx Students, Especially on the Border, Know How to Blur Lines between Expert and Lay Discourses and Languages

My students' experiences creating bilingual materials for their community clients helped me understand how technical communication with Latinx populations (and particularly those living on the borderland) can help our field to continue expanding our notion of accessible languages and designs. For instance, students in my course understood from the beginning that they would need to translate information on their designs to meet the needs of diverse audiences. However, in addition to understanding a need for translation, these students were also able to complete the translation work themselves. Through this process, they exhibited intricate design decisions as they opted to create bilingual materials rather than sticking to more traditional notions of translation. Because students understood that they were designing for Latinx communities living in the U.S., they were able to create materials that echoed the linguistic practices of localized communities. While some of my Mexican National students felt more comfortable speaking and writing in Spanish and some of my students from El Paso felt more comfortable speaking and writing in English, our class conversations revolved around the linguistic practices that we needed to engage in as a class in order to better understand and accomplish work with each other In this way, students in this course on the México–U.S. borderland knew that immigrants in the U.S. have a unique orientation to language and information processing—an orientation that should be honored and represented in contemporary technical designs for those communities. The purpose of successful technical communication, at least for the students in this course, was not about maintaining simple or standardized language and design decisions; rather, the objective was to echo the communicative practices and localized design patterns of cross-cultural communities.

3. Latinx Students on the Border Understand the Need for Research and Cultural Sensitivity in Technical Communication

Perhaps due to their own cultural and linguistic histories and experiences on the borderland, students in this technical communication course made immediate connections between cultural sensitivity and successful technical communication. For example, in their collaborative assignments, students were more interested in asking questions about their community partners, rather than focusing solely on the assignment requirements. That is, rather than focusing on the specific design parameters required to successfully complete a task, students in this course began their projects by learning more about their audience, aiming to understand what it is what I meant by the term "Latinx" when introducing collaborators. In this case, students came into service learning projects with an understanding that concepts like "Latinx" are complex and are often representative of a wide range of cultures, languages, and communities. Thus, in part due to their own cultural orientations, Latinx students on the borderland exhibit expertise in culturally sensitive and rhetorically localized technical communication. Their goal in designing and disseminating documents and designs was not generalized for ambiguous "standard" users, but rather to specify and tailor designs for local communities.

Conclusion

In his discussion of borderland identities, Noe (2009) draws a connection between the term "Latino/a" and Mexican/Mexican-American history. Citing the origins of the term "Latino" in relation to the erasure of Mexican and Mexican-American identities, Noe (2009) explains the importance of acknowledging and recognizing borderland experiences as critical to how we theorize Latinidad more broadly. He explains, "border rhetorics . . . can be used to resist being appropriated by academic discourse through mimicry of the conventions of that discourse as students envision a fluid identity rather than the exchange of one identity for another" (Noe, 2009, p. 604). In other words, if we center conversations about Latinx identity in the borderland experience, we can recognize the multiplicity of language, culture, and history embodied in conceptions of Latinidad, while simultaneously honoring the "hardship, despair, constant struggle, and numerous large and small moments of oppression" experienced by Mexican and Mexican-American communities who are often erased in the broader "Latinx" label (Noe, 2009, p. 604). Furthermore, in technical communication specifically, if we listen to borderland Mexican/Mexican-American experiences and knowledge making practices, we can continue to recognize how "Latino/a students already bring an exemplary discourse into the classroom, one immersed in a quite different rhetorical tradition, one that comes out of a much less conventional language of parents, coaches or other powerful adults than we have hitherto assumed" (Noe, 2009, p. 603). In turn, as scholars such as Gloria Anzaldúa (1987) and multiple Indigenous and Chicanx scholars have been teaching us for decades, discourses on the borderland blur boundaries between languages and cultures, providing examples of fluid contemporary discourses that are now common in both academic and professional spaces, both within and outside of the United States (Torrez, 2013).

Although the evidence shared in this chapter is limited and anecdotal, my ultimate purpose is to share brief examples that can continue helping technical communication researchers and teachers to recognize the experiences of Latinx communities, and of borderland Mexican/Mexican-American communities specifically, as central to the diversity work that we can continue to support and undertake as a discipline. Because students like those described in this chapter have extensive experience navigating multilingual, cross-cultural communication in both United States and international contexts, they hold unique expertise that can be of value to technical communication scholarship and pedagogies. As our field continues to push for increased diversity and new perspectives in teaching, research, and practice, understanding how technical communication is situated and developed on the borderland can help us develop nuanced understandings of technical documentation, translation, and localized design, particularly as they are enacted in the daily experiences students who have historically been excluded from our disciplinary conversations. Furthermore, as technical communication scholarship and pedagogies continue extending efforts toward diversity, we should look closer at the complexity and layers of difference embedded within what we may typically generalize as "non-standard." That is, as we continue acknowledging the difference embedded in all communication design, we should continue moving beyond general labels like "Latinx," to more intricately understand the different cultures, languages, and iterations of Latinidad that are present in and across our communities. In order to do this work successfully, I suggest we continue learning from the expertise of students and professionals who embody border(ed) identities and experiences, as their orientations to technical communication work echo the multiplicity and dynamism that we strive for as technical communicators working in contemporary cross-cultural contexts.

Notes

1. Located on the border of El Paso, Texas, and Juárez, Chihuahua, México, UTEP is the only research doctoral university in the United Stated with a Mexican-American majority student population, hosting an 80% Hispanic student population with 5% of students identifying as Mexican Nationals (https://www.utep.edu/about/about-utep.html).

2. This collaboration was coordinated as part of the Trans-Atlantic and Pacific (TAPP) network organized by Dr. Bruce Maylath at North Dakota State University.

3. For more information about this Language Services Center, please see: http://hispanic-center.org/language-translation-services/

References

Agboka, G. Y. (2013). Participatory localization: A social justice approach to navigating unenfranchised/disenfranchised cultural sites. *Technical Communication Quarterly, 22*(1), 28–49.

Anzaldúa, G. (1987). *Borderlands/La frontera: The new mestiza*. San Francisco, CA: Aunt Lute Books.

Barnum, C. M., & Li, H. (2006). Chinese and American technical communication: A cross-cultural comparison of differences. *Technical Communication, 53*(2), 143–166.

Colton, J. S., & Walton, R. (2015). Disability as insight into social justice pedagogy in technical communication. *Journal of Interactive Technology and Pedagogy, 8.*

Evia, C., & Patriarca, A. (2012). Beyond compliance: Participatory translation of safety communication for Latino construction workers. *Journal of Business and Technical Communication, 26*(3), 340–367.

Germaine-McDaniel, Nicole. (2009). Localizing medical information for U.S. Spanish-speakers: The CDC campaign to increase public awareness about HPV. *Technical Communication, 56*(3), 235–247.

Gonzales, L. (2017). But is that relevant here? A pedagogical model for embedding translation training within technical communication courses in the U.S. *Connexions International Professional Communication Journal, 5*(1), 75–108.

Gonzales, L., & Turner, H. N. (2017). Converging fields, expanding outcomes: Technical communication, translation, and design at a non-profit organization. *Technical Communication, 64*(2), 126–140.

Haas, A. M. (2012). Race, rhetoric, and technology: A case study of decolonial technical communication theory, methodology, and pedagogy. *Journal of Business and Technical Communication, 26*(3), 277–310.

Johnson, J., Pimentel, O., & Pimentel, C. (2008). Writing New Mexico White: A critical analysis of early representations of New Mexico in technical writing. *Journal of Business and Technical Communication, 22*(2), 211–236.

Jones, N. N. (2016). Found things: Genre, narrative, and identification in a networked activist organization. *Technical Communication Quarterly, 25*(4), 298–318.

Jones, N. N., Moore, K. R., & Walton, R. (2016). Disrupting the past to disrupt the future: An antenarrative of technical communication. *Technical Communication Quarterly, 25*(4), 211–229.

Longo, B. (1998). An approach for applying cultural study theory to technical writing research. *Technical Communication Quarterly, 7*, 53–73.

Matveeva, N. (2015). Teaching technical, scientific, or professional communication at Hispanic-Serving Institutions. *Programmatic Perspectives, 7*(1), 3–20.

Medina, C. (2014). Tweeting collaborative identity: Race, ICTs, and performing Latinidad. In M. F. Williams & O. Pimentel (Eds.), *Communicating race, ethnicity,
and identity in technical communication* (pp. 63–86). Amityville, NY: Baywood
Publishing Company.

Noe, M. (2009). The corrido: A border rhetoric. *College English, 71*(6), 596–605.

Pimentel, C., & Balzhiser D. (2012). The double occupancy of Hispanics: Counting
race and ethnicity in the U.S. Census. *Journal of Business and Technical Communication, 26*(3), 311–339.

Savage, G., & Mattson, K. (2011). Perspectives on diversity in technical communication programs. *Programmatic Perspectives, 3*(1), 5–57.

Savage, G., & Matveeva, N. (2011). Toward racial and ethnic diversity in technical
communication programs. *Programmatic Perspectives, 3*(1), 58–85.

Scott, J. B., Longo, B., & Wills, K. V. (Eds.). (2006). *Critical power tools: Technical
communication and cultural studies.* New York: SUNY Press.

St. Amant, K., & Sapienza, F. (2011). *Culture, communication & cyberspace: Rethinking technical communication for international online environments.* Amityville,
NY: Baywood.

Steinberg, E., Bowen, B., & Duffy, T. (1991). Analyzing the various approaches of
the Plain Language laws. In E. Steinberg (Ed.), *Plain language: Principles and
practice* (pp. 19–28). Detroit, MI: Wayne State University Press.

The University of Texas at El Paso. (2018). *About UTEP.* Retrieved from https://www.
utep.edu/about/about-utep.html

Thrush, E. A. (2001). Plain English? A study of plain English vocabulary and international audiences. *Technical Communication, 48*(3), 289–296.

Torrez, J. E. (2013). *Somos Mexicanos y hablamos Mexicano aquí:* Rural farmworker
families struggle to maintain cultural and linguistic identity in Michigan. *Journal
of Language, Identity & Education, 12*(4), 277–294.

Walton, R. (2016). Supporting human dignity and human rights: A call to adopt the
first principle of Human-Centered Design. *Journal of Technical Writing and
Communication, 46(4), 402–426.*

Williams, M. F. (2009). Understanding public policy development as a technological
process. *Journal of Business and Technical Communication, 23*(4), 448–462.

Testimonio 4

English, *Español*, or *Los Dos*

Isabel Baca

> The fact that I
> am writing to you
> in English
> already falsifies what I
> wanted to tell you.
> My subject:
> how to explain to you that I
> don't belong to English
> though I belong nowhere else.
>
> —Gustavo Pérez Firmat

In writing this *testimonio*, I debated what angle to take; there's so much to say, so much to share when you live on the borderlands, where language is in constant flux and culture is so multidimensional and multifaceted. My personal journey as a second language speaker, as a daughter raised in a traditional, double-standard, Mexican home, and as a Latina in higher education teaching in a Department of English and Rhetoric and Writing Studies Program, is full of stories to tell and important lessons to share. However, as a single mother raising a son on the El Paso, Texas–Juárez, México border, I see the urgency, because of my linguistic and cultural upbringing, of sharing my journey as a parent wanting to have her son be an English-Spanish bilingual Latino who is proud of his heritage and roots and be successful and happy in life. Because of my personal experiences as an English-Spanish bilingual Latina scholar and as a parent, I see the need of seeking venues, tools, and strategies that will allow us to honor and value students' home languages and cultural assets, especially when teaching at Hispanic-Serving Institutions.

I am a product of the U.S–México border and am proud of it. I was born in El Paso, Texas, but lived the first years of my life in Juárez, Chihuahua, México. Both my parents are native Mexicans, and both became U.S. citizens later in their lives. I have three siblings: an older sister, a younger sister, and the youngest, a brother. All of us were born in El Paso, but only my older sister and I lived in Juárez and attended school there the first few years of our schooling. All four of us attended private schools from elementary to high school. We were privileged. We are not first-generation students, and we were not a low-income family. Our father is a civil engineer who graduated from college with a Bachelor's degree, and our mother completed high school and attended community college as a returning student once all of us, her four children, were college graduates. My sisters and I grew up speaking Spanish at home, while my brother, ten years younger than I, grew up speaking English. Both my parents are second language learners, with Spanish being their first language. However, the role of English in my parents' lives changed with the birth of my brother.

My parents made it a point to speak to him in English, even though their first language is Spanish. In my family, it is common to hear both languages and code-switching. If my parents are speaking with my brother, they will speak English, even though my brother is bilingual. However, if my parents are speaking with me or one of my sisters, they will speak Spanish. From an early age, I learned that for my parents, English was the language of power, the privileged language, and the language of opportunity. Spanish was the language of la *familia*, the language to be used intimately but not to get ahead in life. Thus, they saw the need for us to learn English. And somehow, in their eyes, my brother had to embrace the language of opportunity while foregoing the language of la *familia*. Even with language, double standards were present in my family.

With only one summer of private, intensive English classes, my parents enrolled me in a U.S. elementary school in the third grade. I stopped attending school in Juárez, México. My best friends became an African-American girl and a German girl; neither knew Spanish. We communicated through signs. My Mexican-American classmates treated me like a foreigner because my English was so limited, and their Spanish was not fluent. Our teacher knew no Spanish. I was forced to learn English the hard way, and I had to learn it fast. Even at this young age, I experienced confusion and conflict with what was the "right" language or the "right" way to speak and talk. I recall having my third grade teacher hit me on the hand with a ruler if I spoke

Spanish in class or in school and having my parents get angry with me if I spoke English at home.

Upon graduating from eighth grade, I had learned English. I knew how to write it. I knew how to read it. I knew how to speak it. The many challenges that came from those years of schooling taught me how important it was to be able to communicate with others and to respect linguistic and cultural differences. From being afraid to speak with an accent to honoring my parents' upbringing, I learned the greatest lesson: If I could not value my home language, culture, and roots, I could not value myself. These challenges strengthened my love for language. Writing became my venue to express this love, and I wrote in English and Spanish. Because I lived the struggles of a second-language student in a U.S. classroom, I knew the importance and value of being bilingual.

In 1996, when I became a mother, I had already promised myself that I was going to raise my children bilingually. I was not going to teach my children that one language was better than the other or that each language had a different place in our lives. English and Spanish are beautiful languages and both open doors for us personally, academically, and professionally. Both have equal places in our lives, and both should be valued and practiced. Both contribute to our identities, and both contribute to our growth as individuals, students, and professionals. So, it is not a matter of English or *Español*; it is a practice of both languages, *de los dos*.

On April 4, 2016, at the 2016 Conference on College Composition and Communication, as a panelist, Alexandra Hidalgo presented "A Video Exploration of the Hybrid Cultural Identities of Bilingual Latina/o Children." Through a discussion and a video that she created, Hidalgo shared her personal journey and how it has affected the way she raises her children linguistically. She says in her video, "I will never be white. I will never be standard." She states, "Spanish is the language of my soul." Hidalgo recalls when her son began rejecting Spanish and spoke more and more English and how this was a painful experience for her. She felt deep shame of having lost so much. He was forgetting his mother tongue. In her video, Hidalgo argues, "We can't give them [our children] fully the culture because we are not fully of the culture ourselves anymore." She poses the question: "How do we let English creep in without taking over?" I wondered if I had let English creep in without taking over in my son's life.

My son, Antonio, or "Toño" as we call him at home, was raised with both languages. I raised him as a single mother with the help of both my parents. All of us spoke to Toño in Spanish; thus, his first language was Spanish, with his first words being *mamá*, *papa* (as in food), and *agua*. But soon after enrolling him in a U.S. elementary school when he was four years old, he grasped English. Television, friends, and school influenced his use of both languages. English overshadowed his first language, *Español*. Before I knew it, his grandparents were speaking to him in English too. As much as I tried speaking to him in Spanish, he replied in English. In the wink of an eye, Toño was losing his mother tongue. I, like Hidalgo, felt shame that my son was no longer practicing his first language and forgetting the language of my soul, *Español*.

Toño is now 22 years old, and his linguistic journey has been more of a rollercoaster than anything else. He fought me, linguistically, throughout his teenage years. I demanded he speak to me in Spanish, only to have him distance himself more and more from his mother tongue. When he entered the university, he chose to study French instead of taking Advanced Spanish. I felt I had lost the language war with my son. But hope crawled in when he chose to major in Creative Writing and Multimedia Journalism. Toño wanted to write, and he wrote. My soul danced when I read his poetry and short stories: His integration of words in Spanish, the references to his heritage and culture, and his reading of the works by Latinx authors announced, in BOLD letters, his love of and connection to his mother tongue and his cultural upbringing.

Soon Toño began his journalism experience when he and other class-mates began an online magazine focusing on local and international artists, musicians, and authors. He conducted interviews in Spanish, and I would see him transcribing these into English late at night. Occasionally, he would pop into my room and ask, *"Como se dice . . . en inglés?"*—asking me to translate different words from Spanish to English. Toño had not, and has not, lost his first language, the language of my soul, *Español*. The language war ended when I stopped fighting.

How I wish there were a magical potion, definite tool, or confirmed strategy that ensures that our children will not lose their mother tongue when learning English! What can we do as parents, as educators, and as scholars to prevent this from happening? What am I doing to honor, recognize, and value students' home languages and cultural assets? My attempts include teaching bilingual writing courses, allowing students to use their home lan-guages throughout the writing process, and sharing my personal journey as an established Latina scholar whose first language is Spanish, and still feels like an impostor when writing, publishing, and speaking in English. I often tell my Latinx students, "If I can do it, you can too. *Sí se puede!*" I know that changes can begin in the writing classroom. *Tengo esperanza*. I have hope. It is not a matter of English or *Español*. It is the recognition, value, and practice of both, *de los dos*.

PART IV

WRITING CENTERS AND MENTORED WRITING

Chapter 9

On Longing and Belonging

Latinas in the Writing Center

NANCY ALVAREZ

> I write to record what others erase when I speak, to rewrite the stories
> others have miswritten about me, about you. To become more intimate
> with myself and you. To discover myself, to preserve myself, to make
> myself, to achieve self-autonomy. To dispel the myths that I am a mad
> prophet or a poor suffering soul. To convince myself that I am worthy
> and that what I have to say is not a pile of shit. To show that I can and
> that I will write, never mind their admonitions to the contrary. And I
> will write about the unmentionables, never mind the outraged gasp of
> the censor and the audience. Finally, I write because I'm scared of writing
> but I'm more scared of not writing.
>
> —Gloria Anzaldúa, "Speaking in Tongues"

The first time I attended the International Writing Center Association (IWCA)
conference in 2012, I was lucky enough to be on a panel with Dr. Harry
Denny, the former director of St. John's University Writing Center where I
am currently a doctoral student. As a tutor who questioned our writing center's ideals, values and practices, I was encouraged by Harry to put together
a proposal for the conference. At the time that I was writing the proposal I
wasn't sure if I would continue in my doctoral program. As one of the few
Latina students in most of my graduate courses and within the writing center,
I felt inexperienced, inadequate, inarticulate, and so very brown. But when
our IWCA proposal was accepted, I felt accepted as well. I felt that I had
found my niche, my people!

Ironically enough, the title of our panel was "Drawing a Line in the Sand: Contesting Everyday Oppression in/through Writing Centers." My presentation was a talk on the role that the Conference on College Composition and Communication's (1974, 2003) "Students' Right to their Own Language" (SRTOL) could play within writing centers. For a Saturday afternoon session, our room was surprisingly packed, and Harry ran out to get more chairs. I set myself up at the front of the room while I waited for Harry to get back. You can imagine my surprise when an older White woman came over to tell me that I was sitting in the wrong place. She said, "Harry Denny's presenting here. You can't sit here." I couldn't process what she was saying to me, so I just stared at her for a bit, and at some point, I managed to say, "I'm presenting with Harry. Check the program." I don't remember if she checked or not, but I remember wondering if she was going to ask me for proper identification to confirm that what I was saying was true.

Harry came back and started his talk, but I don't remember anything he said. I was in shock. I wondered why she thought I didn't belong there, while also knowing in my gut that my brown body had to be enough of a reason why. As I thought about my foolishness for feeling a sense of belonging within this community that I believe cares about writing center tutors and the students they serve, I felt a mix of anger and sadness. The more I thought about her admonition, the more offended I became, and the more I wanted to just go home.

When it was my turn to speak, I put my head down to read my paper and tried to read it quickly, so I could get out of there, but then Harry cleared his throat and poured me a glass of water. I stopped to look at him, and he gave me a look that I understood as saying, "slow down and breathe." I took a breath, sipped my water and decided to slow down. I remembered why I was there, and how what I had to say needed to be heard, especially by that one woman. I finished my talk and people seemed to like it, and they told me how important the topic I was talking about was in our field. For a minute, I felt like a person who did belong, even though it seemed to me that the only people that looked like me at this conference were the hotel maintenance staff.

When I got back to the St. John's University's writing center and looked around, I realized that the truth was that my presence in writing centers, St. John's, and the field as a whole, was complicated. On the one hand, a Latina in the writing center isn't a strange occurrence. I saw plenty of us in the writing center every day—as students who have been sent there by their professors in order to fix their papers . . . and language . . . and maybe even their way of thinking. I thought about how often, when I walked into the writing center during my first and second semesters as a grad student, I was stopped and asked, "Are you here for a session?" I had classes with some of these tutors and during that spring semester, I was working as a tutor as well. And yet, I still came across as a stranger; someone that must be in the writing center for a session and couldn't possibly be one of the many tutors who worked there. It was as if my brown body spoke words that I wasn't uttering. I wondered why a brown body in the writing center was perceived as a body in need of help. On the other hand, I understand that when tutors and administrators aren't used to seeing tutors and administrations of color working at the writing center, they assume we don't exist within the field. I thought about these issues and decided that even though many would see me and think that I don't belong in writing centers as a tutor or administrator, I needed to make a space for myself and people like me, and that I would do that through research, presentations, and, more importantly, through writing.

Latina Tutor Research

I began this chapter with my *testimonio* because I wanted to offer a firsthand account of my experience in writing centers before sharing the experiences of the Latina tutors I interviewed for my dissertation research. Through my research, I was able to capture counter-stories offered by Latina writing center tutors. My research isn't about retention, training or solutions to a supposed problem; it's about listening to a growing population in academia, Latinas, that have stories to share about how they experience a particular part of their academic life—working in the writing center. Through interviews and written *testimonios*, I am able to share different perspectives and unheard stories, which will hopefully broaden the worldview of writing center administrators and tutors. As Daniel G. Solorzano and Tara J. Yosso (2002) write:

> The counter-story is also a tool for exposing, analyzing, and challenging the majoritarian stories of racial privilege. Counter-stories can shatter complacency, challenge the dominant discourse on race, and further the struggle for racial reform. Yet, counter-stories need not be created only as a direct response to majoritarian stories. As Ikemoto (1997) reminds us, "By responding only to the standard story, we let it dominate the discourse" (p. 136). Indeed, within the histories and lives of people of color, there are numerous unheard counter-stories. Storytelling and counter-storytelling these experiences can help strengthen traditions of social, political, and cultural survival and resistance. (p. 32)

Capturing the voices of the Latina tutors is essential to this study, especially because we are multi-marginalized voices. As the Latinx population increases in the United States, the number of Latinx college students increases as well. According to Pew Research Center, "In 2014, Hispanics made up 17.3% of the total U.S. population, up from 3.5% in 1960. According to the latest projections from the U.S. Census Bureau the Hispanic share of the U.S. population is expected to reach 28.6% by 2060" (Stepler & Brown, 2016). The Pew Research Center also provides statistics that show an increase in Latinx college students:

> In 2014, 35% of Hispanics ages 18 to 24 were enrolled in a two- or four-year college, up from 22% in 1993—a 13-percentage-point increase. That amounted to 2.3 million Hispanic college students in 2014. By comparison, college enrollment during this time among blacks (33% in 2014) increased by 8 percentage points, and among whites (42% in 2014) the share increased 5 points. Among Asians, 64% were enrolled in college in 2014, a nearly 9-point increase over 1999 (no data are available for Asians before 1999). (Krogstad, 2016)

Considering the expected rise of the Latinx population in the United States, academic institutions need to be prepared to serve these students. One way of learning about Latinx college students is through research that records their voices, instead of research that only serves to examine how to help or fix Latinx students. With this idea, my research examines how Latina tutors experience higher education and the writing center.

My study focuses on Latinas, instead of Latinx, because, in my short time working in writing centers in New York City, I had only ever met a handful of Latina tutors. Moreover, in a study conducted by Heidi Lasley Barajas and Jennifer L. Pierce (2001) on successful Latinx college students, they discovered that Latinas were less likely to assimilate and were more likely to carve out their own paths to college success through community. I was curious about the role the writing center could and/or does play in providing a community to Latina tutors. Barajas and Pierce (2001) write:

> Young Latinas in this study navigate successfully through and around negative stereotypes of Hispanics by maintaining posi-tive definitions of themselves and by emphasizing their group membership as Latinas. Furthermore, their positive self-definition is reinforced through supportive relationships with other Latinas earlier in high school and now in college. (860)

Through their research, Barajas and Pierce (2001) deduced that because of the Latina's need for community and friendship, she is less likely to fully assimilate, unlike the men they studied, who through sports were more likely to buy into the rhetoric of "hard work" that is prevalent in assimilationist agendas. Their study leads them to make the claim that, "[t]hese successful young Latinas found ways to carve out safe spaces through their relationships with other Latinas and to successfully construct paths through the predominantly white, middle-class space of high school and college" (Barajas & Pierce, 2001, p. 864). After reading this article, I thought about the group of Latina tutors that I had met at St. John's University's writing center in 2014. I was no longer tutoring there, but I admired (and envied) their friendship from afar. I wondered if groups like theirs existed in other writing centers. Were they speaking Spanish in the breakroom, too? Did they tutor in English and Spanish? Did they make non-Latina tutors uncomfortable because of their languages and cultural practices? These questions led me to the questions of this study. I needed to know more.

Over the fall 2015 semester, I collected stories from Latina tutors about their experiences working in writing centers. I wanted to explore how Latina tutors shape and are shaped by their work in writing centers, because of or in spite of the assimilationist practices found at most writing centers across the United States (Grimm, 1999; Villanueva, 2006). Through my dissertation study, I highlight ways that Latinas can battle oppression in higher education through their work in the writing center. Because writing centers support students writing across the curriculum, it is important to consider how writing centers serve to regulate Standard English norms by the choices made by writing center administrators regarding the hiring of tutors to the skills that are valued and/or enforced during tutor training (Greenfield & Rowan, 2011). When the writing center is perceived as a monocultural and/or monolingual space, faculty and students are led to believe that this is the norm—that only White, native-English speakers, who resemble the majority of faculty members at most universities ("The Condition of Education," 2015), have the authority to support writers. If writing centers are viewed as White, English-only spaces and the institution ignores or supports this idea, how does this affect the perception of the institution by multilingual and/or multicultural students? If the writing center reflects the values of the institution in which it is housed, what are Latinas' experiences as tutors in a space that is used to seeing them as "clients?"

Because I wanted to find as many Latina tutors as possible, I decided to focus the site of my research to writing centers operating in Hispanic-Serving Institutions because these institutions serve at least a 25% Latinx student body. To recruit participants for my study, I used a list compiled by the Hispanic Association of Colleges and Universities (hacu.net) as a guide for searching for writing centers operating within HSIs. After compiling an HSI writing center director list, I asked writing center directors to forward my email to all of their writing center tutors, with the hope that Latinas would be given the opportunity to self-identify as Latina. It was important for me to have Latinas self-identify instead of having the directors make assumptions about their gender, race, and ethnicity. Willing participants were asked to fill out a short survey that indicated their interest in being part of my study. Once I received their signed consent forms, interviews were scheduled and conducted through Skype, FaceTime, and Google Hangouts.

I collected seventeen interviews with Latina tutors living in California (9), Texas (6), and Florida (2), ages 18 through 32. The tutors described their nationalities as Mexican-American (9), Mexican (2), Colombian (1), Cuban (1), and "mixed" (4), which the tutors described as being half-White and half-Latina. They described their language abilities as: fluent in both English and Spanish (10), fluent in English and "broken" Spanish (5), and English only (2). Seven of the tutors were graduate students, while ten were undergraduates working on their Bachelor's (8) and Associates' (2) degrees. Their majors included: English (9), Psychology (3), Public Affairs (2), Liberal Arts (2), and Biology (1). The diversity in their backgrounds, languages, and educational interests and experiences made me wonder where I'd find the strongest similarities and greatest discrepancies in their experiences as Latina writing center tutors.

Findings

Through this research, I learned that Latina tutors have much to contribute to the fields of English, literacy learning and teaching, and writing center studies, as many have had to navigate racist, xenophobic and/or misogynistic terrains, drenched in English-only ideals, in order to get to where they are now as students, writers, and tutors. Throughout the interviews, the tutors spoke about a wide range of issues: they had concerns over being the only (or one of few) Latina tutors in their HSI writing centers; English majors worried about being the only (or one of few) Latinx in the English depart-ment; some tutors questioned if, and how, their language ability quantifies their Latinidad; and all of the tutors discussed the role that assimilation has played in their lives as tutors and students.

Coming to the Writing Center

I was eager to find out all of the different ways that they had found their way to the writing center and why they decided to work as tutors. Although the reasons why the tutors decided to work in a writing center vary, there are three main pathways for how the tutors in my study came to work at their writing center:

- They were recommended to work at the writing center by a professor who was familiar with their writing

- Working at their university's writing center was a requirement for their degree

- They were looking for a job on campus and heard about openings at the writing center through a friend or a flyer posted on campus or online.

I wondered if and how these pathways played a role in how prepared the tutors felt upon embarking on their jobs as tutors. From the data, I learned that when the tutors were recommended by a professor to work in the writing center they felt confident, capable, and welcomed. The two tutors who were required to work there for their programs expressed concerns with being in a new and/or different environment rather than having anxiety over their qualifications to do the job. But the tutors who sought out the writing center for work showed more hesitation about their ability to do a good job. They wondered about their accents (in both English and Spanish) and their qualifications, and they expressed concerns over feeling like they belonged in the writing center. My research points to the importance of professors as mentors. A professor's recommendation can feel like validation for a Latina tutor who isn't as confident about her ability to be a good tutor.

Out of the 17 tutors, only seven were invited to work at the writing center by a professor (either an English professor or a professor they met during freshman seminar). Six of these tutors were undergraduate students, and only one was a graduate student. When professors approached these tutors to work at the writing center, or to take the required peer tutoring course in order to prepare to work at the writing center, the tutors often did not hesitate to jump on board. Josephine, an undergraduate student from Texas, was recommended to work at the writing center by an English professor she took a course with during her first year of college. This professor suggested that she could improve her own writing by editing the writing of others. Improving her writing, while also getting to meet new people and gaining teaching experience as a tutor, were factors that encouraged Josephine to apply. At Josephine's writing center, there are faculty tutors and peer tutors. By the time I spoke with Josephine she had been tutoring for three years, so she came across as a confident writer and tutor. Josephine shared that this wasn't always the case:

> *When I just started working at the writing center, I would freak*
> *out whenever I would talk to a professor [faculty tutors] because I*
> *felt like I didn't belong or they would know that I wasn't an English*
> *major. That made me feel different. It wasn't a Latina issue; I think*
> *it was just an inferiority complex.*

Having a professor's recommendation didn't keep Josephine from experiencing what she calls an "inferiority complex," but what many in academia may recognize as "imposter syndrome." Josephine's fear of being found out, or of not belonging in the writing center because of her major, speaks into issues of inclusion within academia. Who belongs in certain spaces, and who doesn't? Josephine wasn't the only tutor in this study who assumed that writing centers only hired English majors. The truth is that most writing centers tend to hire students across disciplines because writers write across disciplines in college. Although Josephine claims that her feeling of "inferiority" was not based on her ethnicity, I wonder if perhaps she was neglecting that as a factor. Even though Josephine experienced concerns about how others may perceive her belonging in the writing center, Josephine never expresses concerns over being able to do her job.

Two of the tutors in this study were required to work in their university's writing centers as part of their programs in the field of education. They were not invited to work in the writing center, nor were they recommended by any of their professors. They both knew of the writing center and wanted to work there, so it worked out that their academic requirements and their professional goals aligned. Annabelle, a graduate student from California, had to apply to work in the writing center in order to fulfill her Master's degree requirements. Annabelle clarifies:

> *It's part of the process in order to become a teacher's assistant at*
> *my university, but I was always kind of interested in being a tutor*
> *because my friends at my previous university worked in the writing*
> *center and it seemed like they enjoyed it. I was curious because I*
> *had tutored in math before at a community college, but I'd never*
> *tutored in English. I always wanted to, so basically I just applied*
> *last year hoping to get in and I got in.*

Once Annabelle started working at the writing center, she was able to start working as a teaching assistant through the writing center. Annabelle's professional goals are supported by her work in the writing center. Her Master's program and its faculty understand how the writing center has the ability of creating a pathway from student to teacher.

Almost half of the tutors sought the writing center for work after hearing about job openings on campus, online, or through friends. Five of the seven graduate students came to the writing center on their own. Valentina, a graduate student from California, came to the writing center for a tutoring session before she applied to work there. She enjoyed her session, but waited until she saw a job ad online before applying:

> I actually saw a thing online that they were hiring and I thought, "Hey! You know what? I love writing. I like helping out people, I might as well apply and just see what happens." They took my application and they were hiring at the time, and then I got interviewed and I got the job.

But the hiring process wasn't as simple as she initially described:

> It was quite a bit of work just because the application is like a packet you have to fill out. It was very detailed you had to fill it out and then you had to submit a writing sample and a cover letter. Then, you had to wait for a bit and had to be interviewed. I was interviewed by all three directors who would now be my bosses. Then I had to wait a little bit just to see whether I was hired or not.

Although she described the hiring process as "quite a bit of work," Valentina felt "fortunate" to get a job at the writing center. At the time of our interview, Valentina was a graduate tutor earning her Master's in Public Affairs. She wants to work for the government and mentioned how for her profession, "you need to know how write critically and concisely." She affirmed that her work in the writing center was good practice for her future job of working with people. Valentina's decision to work in the writing center was strategic and, in many ways, used as a form of professional development.

Thinking about all of the different ways and reasons these seventeen Latina tutors came to the writing center makes me wonder how writing centers can foster a more welcoming environment for tutors of color. Only three undergraduates from my study came to the writing center on their own, without a faculty recommendation. This factor makes me think of the visibility of Latina students, and other students of color, when it comes to faculty mentorship and recommendations.

Language and Identity

Not all of the Latina tutors were fluent in both English and Spanish. They
are all fluent English speakers, but Spanish fluency was a more complex issue
across the interviews. Several mentioned how their Spanish skills affected their
identity, even within the writing center. Five tutors described their Spanish
as "broken," "limited," "a little rough," "fragmented," and "not fluent." Valeria
is an undergraduate student from Florida whose first language, Spanish, was
replaced with English as she grew up. Valeria spoke about the guilt she feels
over the loss of Spanish:

> I do experience some guilt with not being able to communicate with
> them [writing center clients] better. They're like "Oh, you are Latina
> why don't you speak Spanish?" You know? To me, it's inexcusable,
> I'm really ashamed of it. I'm happy that my relatives have come
> here for a better life, and that's why I am an English speaker. At
> the same time, it's like "Oh my God" as generations go by, there is
> something being lost there. I reflect on that quite a bit.

Valeria's guilt and shame over not being a fluent Spanish speaker was echoed
by the other four tutors who aren't fluent in Spanish, as well as by one of
the tutors who only speaks English. Leah, a graduate student from Texas,
was worried that I wouldn't want her for my study because as a non-Spanish
speaker, she sometimes feels like she isn't "Latina enough." We spoke about
how her language affects her role as a tutor:

> At this school, most of the students' native language is Spanish,
> and they need tutors who speak Spanish. It's hard to provide that
> ESL tutoring when you don't know the language. It's very difficult,
> and it's something that I'm trying to work on. I'm really consider-
> ing trying to learn Spanish and have my nana work with me, but
> I just don't know how realistic it is at this point.

Leah had tried learning Spanish in school before, but hadn't been successful.
She seemed defeated by her inability to learn Spanish.

> I've gotten lectures on why I should learn. I think it's interesting,
> because it's stuff that I'm aware of. I had a great-grandmother who
> couldn't speak English, so I wasn't able to communicate with her.
> That's kind of hard when you're in this liminal identity between
> two different cultures, like English language then Spanish. How do

you attend to both? My mom would put us in Saturday classes to learn Spanish, and it just never stuck with me. I just feel like I'm constantly kind of trying to understand how do I identify with these two cultures? What does it mean to be a Puerto Rican who doesn't look or speak the language?

Considering that she is also one of the "mixed" tutors, her pale skin plays a role in how others quantify her Latinidad. I almost felt like Leah was looking for me to provide answers about her identity, but the most that I could do was tell her that I considered her Latina, even if she didn't speak Spanish, and even if she had pale, white skin. Language is part of our identity, but there are so many other factors that play a role as well, such as family and cultural values. But her concerns are valid, and I'm sure other Latinas can relate to the "in-betweenness" that comes with not looking or sounding the part, and all of the stereotypes that come with it.

On a different note, Gina, an undergraduate student from Florida, was the only tutor in this study who spoke English with a hint of an accent. At the time of our interview, Gina had only been tutoring for about two months. She was very happy with her new job, but she surprised me when she shared that her accented English was both a motivator and a concern:

I feel like sometimes I still have an accent, so I feel like that was one of the things that motivated me—how can a person whose first language is not English be a tutor, right? That was one of my concerns. At least in the beginning, I thought maybe students will think that I'm not competent or that I won't be as helpful because English is not my first language. I guess in that sense, I had to be more confident and understand that it's not really a big issue as long as I know the proper rules of the English language.

When speaking with Gina, I barely detected an accent (she came to the United States as a child), but I can understand how she may be overly critical about what she sounds like, as many of us who learn English after our home language are at times. Gina's concerns over her English language skills brought to light a factor that I hadn't considered when organizing this study. I assumed that "looking" brown would play a role in how the tutors perceived their identity as tutors in the writing center, but I hadn't thought about how "sounding" brown could make the tutors feel less confident and more self-conscious about their role as tutors. This factor made me wonder how many students don't apply to work in the writing center for fear that their accent will make them sound unqualified to work at the writing center.

Hacking English

Nine of the participants were English majors, five graduate students and four undergraduate students, aspiring to teach college English. The English majors all expressed a desire to tutor at the writing center because they felt that it would prepare them for teaching. The conversations about their career goals were filled with anxiety about being the only, or one of the few, Latinas in their English courses; feeling like they know enough grammar to be confident in their ability to teach English composition, while also convincing others of their capability to teach English; uncertainty about wanting to teach literature that embraces their heritage; and concern over how they performed their identity as Latina English majors.

Mercy is a graduate student in Texas working toward a Master's degree in English. We spoke about the lack of diversity within her graduate courses in English.

> *That's something that I always think about when I'm sitting in class. I had an experience last semester where we read a Pat Mora poem and it has words in Spanish, and I was immediately singled out to pronounce the words in Spanish. Of course, I find that odd because I don't actually speak Spanish. I have a great accent; I can say things in Spanish but it doesn't mean I know how to speak it. I was thinking to myself after this, "Why am I singled out?" I guess because I am Mexican-American. I'm like, "Where is everyone else? Why am I the only one here?" I think that really made me realize, "ow, I am the only one here in this program."*

Mercy later said that there might be two other Latinas in her program, but that number still felt too small for the amount of Latinx within her HSI university. She described the community outside of the university as being predominantly Latinx, which further adds to the odd feeling of being an outsider within an English classroom, especially when you belong everywhere else outside of that classroom.

During our interview, Annabelle shared an anecdote with me about how she came to realize that she wanted to become a composition professor.

> *I didn't even know I identified as a Latina until I took a Chicano Studies class. That's when I started to realize more so, like, it was there. But I think as I get older, I get closer to my roots. The professor was really good. He wasn't one of those that was like, "We all should be like the Chicano Movement." He was very objective*

and he basically told us, "You have a responsibility as Latinos in college to empower other Latinos." That's the main thing I took with me from that class. And that's when I started to realize I wanted to [teach composition] because before I was like, "I want to teach literature and abstract ideas." And then I started realizing I wanted to be more real. And I actually like teaching writing. I was like, "I don't want to teach Austen in a classroom!" I like her books, but I don't want to teach that. There's no real powerful message behind that.

As she tells me this, Annabelle is speaking about the importance of mentorship; finding yourself within literature; and also, attempting to figure out how your cultural identity will come into play as an educator. Annabelle's message about "wanting to be more real" really resonates with me as I think about what it means to be an English major in 2018. In what ways are Latina English majors made to feel that they have to hide parts of their identity in order to fit in? How do we perform "the English major" and what parts of our heritage are "allowed?" As English majors, we're generally expected to love Shakespeare and to write, speak, and think in Standard Academic English. Even when writing this manuscript, I feel that push and pull about how I want to come across. Can I be "more real," as Annabelle describes above and write in a way that feels true to me, or do I have to sound like a White scholar in order to be taken seriously?

In her book, *Reclaiming Composition for Chicano/as and Other Ethnic Minorities: A Critical History and Pedagogy*, Iris D. Ruiz (2016) writes about not finding herself in composition histories and compares it to not finding herself in Shakespeare. She ruminates, "I can't see myself, and oftentimes, I can't see my friends or those who look like me. We don't look like the authors who wrote them. We are not white men. I can't see my history" (p. 1). When the books we read as students consistently match the race of the professor who teaches these books, how are we, as students of color, supposed to believe that our stories and voices are meaningful, worth listening to, and worth teaching? Several of the English major tutors mentioned never encountering a book written by a Latinx in their English courses. Students of color are paying attention to the identities of the authors that are introduced in their classrooms. Educators of color then have to make a decision about the voices they value within literature and within their classrooms.

I see the writing center as a space where Latina tutors can gain some of the confidence that they need to feel like they belong to English, on their terms. Many tutors expressed how reviewing grammar with students made them feel a greater sense of ownership of the language. What was most significant for me was how through tutoring, these tutors felt like insiders within a space and field that hasn't always seen them as such. They described being able to talk to their peers and writing center administrators about writing and tutoring in ways that made them feel included within the discipline. Tutoring others, especially English language learners, made them feel like they were making a valuable contribution to their university—by helping both students and professors.

Tutor *Testimonios*

After each interview, I sent the tutors an email asking them to provide a post-interview, one-page written *testimonio* where the they briefly shared any advice, stories, or tips with future Latina writing center tutors based on their experiences working in the writing center. In gathering these *testimonios*, my purpose was twofold: (1) to witness and gain insight to how Latinas grow to understand themselves and each other within the university, and (2) to contribute to our understanding of how Latinas are viewed within writing centers and the university at large. Through the interview and *testimonio*, my hope was that the Latinas I interviewed would feel like they were part of a growing community that is important to each of their academic institutions, as well as to academia overall.

In order to add more Latina voices into writing center studies, I'd like to share some of the *testimonios* I collected from the tutors.

Gina offers tips for tutoring multilingual students and gives future Latina tutors permission to tutor in Spanish, while assuring them that the goals of the tutoring session will still be reached. Reading about how Gina conducts her bilingual tutoring sessions gives me hope for the future of writing centers:

> *If the student has a very limited background in English, I would suggest to ask what their native language is. If it's Spanish, welcome them to talk to you in Spanish to ensure that both of you are on the same page (no pun intended) with the paper. In addition, it will aid in the explanation on "how to write." If the student still wants to have the session in English (for practice), go ahead and continue with the session in English. At least now they will feel comfortable asking a question if they are not sure how to translate a word or structure a sentence. It is crucial for the tutor to have a readiness to listen to the student's weaknesses/strengths and make accommodations while still maintaining the overall goal.*

Mercy encourages tutors to embrace their cultural identity because of how our multilayered identities can make other like us feel safe and seen within academia:

> At some point, you may feel as though you need to assimilate in order to feel like you're welcome in the academic environment, and that's okay, but you would be surprised how many students you can connect with based on your cultural background. When students come into the writing center, they often feel exposed and intimidated, and making a connection with their tutor over something as simple as a shared cultural experience can help them feel comfortable and at ease with the whole tutoring process. Embracing your cultural identity with students can also help students feel more comfortable expressing their own unique identities since they now feel that they are not alone in academia.

Jenny, an undergraduate student from California, explains how tutoring is personal and how our complex identities as Latinas can only enhance our tutoring sessions:

> Growing up, I felt stuck between two languages, two cultures, and two worlds. I had a hard time finding the balance between being Mexican and American. When I got to college and started studying TESOL methods, I realized how lucky I am as a Latina woman. I carry all this with me into the writing center. I work with many ESL students, so I have a firsthand look at how hard it can be to write in a second language. I think the fact that I am Latina, and even more so my heart for multiculturalism, has made me an excellent tutor. To be a great tutor, one must have the ability to connect with others on a personal level. Writing is personal, so tutoring must be as well. My background has prepared me well for serving the students that come into the writing center. We connect on a personal level, which leads to great tutoring sessions.

Through these *testimonios*, the tutors were able to reflect on the work that they do as tutors and the positive impact that Latina tutors have in their writing centers. These *testimonios* were written after the interviews took place, which I believe gave the tutors time to process our conversations and reflect on the experiences they value as tutors.

Conclusion

Since conducting this study, I have presented my research at various regional, national and international conferences. I have read the Latina tutors' *testimonios* aloud and have shared their thoughts on the importance of cultural and linguistic diversity. I have tried to speak up at those panels that I find offensive, instead of just quietly stewing in the back row. At these conferences, I have often been approached by writing center directors asking me for advice on recruiting Latina tutors. That's not the point of my research. I'm not advocating for everyone to hire a Latina for their writing center. It's not about fulfilling a quota, or being able to claim that your writing center is diverse. What I really want writing center administrators and faculty to understand from my research is that we, Latinas, exist. Some of us are English majors. Some of us want to be college English professors, just like you. Some of us want to be writing center tutors. Some of us will do a great job tutoring students of every color, even White ones. Some of us will not speak Spanish. Talk with us and ask us about our goals without making assumptions based on stereotypes about our identities. We are in your English classrooms, and there are more of us on the way.

References

Anzaldúa, G. (1983). Speaking in tongues: A letter to 3rd world women writers." In C. Moraga & G. Anzaldúa (Eds.), *This bridge called my back: Writings by radical women of color* (pp. 165–174). New York: Kitchen Table, Women of Color.

Barajas, H. L., & Pierce, J. L. (2001). The significance of race and gender in school success among Latinas and Latinos in college. *Gender & Society, 15*(6), 859–878.

Conference on College Composition & Communication (CCCC). (1974, 2003). Students' right to their own language. Retrieved from http://www.ncte.org/library/NCTEFiles/Groups/CCCC/NewSRTOL.pdf

"The Condition of Education: Characteristics of Postsecondary Faculty." *National Center for Education Statistics.* Nces.ed.gov, May 2015. Web. 31 Mar. 2016. Retrieved from https://nces.ed.gov/programs/coe/indicator_cuf.asp

Greenfield, L., & Rowan, K. (Eds.). (2011). *Writing centers and the new racism: A call for sustainable dialogue and change.* Logan, UT: Utah State University Press.

Grimm, N. (1999). *Good intentions: Writing center work for postmodern times.* Portsmouth, NH: Boynton/Cook-Heinemann.

Krogstad, J. M. (2016, July 28). 5 facts about Latinos and education. *Pew Research Center.* Retrieved from: http://www.pewresearch.org/fact-tank/2016/07/28/5-facts-about-latinos-and-education/

Ruiz, I. D. (2016). *Reclaiming composition for Chicano/as and other ethnic minorities: A critical history and pedagogy.* New York: Palgrave Macmillan.

Solórzano, D. G., & Yosso, T. J. (2002). Critical race methodology: Counter-storytelling as an analytical framework for education research. *Qualitative Inquiry, 8*(1), 23–44.

Stepler, R., & Brown, A. (2016, April 19). 2014, Hispanics in the United States Statistical portrait. *Pew Research Center's Hispanic Trends Project.* Retrieved from: http://www.pewhispanic.org/2016/04/19/2014-statistical-information-on-hispanics-in-united-states/

Villanueva, V. (2006). Blind: Talking about the new racism. *The Writing Center Journal, 26*(1), 3–19.

Chapter 10

Mentored Writing at a
Hispanic-Serving Institution

Improving Student Facility with Scientific Discourse

HEATHER M. FALCONER

The first time I met Ruben[1] it was a cold January Friday, late in the day. He spoke to me via Skype on his dinner break from a construction site in the middle of New York City. The sounds of nail guns and saws merged with honking cars from the other side of new walls, muffling his voice until he found a quiet space where we could talk. At the time, Ruben was a junior at John Jay College of Criminal Justice (JJC), having transferred in the previous year through an articulation agreement with a partnering two-year institution. By many accounts he is considered non-traditional: he is older than many of his student-peers (late-twenties), the first in his family to pursue higher education, a father who works 30 hours per week in addition to attending school part-time, is not a U.S. citizen (though has been in the U.S the majority of his life), and has paid for his education completely out-of-pocket. Ruben is also a Latino attempting to enter a discipline that has traditionally marginalized people of color. Yet, when we spoke that first afternoon, his commitment was palpable: "I think science can benefit society and can also benefit me. I just want to be useful."

In our first conversation, I learned that he was an active reader, enjoying science fiction and historical texts that both carried complex plot lines and utilized mid-level diction and syntax, and spoke both English and Spanish fluently. Though Ruben had successfully passed the requisite upper-level science courses (i.e., organic chemistry) to be eligible for the college's undergraduate research program, it was clear that the science coursework at both JJC and his community college had not prepared him for the reading and writing tasks of *practicing* science. The courses focused on reading textbooks, not journal articles, and writing formulaic laboratory reports rather than engaging with any of the other genres common to science. His mentor, Marta, would later tell me he arrived "as freshman as they come" in research, with little understanding of the purpose or structure of the research proposal, no knowledge of scholarly databases or how to find literature, and having never read a peer-reviewed journal article. What Ruben *did* have was a desire to learn and an affinity for his mentor as both a scientist and a person.

In this chapter, I explore how the use of mentored writing in an undergraduate research program helped Ruben, a non-traditional student and underrepresented minority in science, develop facility with scientific discourse despite social conditions disrupting that development. Mentored writing—writing that is explicitly directed and supervised by a more practiced writer—is not commonly practiced in disciplinary arenas. Though the field of science has a long history of collaborative scholarship, it often falls to one or two members of the team to do the actual writing. Here, I show how pairing collaborative scholarship with the explicit instruction of writing in the sciences contributes to a refined view of the nature of scientific knowledge and improved performance with scientific genres. On one hand, Ruben's case provides insight into the effectiveness of mentored writing with undergraduate science students, particularly (but not limited to) those engaged in undergraduate research. On the other hand, it offers a deeper understanding into the different factors that mediate student engagement with disciplinary genres. In the spirit of work by Cope and Kalantzis (1993), Clark and Ivanič (1997), Kapp and Bangeni (2005), and Wilder (2012), this research demonstrates the importance of why "genre teaching [should] go beyond focusing on how texts function to teaching the ideological underpinnings of form (the "why")" (Kapp & Bangeni, 2005, p. 111). The work presented in this chapter serves as an exemplar of how, as David R. Russell (1993) argued, writing can be effectively learned in conjunction with "the problems, the habits, the activities—the subject matter—" of the disciplinary group itself (p. 194).

Ruben's story is one part of a larger, longitudinal case study of the Program for Research Initiatives in Science and Math (PRISM), a unique undergraduate research program housed within John Jay College of Criminal Justice, a senior college within the City University of New York system and the largest Hispanic-Serving Institution in the northeast. What makes this program particularly interesting is not simply its structure (it conducts real-world research in science), but that the majority of the students participating in it are students of color—predominantly Black and Latinx; populations largely underserved nationally in higher education. Since its inception in 2006, the program has had great success in placing students in graduate programs (particularly PhD, MD, and MPh programs)—something that was virtually unheard of for graduates of the science major before its creation. In more recent years, the number of Research-1 institutions comprising these acceptances has also increased, likely as a result of the professionalization that occurs as part of the program (e.g., publishing research and presenting at scientific conferences).

In this chapter, I have chosen to present Ruben's case chronologically in narrative. This approach, I believe, allows for a better understanding of Ruben's growth over time and the social factors that influenced the speed of that growth. It also allows both Ruben and Marta's voices to drive the discussion, privileging their lived experiences over my external observation.

Engaging with the Research Proposal

The genre of the research proposal, as Greg Myers (1990) has described, is "the most basic form of scientific writing: the researchers must get money in the first place if they are to publish articles and popularizations, participate in controversies, and be of interest to journalists" (p. 41). While its purpose is to acquire funding to allow an inquiry to take place, it forces the writer to argue for certain assumptions about the proposed research and to do so through the use of multiple genres common to the community of practice. In many ways, the research proposal is a sophisticated genre that requires writers to understand rhetorical purpose and disciplinary conventions while being firmly rooted in, and facile with, disciplinary content.

All students who have been admitted to PRISM are required to submit a research proposal as a first step toward working in a laboratory. The program provides students with a formal "call" each semester, outlining the expectations and, to some extent, genre conventions of the proposal. Proposals must include a review of the literature, methodology for the project, a discussion of how it contributes to the larger body of scientific knowledge, and the amount of time and resources required to complete the study. Though there are no requirements that mentors work with their students in the writing of these proposals, mentors are expected to assist students in identifying an appropriate research question. Following the peer-review process in science, proposals are carefully reviewed by the Program Coordinator, who often provides written feedback. Accepted proposals are awarded a stipend to help offset the costs of engaging in extracurricular laboratory work, intentionally mimicking the genre engagement and exchanges that take place in the professional scientific community.

Clearly, such a process serves a gatekeeping function. Most students enter the research experience with no prior knowledge of or exposure to scientific genres other than the laboratory notebook and, occasionally, a scientific article pulled from a non-peer-reviewed source (most often Google searches). For this reason, explicit instruction and mentored writing in the proposal genre becomes even more crucial. When Marta, an early-career faculty member at the college, agreed to mentor Ruben in her toxicology laboratory, she found his understanding of the proposal genre was nearly nonexistent. He came to her office armed with the template PRISM provided and the agreed-upon research topic, but was otherwise unsure where to start, expecting her to write the proposal with him from scratch. Fortunately, her approach to teaching and mentoring embodies many of the best pedagogical practices we know help students of all types improve: She presents disciplinary writing as a dynamic, situated process that requires time and consideration of audience, as well as something that can serve a heuristic role ("Statement of WAC Principles," 2014). As Marta explained, when Ruben came to her, "he had no idea."

> [I said,] "You do the work, and I *review* the work. But I'm not starting with a blank page. *You* start with a blank page." So, he was like, "Oh, but I don't know how," and I said, "Well, I mean, you have to start with PubMed," and he didn't know what that was. So I said, "Ok, let's back up. Just to make your life easy for the proposal, I am sending you three papers. I want you to read these three papers . . . they are very related to your project, and then you write [a draft] of the proposal."

Though Ruben was left to his own devices at this initial stage, with the PRISM template and the articles Marta gave him his only resources, he managed to generate a five-page document. A review of the initial draft shows a student attempting to engage with the discourse of science, but unsure of his audience's knowledge base and uncomfortable with the toxicology jargon. In places his writing is unnecessarily specific, while in others overly general, and he demonstrates no clear understanding of the rhetorical structure employed in such a text (see figure 10.1).

In the Abstract and Introduction, for example, there is no real sense of the significance of the research in the larger sphere of forensic toxicology, and no hypothesis stated. The methodology is vague, while the listing of metabolites is overly specific. These errors are common, however, to novice researchers and according to Marta that first draft was "pretty decent"—particularly coming from an undergraduate student who had never encountered the genre before. At the same time, it gave her a clear indication of the writing instruction she

Liquid chromatography tandem mass spectrometry will be tested for its sensitivity to detect Tetrahydrocannabinol (THC) and its metabolites which are, 11-Hydroxy-THC (THC-OH), 11-nor-9-THC-9-Carboxylic acid (THC-COOH) and 11-nor-9-THC-9-Carboxylic acid glucuronide (THC-COOH-glucuronide). These metabolites are found in hair in very small concentrations. THC will be in ng/mg and THC-OH, THC-COOH, and THC-COOH-guluronide will be in pg/mg range. The research will consist in analyzing two groups of samples, one group will be of free drug hairs and the other group will be hairs of people that consumed Cannabis regularly. THC and its metabolites get into the hair via passive diffusion from blood capillaries and from surrounding tissues into growing hair cells. Once drugs are deposited in hair, they remains there for a long time in contrast to the short time drugs remain in urine and blood [3]. The first part of this research will concentrate in isolating and quantifying THC metabolites from hair samples using liquid chromatography tandem mass spectrometry. Depending on the results and the sensitivity of liquid chromatography tandem mass spectrometry we will continue with a second part of this project.

Rather than situate the research in the larger body of scientific knowledge, the first sentence presents the research question. Further, this question suggests the technique itself is under scrutiny, not the detection of metabolites. The listing of metabolites, here, is also awkward.

Scientific Abstracts should introduce the topic, present the hypothesis/research question, then succinctly outline the methods to test the hypothesis. This is followed by expected results and the implication of the research for the field. This Abstract does not offer these elements in a way that is clear or specific enough.

Figure 10.1. Ruben's first attempt at the proposal Abstract, with author's annotations.

would need to offer Ruben as a member of the laboratory. Marta decided to approach Ruben's scientific writing instruction in two stages: First, she would provide explicit guidance on the proposal, so it could be submitted on time and have a chance of being funded; second, she would assign scaffolded tasks to help him develop content knowledge, as well as skills in critical thinking and synthesis. In her approach, exposure to scientific texts would need to be intentional and frequent so as to build familiarity and comfort, but not fatigue.

The First Proposal

"It was challenging because I didn't know."

After reviewing Ruben's first proposal draft, Marta took a formative approach to providing feedback. First, she reworked his abstract, so it more clearly mirrored the rhetorical conventions of the scientific community (see figure 10.2 on page 218). Ruben's research was going to be focused on developing a method for detecting *Cannabis* in hair, so Marta began by introducing the drug being researched (*Cannabis sativa*), as well as providing an explanation for the use of hair as a matrix. This was followed by identifying the purpose and methodology of Ruben's research project. The abstract concludes with a statement regarding the significance of the project to forensic toxicology broadly to situate the research. Though Marta heavily rewrote the abstract,

Situates the topic in the scientific and public spheres. Also makes clear why hair is an important matrix for study.

Edits clarify that the LC-MCMS will be the *technique used* to study detection, as opposed to being under study itself.

Cannabis is the most commonly used illicit drug worldwide. According to the United Nations, 170 million people smoke at least once a year. Hair is an alternative matrix in forensic toxicology that allows the detection of past drug exposure. Once drugs are deposited in hair, they remains there for a long time in contrast to the short time drugs remain in urine and blood. In the case of cannabis, the active drug delta-9-tetrahydrocannabinol (THC) and its metabolites 11-Hydroxy-THC (THC-OH), 11-nor-9-THC-9-Carboxylic acid (THC-COOH) and 11-nor-9-THC-9-Carboxylic acid glucuronide (THC-COOH-glucuronide), get into the hair via passive diffusion from blood capillaries and from surrounding tissues into growing hair cells. The objective of the present research is to develop a method for the determination of THC and its metabolites in hair samples by **liquid chromatography tandem mass spectrometry (LC-MSMS). This technique will be tested for its sensitivity to detect these compounds.** THC metabolites ~~tetrahydrocannabinol (THC) and its metabolites which are, 11-Hydroxy-THC (THC-OH), 11-nor-9-THC-9-Carboxylic acid (THC-COOH) and 11-nor-9-THC-9-Carboxylic acid glucuronide (THC-COOH glucuronide). These metabolites~~ **are found in hair in very small concentrations. THC will be in ng/mg and THC-OH, THC-COOH, and THC-COOH-guluronide will be in pg/mg range.** The addition of the metabolites detection will allow to differentiate between external contamination and actual exposure.

Using some of the original text, Marta demonstrates how to present the drug and its metabolites in a way that makes sense to scientific readers, ultimately setting the reader up for understanding the research question/purpose.

Concludes with the significance of the research to the field.

Figure 10.2. Marta's revision of Ruben's abstract, following the rhetorical approach of a condensed Introduction, Method and Materials, Results, and Discussion.

the rest of the proposal, instead, included prompts for revision that mirrored the rhetorical outline of the abstract. In the introduction, for example, she commented: "You should start the introduction talking a little about cannabis (prevalence of consumption, basic pharmacology)."

Importantly, Marta didn't leave the feedback to written comments alone; Ruben was required to go to her office and talk through the edits. This allowed her to gauge firsthand whether he understood what she was asking and the rationale behind such changes. It also provided her an opportunity to show him what he was doing *well*. This combined written and oral feedback was effective for Ruben:

> It was challenging because I didn't know . . . In the beginning I
> wasn't sure what to write, and if it was fine what I was doing, but
> I [did what I could] and I showed it to Marta and she made some
> fixes. Then she explained, you know, 'do this, do this . . .' It was a
> challenge, but her [approach worked] . . . People whose mentors do
> it for them and say, "Here, submit . . ." *eh*. She actually made me
> do it. It was challenging, but I like this. It was great way to learn.

The opportunity to meet and revise was also effective in helping Ruben work through the technical jargon he was encountering in his reading. The jargon, as well as the instruments and techniques discussed, slowed down his understanding of the research he would be conducting and how it fits into the larger conversations in forensic toxicology.

It is important to note that, at this point, Ruben was relying on Marta to tell him what to do and how to do it. He also relied strongly on PRISM's proposal template to guide his writing. Such approaches to learning are not unheard of for first-generation college students and can, unfortunately, be misinterpreted as a lack of initiative or motivation. Whether it was a fear of crossing boundaries, not understanding expectations, or simply the result of being overextended personally with work and family is unclear. However, the revisions of this first proposal consisted largely of accepting Marta's changes and adding the least bit of information required to reach an acceptable version for submission to PRISM for funding. The final version was improved, but not as comprehensive as it could have been. It was funded, however, and Marta began the implementation of Stage 2.

"Reading always helps your writing."

Once Ruben's proposal was successfully approved, Marta told him that they would take some time before beginning experiments to orient him to the project and laboratory. "The first thing he's going to do . . . it's going to be reading," she explained.

> I told him not to be afraid of that, or don't be frustrated because I'm sure he's not going to understand half of the paper. So I said, "Don't expect that this is a novel; you're not going to have a great time. You're not going to understand a lot of things, but this is normal. But you need to do it.

This reading instruction came with even more explicit direction on how to use search engines such as PubMed and identify appropriate keywords, how to look for information and parse through that data for relevant material, and then specified tasks for putting together a review of the literature. At this early stage, though, Marta had not yet explained what literature reviews are or their purpose in scientific work but *did* emphasize that learning to read and understand scientific material is integral to learning how to write it. She encouraged Ruben to keep a notebook where he could write down questions about the readings, key terminology and jargon with definitions, as well as to note how the authors were conveying information. This notebook became an important reference during his time in the laboratory.

A review of this early assignment reveals a student scientist grappling with understanding what he was reading and tackling the writing request given him from his mentor (see figure 10.3). Leaving aside the incomplete sentences and mechanical errors, this early 'review' of the literature demonstrates a reporting of information pulled from the research that does not question the material, rather presents it as fact. There is no summary of what was done, nor is there synthesizing of information with prior knowledge or other research papers. The presence of the articles' authors as rhetors is completely absent, though there are some technical questions posed. Ruben described this early writing experience as "confusing" and "challenging" because, like the proposal, it was a style that he had never before encountered. When asked what he saw as the purpose of the assignment, he said that he saw it as "a sort of test. I think she just wanted to see if I was reading the papers." At this stage, where he had not received any instruction on the rhetorical function of the literature review, he viewed it as an assessment absent of any other purpose, except possibly for Marta to use as a quick reference should she wish to look up an article in the future. His instincts were not entirely incorrect. For Marta, this first assignment was about seeing how he was reading the texts and what parts he identified as important. In many ways, it *was* an assessment, though not in the way Ruben believed.

Contrast this to the same type of assignment completed by him two

Article 2012 september
Monitoring chronic cannabis abuse

- Analyzed compound : THC and THC-COOH

- Internal standard: THC-Deuterated, THC-COOH-Deuterated

- Mobile phase: Mixture of .1% aqueous formic acid and acetonitrile

- Washing procedure: Different solvents were employed like methanol for 5 minutes. The best combination for extractive incubation was found to be 60C for 23 minutes using 2.5 M NaOH.

-Limit of detection: 1 pg/mg for THC and THC-COOH

Limit of quantification: 3 pg/mg for THC and THC-COOH

" LOD and LOQ is too high for TCH-COOH according to society of hair testing"

- Questions:

What is parent and daughter signal in the result (chromatogram) ?

Why is derivatisation procedure when using GC-MS/MS and why is time consuming and expensive?

hydrophobicity of Cannabis is important when setting up chromatographic condition

Article 2013 August
Simultaneous determination of THC, Cannabidiol, Cannabinol, and THC-COOH in hair by LC-MS/MS

Figure 10.3. The first reading and synthesis assignment.

No citation information

No narrative or summary about the research; simply presents facts without context. Questions relate to understanding the science rather than critiquing the research findings themselves.

months later, this time following explicit direction on what to read for, where to look in the papers for information, and then how to present that information coherently. Ruben was told to research what is known about the metabolism of cannabinoids in the human body, and then present what he had learned in narrative form. This narrative, Marta told him, would help him to understand the role of his research—or, as she explained to me, to "situate it in the larger scientific discussion." In figure 10.4, we see Ruben has not only begun to understand the material he is reading better, but he is attempting to synthesize it in a way appropriate to the scientific community. Many of the mechanical issues in the earlier drafts are absent, and rhetorical moves such as hedging and third-person point of view become more apparent. Even citation conventions improved because Marta talked him through the function and purpose of citations. In this assignment, Ruben understood that the writing he was doing had a purpose other than assessment. This change suggests that he had begun to shift from taking scientific research at face value toward critiquing it in order to determine whether the results are supported by the reported methodology, as well as if there are unanswered questions that might point to a new research trajectory.

At the time he was instructed to write this review, Ruben was told to familiarize himself with proposals by the master's students who were also working in Marta's lab. In this way, he was receiving implicit instruction through exposure to the ways professional scientists communicate their ideas and set up answerable questions—something he could compare and contrast with the genre of the scientific paper. This exposure, Marta explained to me, was to help Ruben see the connections between the genres, as well as to provide a referent for their future discussions on writing his research poster (another, later, writing requirement of PRISM students). Reviewing these proposals provided an important orienting function to Ruben in the laboratory. He was able to understand Marta's research, see how the Masters students in the laboratory were supporting and complementing that research, and then identify how his own work fits into the larger scheme.

The Second Proposal and Beyond

Because students must submit proposals for each semester they wish to receive funding from PRISM, Ruben was required to submit a proposal the following semester. While he took a passive approach to this task, simply recycling the first proposal's text, he effectively engaged with the required Appendix, providing a thorough update on his research. In addition to a thoughtful collection of images representing data (including chromatograms and opti-

Distribution and Absorption

THC is highly lipophilic and it is rapidly taken up by tissues and lungs, heart, brain, and liver. Very little THC is retained in the brain in contrast to human fat when prolonged exposure occurs. It is suggested that fatty acid conjugates of THC and THC-OH may be formed which increases the stability of these compounds in fat [1] Detectable concentrations of THC have been found in fat biopsies obtained more than 4 weeks after smoking.

In an experiment done with large pig model due to similarities with human biotransformation including enzymes and isozymes of drug biotransformation. Eight pigs were injected with 200mg/kg intra-jugular THC injections and two were sacrificed after 30 min, 2,6, and 24 hours later. The fastest THC elimination was noted in liver where concentration fell below measurable levels by 6 hours. Brain concentration was approximately twice the blood concentration at 30 minutes with highest values in the cerebellum and occipital and frontal cortex. THC concentrations decreased in brain tissue slower than in blood. In fat tissue THC concentration decreases very slow [1].

Disciplinary-appropriate structure

More effective synthesis of scholarly literature

Appropriate use of hedges (underlined), which leaves room for error or alternate findings.

Figure 10.4. Ruben's second engagement with the scholarly literature demonstrating a much clearer understanding of the literature and closer alignment with disciplinary conventions.

mization tables), the written text demonstrates a clarity of thinking that was not present in the earlier work. The Appendix opens with a reminder of the purpose of the research and how it is being conducted, and then follows with a stage-by-stage description of what Ruben did and what was found (see figure 10.5). His comfort level with the jargon, techniques, and instruments of the forensic toxicology laboratory was markedly improved and the conciseness of the writing was far more proximal to the discourse conventions of science than his earlier attempts. Even more, there is a sense of confidence in the text that was previously absent.

During this semester, Marta was preparing Ruben for writing the scientific poster that he would be required to present at PRISM's end of year conference. Though his rhetorical awareness and engagement with disciplinary conventions had begun to improve, she was still slightly concerned about the quality of his writing—seeing it as often naïve and simplistic for his level. She was also concerned that Ruben might not be improving fast enough with his critical thinking, though she largely attributed that to his not yet having had the highest level toxicology courses that would provide the deeper context for what he was reading and doing. But for Ruben, he was only just beginning to feel confident in his own research and was testing the waters with independent thinking. Though he appreciated Marta's desire for the students to "basically work on [their] own," the subtext of our conversations was that he still wasn't confident enough in his abilities as a scientist to work without strong direction: "I try to think on my own before I go to her because . . . I know she will ask me first, and then if she sees that I can't answer or something, then she will take the lead. But I should try to do my own thinking before I go to her so that I don't look at her and expect her to do everything."

Ruben was navigating that liminal space between advanced beginner to competent practitioner at the same time he was making decisions about his career path. While all students who participate in PRISM are highly encouraged to pursue postgraduate work, Ruben had already decided that he wanted to work as a technician in a toxicology laboratory. Marta confessed a concern that family and friends were influencing this career path, as well, challenging Ruben's allegiances. Though he had been doing the work required, she noticed that his motivation and engagement had been on a steady decline. His presence in the laboratory was not frequent or long enough to really achieve the results needed, and they had had some conversations about the value of the degree he was earning. What was the point, really, if he could earn more money on the construction site?

In our conversations, Ruben clung to his identity as a carpenter and his interest in postgraduate work extended only to a possible Master's degree at

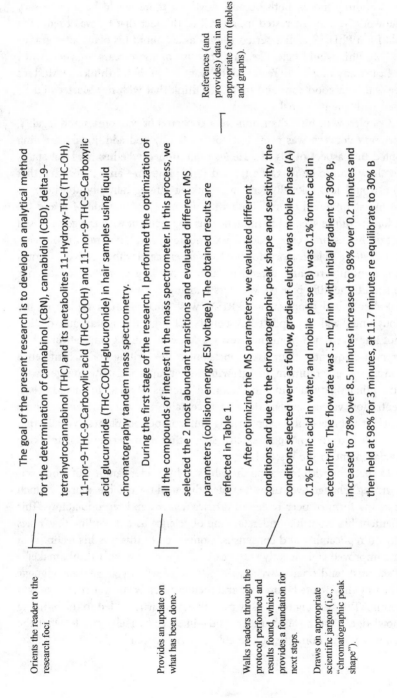

The goal of the present research is to develop an analytical method for the determination of cannabinol (CBN), cannabidiol (CBD), delta-9-tetrahydrocannabinol (THC) and its metabolites 11-Hydroxy-THC (THC-OH), 11-nor-9-THC-9-Carboxylic acid (THC-COOH) and 11-nor-9-THC-9-Carboxylic acid glucuronide (THC-COOH-glucuronide) in hair samples using liquid chromatography tandem mass spectrometry.

During the first stage of the research, I performed the optimization of all the compounds of interest in the mass spectrometer. In this process, we selected the 2 most abundant transitions and evaluated different MS parameters (collision energy, ESI voltage). The obtained results are reflected in Table 1.

After optimizing the MS parameters, we evaluated different conditions and due to the chromatographic peak shape and sensitivity, the conditions selected were as follow, gradient elution was mobile phase (A) 0.1% Formic acid in water, and mobile phase (B) was 0.1% formic acid in acetonitrile. The flow rate was .5 mL/min with initial gradient of 30% B, increased to 78% over 8.5 minutes increased to 98% over 0.2 minutes and then held at 98% for 3 minutes, at 11.7 minutes re equilibrate to 30% B

Orients the reader to the research foci.

Provides an update on what has been done.

Walks readers through the protocol performed and results found, which provides a foundation for next steps.

Draws on appropriate scientific jargon (i.e., "chromatographic peak shape").

References (and provides) data in an appropriate form (tables and graphs).

Figure 10.5. Appendix from Ruben's 2nd proposal showing improved engagement with the tone and jargon of forensic toxicology.

JJC and nothing more—both because anything more would be unnecessary for the work he was interested in, as well as the fact that he was tired. "I'm too old for a PhD," Ruben asserted when I asked about his plans after graduation; "My PhD would take, like, probably five or more years, maybe? And I can't. I can't any more . . . Yeah, I don't want to do that. I think the Master's degree will be a good spot and that's it. I think that with my Master's I'll be satisfied with my life's goal."

Coupled with his exhaustion were concerns of economics and legality. His primary concern was providing for his family and additional schooling disrupted that aspect of his life. He also questioned whether his legal status would allow him to be part of a funded PhD program—and, if so, what that income would look like. Ruben was thinking strategically about where he would invest time and energy, both within school and outside of it and his plans for the future seemed to influence his engagement with the genres used as part of the research experience. Task-oriented genres, like reports on what was completed and laboratory notebooks, were engaged with effectively. Genres more common to research scientists, such as funding proposals, conference posters, and scientific papers, were less enticing.

Ruben's final proposal for PRISM was, once again, a replica of the previous ones, with an updated Appendix. Though the syntax and diction did not improve much from the previous Appendix, and grammatical errors still appear frequently, there is a concision to the writing and a confidence that supports an argument for growth. Ruben appropriately engages with the disciplinary jargon and the rhetorical choices of what to include (e.g., concentration values, explanations of acceptable percentages) and exclude (e.g., using abbreviations over writing out compound names, visuals that don't speak directly to the research), suggesting a higher level of thinking and engagement in the research.

In speaking with him about how he saw his understanding of "good science writing" change over time, he noted the need for reliable sources, which came in the form of peer-reviewed articles, clarity, and reproducibility. This last element hinted at his understanding of science as a discipline that relies heavily on replicability and consensus. Connected to this was his feeling that writing improved significantly with reading: "Reading a lot, I think, makes a good scientist [and science writing] . . . Because when you see the language and the way they wrote before . . . and then eventually you get your own way of writing." This reading (of mostly peer-reviewed articles) led to the building of knowledge: "You have to understand—like, really, really good—what the experiment you're doing [is] to be able to write it well."

What Does Ruben's Experience Teach Us?

As noted in the introduction to this chapter, Ruben's story provides insights into two different, yet important things. First, his case offers an understanding of the potential effectiveness of mentored writing with undergraduate science students, particularly underrepresented minorities. Second, it offers a deeper understanding into the different factors that mediate student engagement with disciplinary genres. Though other students in my larger, longitudinal project have had outcomes that are more in line with our hopes for mentored writing and explicit instruction, I chose Ruben's story to explore because it highlights the various borders (discourse, economics, competing demands, etc.) that many students at Hispanic- and Minority-Serving Institutions grapple with. Ruben did not leave the program an expert scientific writer, in part because such expertise did not fit with his professional identity. His understanding of discourse conventions (e.g., why scientific writers use passive voice) remained tacit despite Marta's efforts at explicit instruction, he had no interest in collaboratively writing a journal article, and his reading practices outside of the required reading for classes and the lab were focused on Literature and History rather than scholarship. But important improvements were made and his facility with the discourse, in the end, was developed enough that he was recognizable as a junior member of the scientific community. More importantly, the experience helped him solidify what *type* of scientist he wished to be.

As Kapp and Bangeni (2005) have argued, "the process of learning/ acquiring a new discourse must include space for students to explore who they are and who they are becoming" (p. 124). It also has to account for the fact that whom our students choose to become is separate from our own hopes and expectations as teachers and mentors. Marta hoped Ruben would be more motivated and engaged with the work of the professional researcher—the kind that pursues a PhD and creates and leads their own experiments—but the affinity that Ruben held for the work of technicians was much stronger. This is in no way a "failure;" rather, it demonstrates the important role in identity formation mentorship can have. At the same time, Ruben's case shows us how we need not wait until students have reached the graduate level of academia to engage them effectively in the reading and writing practices of professional discourses. Though content knowledge is critical in being able to effectively communicate in disciplinary realms, it is not necessarily a prerequisite. Explicitly teaching the genre and discourse conventions in tandem with content can help students to understand the work they are engaging with, as well as develop their own communicative skills. Just as Kamler (2008) argues to rethink co-authorship as a pedagogic practice with doctoral students, so too should we think of mentored writing at the undergraduate level as a pedagogical tool to acculturate newcomers to disciplinary discourse.

This brings to mind questions posed by Freedman (1993): "Is explicit teaching [and by extension, mentored writing] necessary," or even "possible" (p. 224)? Who benefits, and when? In Predominantly White Institutions, with predominantly middle- and upper-class students, maybe explicit teaching *isn't* necessary to the degree that Marta enacted with Ruben. However, if we take a critical approach and think of the scientific community as an institution, we can approach these questions by asking: Who is allowed to speak? When? Who is expected to understand what is being said? And what are the connections of these affordances and constraints to societal categorizations such as class, race/ethnicity, and gender? As Fairclough (1989) explains,

> Institutional practices which people draw upon without thinking often embody assumptions which directly or indirectly legitimize existing power relations. Practices which appear to be universal and commonsensical can often be shown to originate in the dominant class or the dominant bloc, and to have become *naturalized*. (p. 33)

In this way, not only is discourse functioning ideologically, it is also functioning politically. Access to language—particularly the standardized forms of language—United States are unequal because of where these languages are located. The association of standardized American English, for example, with "the most salient and powerful institutions" of the U.S. (higher education and the legal system, for example) means that this form of English has become "the language of the politically and culturally powerful," and *non-standard* forms (as well as the groups associated with them) have been "stigmatized" (Fairclough, 1989, pp. 56–57).

Within the context of this research, we can view scientific discourse as a standardized form of disciplinary communication with a high barrier to access. Facility with scientific discourse (including genres and conventions, as well as jargon) is an asset, a form of cultural capital, because its use serves as a "passport" to well-paying jobs, further academic opportunities, and "positions of influence and power in national and local communities" (Fairclough, 1989 p. 57). It is also a discourse to which access is restricted—through literacy practices, educational opportunity, and economics. This restrictedness helps reinforce a narrative of exceptionalism that often places scientists in opposition to laypeople, and makes science as a career seem out of reach to so many (hence the disparities in STEM with regard to race/ethnicity and gender).

To engage successfully with scientific discourse requires a high level of reading and writing proficiency, particularly in English; it requires the ability to reach the later stages of higher education, as most individuals do not begin reading scientific papers until their 3rd and 4th years in undergraduate coursework (if then), or writing such genres until they reach the postgraduate level; and it requires not only the economic ability to pay for higher education for many years, but also the ability to attend institutions that grant access to scientific publications (and if not, the ability to purchase access for oneself). Thus, the exceptionalism that is embedded in science is not necessarily one of innate brilliance and daily breakthroughs, but of *access*. Once through these gates, however, engaging successfully means negotiating the power relations and ideologies embedded in the discourse itself.

The students in this larger, longitudinal project, like Ruben, have acquired a certain level of access. They are enrolled in a four-year, degree-granting institution, as well as have access to direct mentorship in an undergraduate research program. However, simply being present does not break down the institutional *discursive* barriers that exist—which is where mentored writing can play an important role. By recognizing scientific genres and language as something not natural, but rather as unique forms of disciplinary communication that have been shaped over time by the members of the community, this approach opens the doors for students of color to gain further access and may work to remediate some of the disparities in STEM persistence and retention that is of great concern in the United States. Minority- and Hispanic-Serving Institutions, because of their student populations, will by default play a critical role in this success.

Note

1. All names used are actual; both Ruben and Marta desired to use their real names rather than pseudonyms.

References

Clark, R., & Ivanič, R. (1997). *The politics of writing*. London, UK: Routledge.

Cope, B., & Kalantzis, M. (Eds.). (1993). *The powers of literacy: A genre approach to teaching writing*. London, UK: Falmer.

Fairclough, N. (1989). *Language and power*. New York: Longman.

Freedman, A. (1993). Show and tell? The role of explicit teaching in the learning of new genres. *Research in the Teaching of English, 27*(3): 222–251.

Kamler, B. (2008). Rethinking doctoral publication practices: Writing from and beyond the thesis, *Studies in Higher Education, 33*(3): 284–294.

Kapp, R., & Bangeni, B. (2005). "I was just never exposed to this argument thing": Using a genre approach to teach academic writing to ESL students in the humanities. In Herrington, A., & Moran, C. (Eds.), *Genre across the curriculum,* pp. 109–127, Logan, UT: Utah State University Press.

Myers, G. (1990). *Writing biology: Texts in the social constructions of scientific knowledge.* Madison: The University of Wisconsin Press.

Russell, D. R. (1993). Vygotsky, Dewey, and externalism: Beyond the student/discipline dichotomy, *Journal of Advanced Composition, 13*: 173–194.

Statement of WAC Principles and Practices. (2014). *The WAC Clearinghouse.* Retrieved from http://wac.colostate.edu/principles/

Wilder, L. (2012). *Rhetorical strategies and genre conventions in literary studies: Teaching and writing in the disciplines.* Carbondale: Southern Illinois University Press.

Testimonio 5

The Invisibility of a Lack of Privilege and the Homelessness of a First-Generation Latina Student in Higher Education

KAYLEE CRUZ

First-generation Latina student. This is the demographic profile used as my identity marker as a college student. It defines, in part, my academic status, my financial aid, and my official identity at my school. For those looking at my records, I could be assumed to possess characteristics rooted in my family and background that are associated with risk for attrition, such as being from a "low-income family" and having "lower achievement and degree aspirations" (U.S. Department of Education, 1998). But for me, it was an unknown.

I became aware of my position in the social structure of higher education through my role as a tutor at my institution's writing center. As the University of La Verne is a Hispanic-Serving Institution, the realization that I was not an average American student was nonexistent until attending the 2015 National Conference on Peer Tutoring in Writing, held in Salt Lake City, Utah. Describing the writing center community in higher education, Nancy Grimm (2011) notes, "the small but significant presence of people of color" (p. 77). What I saw at this conference was more "small" than "significant." Whiteness dominated the conference, and I felt uncomfortable, alienated, and intimidated, a feeling I was not used to. During all of the workshop sessions I attended, I remained quiet, withholding any comments and questions, so I could be invisible; I longed to offer my input because of my interest in a majority of the topics, but I refrained from talking due to some internal force. I lacked the courage to overcome the fear of how the White community, the "mainstream," would react to my perspectives on the topics. I worried that they would see me not as an equal but as an *other*, which was how I suddenly understood myself.

The conference continued to yield situations where I became aware of my ethnicity, especially as it affected my academic identity. While attending a presentation entitled "Meeting of the Special Interest Group (SIG) on Anti-racism Activism," I started up a conversation with a female and male student from a large public university in a predominantly White area of the Midwest. Both of the students were White and expressed their willingness to better understand issues involving race, especially because the topic, they said, was not ever discussed where they were from, as their university is ~95–97% White students. While talking, I realized the polarized backgrounds we came from, practically different worlds, though we were only a year or so apart in age. The female tutor shared how racial issues were never discussed throughout her life, and the only reason she was exposed to such situations was because of a class she was enrolled in. That this could be true shocked me.

And I was shocked too to realize that race and ethnicity had been at the center of my experiences in higher education, without me being aware. Though I had been a high-achieving student in high school, at the start of college, I was struggling in my courses and was placed on academic probation. I was unaware of the resources available to help me and did not feel connected to my campus. This is not surprising, considering the fact that nearly 50% of undergraduate Latino students, like me, are considered first-generation, meaning their parents have either never enrolled in or completed college (Liu, 2011); because my family is unaware of the challenges faced in higher education by first-generation students, I was unable to receive the support I needed at home, as well as at school. In my first semester, I failed chemistry, which is a requirement for my major. My advisor immediately tried to persuade me that the major I had chosen was not a good fit for me. Looking back, I wondered: would she have been so quick to tell a White student they couldn't succeed in their chosen major? At the time, I had to reassure her that I would have passed the class were there not other factors affecting me, things outside of school. But after that, I became terrified of school, terrified of failing, and strayed away from enrolling in my major courses. I was unexpectedly thrown into a gyre and my academic identity, for the first time in my life ever, was in flux. This inability to feel secure in who I was as a student hounded me. I questioned my major, my career path, and myself overall. Still, I was left to navigate college on my own.

This experience of transforming from a high-achieving student to a student on academic probation made me realize something that had been invisible to me: my high school education did not prepare me for college. I was not prepared because I was not coming from a White upper-middle class context, and that was only visible to me as a lack once I was put into the context of higher education. I genuinely believed I had lived a privileged life, but it was clear this was not the case in terms of the academy. Because I was raised in Montebello, a diverse working-class community outside of Los Angeles, I did not have the privilege of students who attended high schools that would make for an easier transition, high schools where students went to college prepared to succeed. Comparing the school district I went through to that of a more affluent community just 35 miles away, shows the difference. My school district was made up of 96% Hispanic/Latino students, whereas the other consisted of only 10% Hispanic/Latino students. The districts' average Academic Performance Index scores are 663 and 897, and the median household incomes are $46,316 and $87,830, respectively. It is not surprising that these disparities affect the educational performance of students who live in lower socioeconomic status communities. I lived this difference. Thinking back to my conversation with the White tutor at the conference, I realized that she too was blind to the reality of these statistics; the only difference between us is her ability to preserve her privilege to not have to see the reality of the correlation between these factors. For her, race and ethnicity were just topics in a class.

For me, the paradoxical structure of my dual identity was becoming clearer. I can now see that as a Mexican-American first-generation student, I self-identify as being two distinct individuals—one at home and one at school. As a student, and, especially as a writing tutor, I engage in academic discourses and generate dialogues to help other students navigate their thinking processes. At home, school lingers in the background and family takes the forefront. How I talk changes. I rarely mention what I am studying at school or my work as a tutor because my family members do not understand. Family is my past, but school leads to my future. Balancing the two takes a major toll on me. It is a constant battle between becoming the first to carry on the family name successfully and being accused of thinking I am "better" than everyone else. It is a constant battle of praise and jealousy. It is a constant battle of being the "perfect" and "favorite" child and of having your achievements put down as the result of some external factor rather than the hard work you put in. It is heartbreaking to be the point of comparison for other family members when they are not succeeding. I am accepted for who I am, but I am still seen as drastically different. Although my family wants to see me succeed, their reasons are not always kind. It is difficult coping with the stress that comes along with a grandma who only loves you because you make her look good and cousins and extended family that marginalize you. Because education is a significant part of my identity, I am forced to hide my true self and constantly struggle with being the black sheep, which provokes loneliness and isolation. It is difficult for me not to be able to express my intellectual and creative side with the people I love the most. Additionally, family taking precedence over school and work is not an option. With a mom who recently recovered from breast cancer and is the only income source for the family, a dad with a recent kidney failure and ongoing dialysis, a 9-year-old nephew and a 3-year-old niece who need attention and care, and a 15-year-old adopted cousin who is struggling with the absence of her parents and her own identity, I am expected to help out at home in order to make life a little easier for everyone. In the end, who am I? Does "first-generation Latina student" cover all this?

References

Grimm, N. M. (2011). Retheorizing writing center work to transform a system of advantage based on race. In L. Greenfield & K. Rowan (Eds.), *Writing centers and the new racism: A call for sustainable dialogue and change* (pp. 75–100). Logan: Utah State University Press.

Liu, M. C. (2011). Investing in higher education for Latinos: Trends in Latino college access and success. In *Proceedings of National Conference of State Legislatures.* Denver, Colorado, 1–12.

U.S. Department of Education. (1998). National Center for Education Statistics. *First generation students: Undergraduates whose parents never enrolled in postsecondary education*, NCES 98-082. Washington, DC.

Contributors

Nancy Alvarez is a PhD candidate in the English Department at St. John's University in Queens, New York. Her dissertation is a qualitative study of the experiences of Latinas tutoring in writing centers housed within Hispanic-Serving Institutions across the United States. Her research interests include writing center studies, writing pedagogy, digital literacies, language rights, and issues of access and equity for Latinx in Higher Education.

Steven Alvarez is the author of *Brokering Tareas: Mexican Immigrant Families Translanguaging Homework Literacies* published by State University of New York Press and *Community Literacies en Confianza: Learning from Bilingual After-School Programs* published by the National Council of Teachers of English. He is Assistant Professor of English at St. John's University.

Isabel Baca is Associate Professor of English, Director of the Community Writing Partners Program, and Director of the Bilingual Professional Writing Certificate Program at the University of Texas at El Paso. She edited *Service-Learning and Writing: Paving the Way for Literacy(ies) through Community Engagement* (2012) and *Borders* (2011). She is a 2017 University of Texas System Regents' Outstanding Teaching Award recipient and a 2018 National Endowment for the Humanities (NEH) Humanities Initiatives at Presidentially Designated Institutions Grant recipient. Her research interests include service-learning in writing studies, bilingual professional writing, second-language writers, and community engagement in higher education. Her chapter "It Is All in the Attitude—The Language Attitude" was published in *Teaching Writing with Latino/a Students: Lessons Learned at Hispanic-Serving Institutions* (Kirklighter, Cárdenas, Wolff Murphy, 2007).

Lucas Corcoran is a doctoral candidate at the Graduate Center, CUNY, where he is completing a dissertation that centers on the relationship between rhetoric and translingual language and literacy practices.

Kaylee Cruz graduated from University of La Verne, a Hispanic-Serving Institution, in Southern California in 2018 with a Bachelor of Science in Biology. She is a first-generation Latina student and was born and raised in Los Angeles, California. During her undergraduate career, she presented at seven regional and national conferences, speaking about writing centers. Her *testimonio* reflects on one such experience and highlights how she became increasingly aware of her identity through her role as a writing tutor.

Candace de León-Zepeda is the Chair of the Department of English, Mass Communication and Drama and Director of the QUEST First Year Writing Program at Our Lady of the Lake University in San Antonio, Texas. Her field of study is in both Latino/a Literary & Cultural Studies and Rhetorical and Written Studies. Her scholarship is currently focused on how Hispanic-Serving Institutions can better "serve" students of color with inclusive program design, curriculum, assessment, and culturally relevant pedagogies. She is currently co-editing a book related to teaching practices for students of color.

Erin Doran is an Assistant Professor of Higher Education in the School of Education at Iowa State University. A native of El Paso, she is a proud graduate of the University of Texas at San Antonio, one of the largest 4-year HSIs in the state. Her doctorate, conferred in 2015, is in Educational Leadership, and her dissertation was named Dissertation of the Year by the Council for the Study of Community Colleges in 2016. Erin's research focuses on issues of student success and access of Latinx students in community colleges, especially those in developmental education, and Hispanic-Serving Institutions.

Aydé Enríquez-Loya is an Assistant Professor of rhetoric and composition, with a specialization in Chicanx/Latinx Rhetoric in the English Department at California State University, Chico. She teaches courses in technical writing, rhetorical and decolonial theory, composition, and Chicanx literature and rhetoric. Her ongoing research varies between femicides of Mexican/Mestiza women on the U.S.–Mexico border and decolonial pedagogical practices.

Heather M. Falconer is a Assistant Professor of Writing at Curry College and Associate Editor for the *Perspectives on Writing* book series (The WAC Clearinghouse). Her research has appeared in *The WAC Journal, Journal of Research in Science Teaching, Written Communication,* and *Journal of Hispanic Higher Education.* She received a 2016 CCCC Emergent Research/er Award for her research with underrepresented minorities in science.

Christine Garcia is a mother, wife, writer, and Assistant Professor of Rhetoric and Writing at Eastern Connecticut State University. She pushes boundaries, advocates for kinder, more inclusive spaces, dreams and enacts empowering and challenging pedagogies, molds critical thinkers, and writes like a *chingona.*

Romeo García is an Assistant Professor in the Department of Writing and Rhetoric Studies at the University of Utah. His pedagogical practice remains focused on the visibility of marginalized students and critical approaches to working with students in institutional spaces. García is author of "Unmaking Gringo-Centers," published in *The Writing Center Journal* and "On the Cusp of Invisibility," published in *Open Words.*

Laura Gonzales is an Assistant Professor of Rhetoric and Writing Studies at The University of Texas at El Paso. Her work highlights the intellectual work that multilingual communicators engage in as they translate information for their communities. She is the author of *Sites of Translation: What Multilinguals Can Teach Us About Digital Writing and Rhetoric* (University of Michigan Press, 2018).

Marcela Hebbard was born in Mexico City but moved to the United States 23 years ago. She holds three MA degrees and is currently working on a doctoral degree in Women's Studies. She believes that instructors should become life-long learners. She currently is a Lecturer at the University of Texas Rio Grande Valley where she teaches First Year Composition and linguistic courses. Because of her background, she identifies with the challenges that incoming freshman and multilingual writers bring to the classroom. As a result, she integrates different methodologies to serve the needs of diverse students. Her goal as an instructor is that students in her courses grow in self-knowledge and self-efficacy about their own linguistic and literacy processes.

Yndalecio Isaac Hinojosa is an Assistant Professor of English at Texas A&M University–Corpus Christi and co-editor of *Open Words: Access and English Studies.* His work focuses on intersections between Chicana third space feminist theory and Writing Studies under the lenses of border theory, gender, sexuality, nationality, and race. He is author of "Localizing the Body for Practitioners in Writing Studies" in *El Mundo Zurdo 5* and "The Coyolxauhqui Imperative in Developing Comunidad-Situated Writing Curricula at Hispanic-Serving Institutions," coauthored with Candace de León-Zepeda in *El Mundo Zurdo 6.*

Cristina Kirklighter is a retired Professor of Rhetoric and Composition at Texas A&M University–Corpus Christi, a Hispanic-Serving Institution. Kirklighter published numerous articles and books throughout her career. She co-edited with Diana Cárdenas and Susan Wolff Murphy, *Teaching Writing with Latino/a Students: Lessons Learned at Hispanic-Serving Institutions* (2007). From 2011 to 2017, she was managing editor of *Reflections: A Journal of Public Rhetoric, Civic Writing, and Service Learning,* a peer reviewed community engagement journal. She served as co-chair of the NCTE/CCCC Latin@ Caucus from 2009–2015 and on numerous NCTE/CCCC committees throughout the years. Today, she owns a jewelry business and is working with a Mayan master to better understand her indigenous roots.

Heather Lang was born and raised in Farmington, New Mexico, and completed her BA and MA degrees at New Mexico State University prior to completing her PhD in English—Rhetoric and Composition—at Florida State University. She is currently appointed as an Assistant Professor of Digital Publishing and Writing at Susquehanna University in Selinsgrove, Pennsylvania, where she pursues research in two areas: digital activism and writing center administration.

Kendall Leon is an Assistant Professor of Rhetoric and Composition, with a specialization in Chicanx/Latinx/@ Rhetoric in the English Department at California State University, Chico. Her teaching and research interests include cultural and community rhetorics, professional writing, service learning pedagogies, and writing program administration.

Jens Lloyd is a Visiting Assistant Professor in the English Department at Drew University, where he also serves as the Director of First-Year Writing. He completed his PhD and the research that led to his contribution in this collection at the University of California–Irvine. Specializing in spatial and ecological approaches to composition theory and pedagogy, he plans to study further the co-curricular dimensions of campus life and how these dimensions intersect with rhetorical education. You can read his scholarship in *Literacy in Composition Studies* and *Present Tense: A Journal of Rhetoric in Society.*

Beatrice Mendez Newman, Professor in the Writing and Language Studies Department at The University of Texas Rio Grande Valley, teaches first-year writing, rhetoric, and literacy classes. Her research, focused on translingualism, translanguaging, and pedagogy, appears in several collections and in the *Writing Center Journal, Praxis: A Writing Center Journal,* the *English Journal, Voices from the Middle,* and *HETS Online Journal.* She has also published several books on preparation for Texas educator certification exams.

Susan Wolff Murphy is Professor of English and Associate Dean of the College of Liberal Arts at Texas A&M University–Corpus Christi. She co-authored a chapter with Mark Hartlaub in *Retention and Resistance: Writing Instruction and Students Who Leave.* She co-edited *Teaching Writing with Latino/a*

Students: Lessons Learned at Hispanic-Serving Institutions (2007) and has published articles in *Writing Center Journal* and other publications. She serves as a CompPile.org editor, and her research interests include developmental and first-year writing, writing centers, and learning communities.

Nicole Nicholson received her MA in Teaching English as a Second Language from Arizona State University (ASU) in 2006. She has taught in a variety of educational settings, including providing language support at an elementary school in Compton, California; freshmen composition courses for international students at ASU; all levels of English language courses for an international student population at a Phoenix, Arizona, high school; and English language and composition courses at the University of Puerto Rico. She is currently a lecturer at the University of Texas Rio Grande Valley where she incorporates *Familismo* and multilingual techniques in her FYC classrooms.

Yemin Sánchez obtained her MA in ESL from The University of Texas Pan-American. She has taught ESL, English language and composition at HSIs for over a decade. She has served Hispanic students from various backgrounds, ages, and levels of English proficiency. Currently, she is a lecturer at the University of Texas Rio Grande Valley.

Caroline Wilkinson is an Assistant Professor in English at New Jersey City University in Jersey City, NJ. She studies the transition from high school to college for FYC students and the role of dual enrollment in composition. She teaches composition, linguistics, and dual-enrollment courses.

Index